C000180287

the
WAINWRIGHT
companion

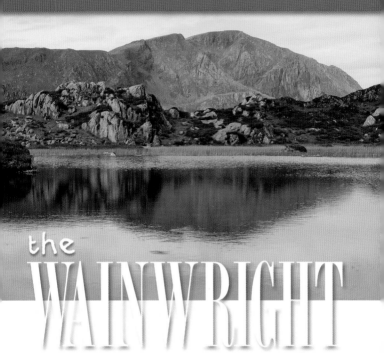

the
WAINWRIGHT
companion

being an illustrated collection of fascinating facts,
statistics, trivia and opinion – based on the
guidebooks to the English Lake District of

AWainwright

CLIVE HUTCHBY
Photography by Sean McMahon
Special contribution by Ken Garland

Dedicated to A. Wainwright, for the inspiration,
and
Roy Lomas, for giving me my first job.

Frances Lincoln Limited
4 Torriano Mews
London NW5 2RZ
www.franceslincoln.com

First published by Frances Lincoln 2012

Printed and bound in China.

A CIP catalogue record is available for this book
from the British Library

ISBN 978 0 7112 3382 9

9 8 7 6 5 4 3 2 1

FOREWORD

By ERIC ROBSON, Chairman, The Wainwright Society

Wainwright fans will never be short of a one-liner ever again. Thanks to Clive Hutchby's obsessional ferreting, here is everything you ever wanted to know about AW's books but were either afraid or too busy to ask. When you want to find out which is the 50th-highest Wainwright fell (as one day you will), there it is on page 46. More precisely there *they* are because Grey Friar shares the spot with Sail at 2536 feet. And while you're at it, did you realise that there are 70,649 feet of fells in Book Seven of the Pictorial Guides?

Now the problem with most miscellanies is that they're – well, miscellaneous. This one is different; opinionated, challenging, even a bit heretical. It says that some of the Pictorial Guides are better than others – right there in black and white on page 34. It also has the clearest explanation I've ever read of why Wainwright's interpretation of mountain landscapes is better than any other.

Like all AW's books, *The Wainwright Companion* has a wealth of detail leavened by digression and all illustrated with the work of one of the great photographic interpreters of Lakeland, Sean McMahon. So, which fell suffers from *extreme dreariness and universal swampiness*? And of which fell did AW say there were very few fells not worth climbing but.......... *is one of the few*? Get digging - there will be tests.

Broadcaster Eric Robson is well known for his series of TV programmes with AW in the mid-1980s which looked back over the writer's life. He lives in Wasdale, where he farms at Crag House Farm, and with his wife he runs a mail order company (www.stridingedge.com) specialising in DVDs, maps and books.

THE WAINWRIGHT SOCIETY: Set up in 2002 to celebrate the work of AW, the society publishes a quarterly newsletter and organises an annual memorial lecture by a guest speaker. There are also occasional Lakeland walks. For full details of events and information on how to become a member visit *www.wainwright.org.uk* or write to the Membership Secretary at: Kendal Museum, Station Road, Kendal LA9 6BY.

CLIMB UP HEAVENLY VALLEY: The path to Upper Eskdale, with Ill Crag ahead and Scafell Pike peeping around the corner. AW considers Eskdale to be the finest valley of all for walkers, and Scafell Pike to be Lakeland's grandest fell.
25/6/09

6

PREFACE

The man, the plan, the collaboration

Alfred Wainwright (1907-91), was the Borough Treasurer of Kendal when, on Saturday, 9 November 1952, he began his 13-year odyssey to document all the main summits of the English Lake District in a pictorial guide. His highly ambitious plan was to write himself an extended 'love letter' so that, when he was too old and frail to climb the mountains he loved so much and was forced to swap walking boots for slippers, he could still relax in their company in front of a nice warm fire.

Here's how he put it in his book MEMOIRS OF A FELLWANDERER:

It was total love of the fells, a desire to escape from the common round, my long-standing fascination with maps, an acquired interest in drawing, an insatiable urge to look round the next corner on a trodden way if I could find one and it didn't matter if I couldn't – it was these things that caused me . . . to pen my first page in what I intended to be a series of seven guidebooks to the Lakeland fells, each covering a defined area, and, if you are interested, the first page I did depicted the ascent of Dove Crag from Ambleside. I forgot to mention earlier that I have patience. I knew the work would take all my spare time for the next thirteen years, but it was a prospect I smacked my lips over. Somebody once said (it would be a Chinaman, of course) that a journey of a thousand steps starts with the first step; 9 November 1952 saw my first step. It was a good evening for me. It was a winter's night, but I spent it going up Dove Crag and was lost to all else. And the nights that followed were equally good. At the time I had no thought of publication. I was working for my own pleasure and enjoying it hugely. I was gathering together all my notes and drawings and a host of recollections, and putting them into a book so that when I became an old man I could look through them at leisure, recall all my memories, and go on fellwalking in spirit long after my legs had given up.

However, a love of the lakes didn't start with AW (as he is usually known these days and how he will be referred to in this book). Back in the late 18th/early 19th century **William Wordsworth** and his fellow 'lake poets' **Samuel Taylor Coleridge** and **Robert Southey** first popularised the English Lake District with their poetic descriptions of its beauty (Wordsworth's *Guide To The Lakes* was first published in 1810 and by 1835 had reached its fifth edition). This movement undid the damage inflicted on the area (tourism-wise) by **Daniel Defoe's** book *A Tour Thro' the Whole Island of Great Britain* (1724) in which he described Westmorland as follows:

The wildest, most barren and frightful of any (county) that I have passed over in England, or even Wales itself; the west side, which borders on Cumberland, is indeed bounded by a chain of almost unpassable mountains which, in the language of the country, are called fells.

There followed the Victorian age of exploration, fuelled by the

SCHOOL'S OUT: The spectacular view from School Knott over Windermere makes this outlying fell one of the more popular short walks in Lakeland. 4/11/11

opening of the **Kendal-Windermere railway** in 1847, and, in 1886, by the birth of rock climbing following the first ascent of Napes Needle on Great Gable by **Walter Parry** (W.P.) **Haskett Smith**. Next it was the turn of the **Abraham brothers – George** and **Ashley**, who lived in Keswick – to further popularise the sport (and Lakeland) with a series of photos of rock-climbing pioneers between 1890 and 1920. These included the mercurial **Owen Glynne Jones**, with whom they forged a close partnership in the three years before his death in 1896.

About the same time as the Abraham brothers were 'snapping', the splendidly named **Mountford John Byrde** (M.J.B.) **Baddeley** was writing. His *Thorough Guide to the English Lake District* (first published in 1880) was continually revised and re-issued up until at least 1978. It was of a traditional format for a guidebook, with text backed up by Bartholomew maps. Next, another gifted photographer, **William Arthur** (W.A.) **Poucher** – known to his friends as Walter – produced the excellent *The Lakeland Peaks* (1960), with high-quality black-and-white photographs featuring over-printed lines (in black or white) that marked the suggested ascents.

By then of course AW had already produced four of his planned seven-book Lakeland series known as THE PICTORIAL GUIDES, and by 1966 the 'set' had been published. This book is about those books and the later THE OUTLYING FELLS OF LAKELAND (1974).

When AW sat down to start BOOK ONE on Saturday, 9 November 1952, **Sir Winston Churchill** was Prime Minister; seven years after the end of the Second World War, the UK still had **rationing** in place (petrol rationing ended in May 1950, but sweets were rationed until February 1953, sugar until September 1953, and all food rationing didn't end until July 1954 with meat the last to be freely available); **Newcastle United** were the FA Cup holders; **Queen Elizabeth II** had acceded the throne following the death of her father, King George VI; **Gary Cooper** had won the Best Actor Oscar for his role in *High Noon*; **The Great Smog of London** had killed an estimated 4000 people; and **Agatha Christie's** play *The Mousetrap* had started its run at the New Ambassadors Theatre in London. The last point proves that *some* things never change – as this book went to press in May 2012 it was still running to packed audiences, now at St Martin's Theatre.

AW's plan to research, to write, and to illustrate and design – ALL BY HAND – a seven-book series over 13 meticulously mapped out years was astonishing . . . considering he had no car and insisted on using only public transport; considering he was holding down a full-time job throughout this period; and considering he had no formal training in graphic design. When he was persuaded to publish BOOK ONE, which, despite a rocky start because of a rail strike in 1955 that hit distribution, went on to be a success that had several publishers knocking on his door, the pressure mounted. Now he truly WAS committed to the books (although we now know from his later writings that there was never any doubt about *that*!).

I first came across THE PICTORIAL GUIDES during my first visit to the Lake District in the summer of 1968, and even as a not-then-teenager I appreciated his craftsmanship, his eye for detail, his quirky humour and his mastery of the English language (you'll find more about this moment in my life in *Some personal notes in conclusion* starting on page 345). I later went on to become a journalist – first as a reporter and then as a designer; the latter 'string to my bow' brought me into contact with the wonderful world of typography (as opposed to topography), which made me appreciate AW's great achievements even more. Fast forward to October 2010 when I made my first visit to the Lakes for several years, and naturally I strolled on down to the George Fisher store to check out these second-edition guidebooks I'd read so much about on the internet. I returned with a heavier backpack after buying all seven of the Chris Jesty-revised series (and let me say here and now what a splendid job he has done). Back home after my flying visit, I settled

ARTWORK FROM THE GUIDEBOOKS

All the original artwork from the guidebooks used in this book comes from the FIRST EDITIONS of the books – so don't expect any red lines on ascent diagrams and, because of the number of changes, please do not use these diagrams on your walks. You will need to buy SECOND EDITION guidebooks for that (advt).

RARE SIGHT: Light from a setting sun shines on a deserted Coniston Old Man summit. It's deserted because when this picture was taken there was barely thirty minutes before darkness set in – Sean McMahon is a photographer who loves being in the right place at the right time.   20/1/11

down with the books . . . and once again I was captivated by their whole *scope*. And that's the moment when I came up with the idea for this book – a compendium of stuff (I love that word) from all of AW's Lakeland fellwalking guides (ONE to SEVEN plus THE OUTLYING FELLS); of trivia; of stats; of facts and figures; of conjecture and supposition; of legend and poetry (haven't I read that somewhere before!). I wanted to do this book the AW way, but moved forward 60 years to the 21st century . . . to do it by myself: writing and designing, right up to the moment my finished pages are presented to the printer.

But there was one drawback (a very apt word): I CAN'T DRAW! However, I can take photos, and I soon contemplated the not-unwelcome task of spending several weeks on the fells shooting the shots that I wanted to illustrate this book. Then I realised that someone I know (a cyber pal at that stage) had been doing this since the early 2000s. I'd been following the exploits of **Sean McMahon** and his trusty sidekicks (the late **Angus, King of the Fells**, **Casper** and **Dougal** – all bearded collies) from afar while I was in 'exile' thanks to his excellent Lake District photo diary **www.stridingedge.net**. Over the years (especially the last four or five) Sean has become a terrific photographer – but so are plenty of people who have taken pretty shots of Lakeland from the usual places. The thing is, Sean doesn't go to the usual places, nor at the usual times. Sometimes when he's on a walk he'll just go where the (good) weather takes him. Very often, he'll make a crack-of-dawn start and be up on the fells (and above the crowds as the sun comes up) and take superlative pictures while 99 per cent of the good folk of Keswick and Bowness and Coniston are asleep and tourists are still an hour away from their B&B breakfast. Which is why I asked him to collaborate with me on this book (in effect, to be the 21st-century 'sketch artist') and I was delighted when he agreed to come on board. Then it struck me that the medium used by

ABOUT TENSES...

When looking back on the guidebooks with a historical perspective, I have used the **past tense**. But for the specific content of the guidebooks, I use the **present tense** – AW *writes* enthusiastically about this climb, etc.

www.stridingedge.net was the true 21st-century medium, and that this book simply had to reflect that. Which is why, at the end of every picture caption, you will see a date, like so: *9/11/12*. This indicates the date the picture was taken, which enables you – by going to **www.stridingedge.net** – to access all Sean's walking diaries going back to 2003. All you have to do is find the relevant date, and you can click your way through the route and see a whole lot of other great pictures.

The chapters in this book are set out in a similar way to those in the 'seven' series, although there are some starting on right-hand pages instead of the traditional AW way of all fell chapters starting on a left-hand page. (Did you know, only two fell chapters among the 214 concluded on a left-hand page? They are **Ullock Pike**, BOOK FIVE, and Yewbarrow, BOOK SEVEN). You will notice that both these fell names have been coloured to represent the colours used in AW's first-edition Lakeland guidebooks. These colours will be used throughout this book, thus ruling out the necessity of indicating in which guidebook a particular fell appears. They are as follows:

BOOK ONE: The Eastern Fells
BOOK TWO: The Far Eastern Fells
BOOK THREE: The Central Fells
BOOK FOUR: The Southern Fells
BOOK FIVE: The Northern Fells
BOOK SIX: The North Western Fells
BOOK SEVEN: The Western Fells
THE OUTLYING FELLS OF LAKELAND

Those of you with an eye for colour will spot that the colour for BOOK SIX is more golden than the yellow in the first-edition book – which is because such a shade would be impossible to read. Because of this, BOOK FOUR is a little browner. Likewise, THE OUTLYING FELLS (which was also a shade of yellow in its first edition) has been modified to a kind of 'gherkin' green. Others among you may look at the font used on these pages and wonder: is that a modern-day version of AW's hand-drawn font? It isn't. This font is an Apple-created font called Chalkboard and I've chosen it for this book because it is very effective in *italic* and when used in **bold** for emphasis, and . . .

I didn't want it to be typeset in Times New Roman or some other similar font (too boring!), nor some font such as Gill Sans (too thin!). Neither did I want it to be set in the font, which was created by the publishers of the guidebooks to enable Chris Jesty's revisions to be made in as unobtrusive fashion as possible. The font, known as Lakeland, will, however, be used in selected places in this book (including the jacket and chapter headings) to give it the same 'family feel' as an original AW guidebook. That's the aim anyway.

Now, enough about this book . . . Time to get on to the eight great guidebooks that have been a part of Lakeland life for two generations.

Clive Hutchby, May 2012

This book is split into eight MAIN SECTIONS, and interspersed between them are three MINI-SECTIONS scattered throughout the book. The idea is to break up the longer, main sections, thus maintaining interest (and surprise) as you turn the pages. These MINI-SECTIONS are as follows:

QUIZZES

There are eight of these, all one-page chapters, each with ten questions (all the answers can be found in the guidebooks). They can be found on pages 86, 108, 137, 159, 205, 216, 239 and 259. The answers are on page 344 (no cheating, try the quizzes first!).

PORTRAITS

Eight of these, too (example, left), all one-page chapters, each looking at one of AW's portraits of himself. The first seven cover the main portraits in THE PICTORIAL GUIDES, the last one features the 'eighth portrait' (the dog nipping AW's heels) and two other possible portraits – isn't that intriguing! You will find AW's drawings of himself on pages 68, 96, 130, 152, 179, 210, 217 and 250.

OFF-TRACK

These are short chapters dealing with certain aspects of the guidebooks that don't fall into the main categories. For instance, there is an OFF-TRACK feature about That Kirk Fell ascent (see image, left) described in BOOK SEVEN (you will find this on pages 142-144). Another one deals with The Roadblocks – problems on two major footpaths found at Broad Stand and the Bad Step. That you will find on pages 83-85. Here are the rest:

THE MAIN SECTIONS are outlined **on the next two pages:** THE BOOKS | THE FELLS | THE ARTWORK | LANDSCAPES | STATS & TRIVIA | THE HAND OF MAN | INDEX TO THE GUIDEBOOKS | and SOME PERSONAL NOTES IN CONCLUSION.

THE BOOKS
Design, Typography
How AW designed THE PICTORIAL GUIDE. *The text of renowned 20th-century designer Ken Garland's famous talk in 1996, plus . . . AW's typographical mastery.*

Development
How the guidebooks changed, book-by-book (and why those 'silhouette' summit views didn't last long!).

THE FELLS
A Pictorial Guide
All 214 fells from BOOKS ONE *to* SEVEN *in height order – plus masses of other stats and trivia.*

The Outliers
All 56 chapters (a total of 116 fells including those without a name) from THE OUTLYING FELLS OF LAKELAND *in height order – plus, a profile of Black Combe and analysis of why this guidebook was so different.*

Space allocation
Which fells got how many pages – and why.

Super ascents
AW's favourite ways up – our own star rating (up to five stars) for every one of them.

An ascent of Scafell Pike
The best way up, according to The Oracle.

Super summits
The other tops that impressed him.

Views
Every single view that AW described – in one chapter.

Super ridges
More great high-level routes.

The 'dull' ones
The dreary fells (we still love 'em!).

Top twenty
AW's first-choice eleven, plus nine more.

More exciting places
After the top six – the rest of the best.

GAP IN THE FELLS: Great Door on Yewbarrow – page 156

THE TWIN TARNS – page 194

...AND THE INFAMOUS

This is a typical OFF-TRACK chapter. It is not very long (just two pages) and is slotted in at random, between the main sections, purely to keep you 'on your toes', so to speak! You will find lots of them, dotted around the book. This 'OFF-TRACK' is about some of the famous (and infamous) people associated with Lakeland who are mentioned in the guidebooks. Many of the references were added by Chris Jesty for the second editions, often to replace text that had become dated or to fill up a significant blank white space. These second-edition references are indicated by an asterisk.*

● **William Wordsworth** (1770-1850) – Nab Scar: The poet lived at Dove Cottage (1799-1808 and Rydal Mount (1813-50), which were linked by a path known as the Coffin Route.* Loughrigg Fell: Wordsworth's daughter Dora and son William once lived at nearby houses called Loughrigg Holme and Stepping Stones respectively.* Silver How: Allan Bank was a temporary home (1808-11) for Wordsworth. Grey Friar: The River Duddon was the favourite river of Wordsworth, who wrote a number of sonnets about it, published in 1820.*

The FRATERNAL FOUR: Looking towards Base Brown.   29/1/07

Scafell Pike: Wordsworth's 'Fraternal Four' (four yew trees) indicated on an ascent diagram. 'Yew Trees' was a poem published in 1803: 'Are those fraternal Four of Borrowdale, /Joined in one solemn and capacious grove.' Latrigg: The River Greta was the subject of a poem written by Wordsworth.*

Black Combe: He wrote of the view: 'The amplest range of unobstructed prospect may be seen that British ground commands'.

HOLY MOSES

MOSES RIGG was a notorious quarryman, a smuggler and a bootlegger who was well known in the Seathwaite area of Borrowdale in the 18th century. His high-level route from Honister Pass through to Wasdale, Moses' Trod, is featured in the Great Gable chapter.

● **Beatrix Potter** (1866-1943) – Troutbeck Tongue: She purchased Troutbeck Park Farm and Troutbeck Tongue and bequeathed them to the National Trust in 1923.* Holme Fell: She bought four farms in the 1930s which she bequeathed or gave to the National Trust.* Catbells: The climb from Hawse End crosses the path to Lingholme, where she spent many holidays. 'The Tale of Peter Rabbit' is set in the locality.* Claife Heights: Potter lived in Near Sawrey, which was the setting for many of her illustrations.*

● **Arthur Ransome** (1884-1967) – Coniston Old Man: The mountain named as Kangchenjunga in *Swallowdale*, one of the Swallows and Amazons series of

THE MAN IN THE CAVE

The reclusive MILLICAN DALTON (1867–1947) – famous for spending his summer months in a cave on the slopes of Castle Crag – was a self-styled 'Professor of Adventure'. He was born in Alston, Cumberland, but moved to Essex and became an insurance clerk in London. In his 30s he moved to Lakeland, spending his summers in Borrowdale, and moving south to live in a wooden shed in Buckinghamshire during the winter. Dalton lived in his cave for nearly half a century, and he even carved his own motto into the wall above where he slept: 'Don't Waste Words, Jump to Conclusions.'

books.* **Wetherlam:** Low Yewdale is Dixon's Farm in the novel *Winter Holiday.** **Top o'Selside:** Peel Island, on Coniston Water, was one of the inspirations for Wild Cat Island; Octopus Lagoon was Allan Tarn.*

● **Sir Walter Scott** (1771–1832) – **Watson's Dodd:** Castle Rock is used as the setting for the principal scene in the poem 'The Bridal of Triermain': 'midmost of the vale, a mound arose, with airy summits crown'd . . . and mighty keep and tower . . .'

● **Robert Southey** – Grange Fell: Waterfalls described in the poem 'The Cataract of Lodore'.*

● **Sir Hugh Walpole** (1884–1941) – **Great Crag:** A plaque proclaims that Fold Head Farm was Judith Paris' home in the eponymous novel by Walpole.* **Great End:** Sty Head area described in *Rogue Herries.** **Catbells:** Memorial seat (to the author, who lived in Brackenburn, the house below).

● **Thomas de Quincey** (1774–1843) – **Loughrigg Fell:** The poet once lived at Foxghyll, near the River Rothay.*

● **Donald Campbell** (1921–1967) – **Coniston Old Man:** Broke world water speed record on Coniston Water (10 November 1958) and again in May 1959. In January 1967 he died making a further attempt to better the record.*

● **Richard Adams** (b. 1920) – **Harter Fell:** Farm called Grassguards featured in *The Plague Dogs*, for which AW contributed a number of hand-drawn maps. Adams also wrote *Watership Down.**

● **Matthew Arnold** (1822–88) – **Loughrigg Fell:** The poet and cultural critic owned Fox Holme, near the River Rothay.*

SLEE'S A JOLLY GOOD FELLOW

LANCELOT 'LANTY' SLEE (1800–78) was by day a farmer in Little Langdale, by night a brewer of illegal whisky from a cave on Wetherlam. He delivered his moonshine in pigs' bladders – believed to be the origin of the phrase 'had a skinful' – and among his customers was a local magistrate. Rather amazingly (or perhaps not) whenever he was up before the bench the fines were said to be remarkably low.

The Abominable Snowman? No, only the footsteps of Sean McMahon and his dog Casper in snow near Gray Crag. 5/3/09

A LANDMARK...
REMARKABLE

GRAPHICS MAN: Ken met AW several times to unearth the secrets behind the design of the Pictorial Guides.

so says **KEN GARLAND**, one of the most celebrated British designers of the latter part of the 20th century. Ken is a graphic designer, author and game designer who, in 1963, wrote the famous 'First Things First' design manifesto. He is the author of the 1994 book *Mr. Beck's Underground Map*, about the man who designed the London Underground diagram. More recently, Ken has written, illustrated and designed a series of books produced by his own publishing company, Pudkin Books. He spent many hours delving into AW's methods of producing his guidebooks during a number of meetings with the author in the early 1980s, and gave a famous talk to the British Cartographic Society's Annual Technical Symposium at Reading University in 1996, entitled: ***Passionate Physiographer: The Design and Execution of A. Wainwright's Pictorial Guide to the Lakeland Fells***. It is reproduced here in full. Ken summed up his view of AW's achievement in two words: 'Simply remarkable.'

KEN GARLAND'S 1996 TALK ABOUT THE PICTORIAL GUIDES

His text in *italics*, my notes in **bold**.

He places the guidebooks in context as a publishing phenomenon.

Pondered on since 1950, begun in earnest in 1952 and concluded with the publication of BOOK SEVEN *in 1966, A. Wainwright's A PICTORIAL GUIDE TO THE LAKELAND FELLS was one of the most remarkable happenings in publishing history since the Second World War. It incorporated over 3,600 illustrations – maps, bird's eye views, diagrams, panoramas and representational landscape drawings – all based on his own direct observation. Not only was every word of the text written by Wainwright but it was also drawn by him: there is no typesetting whatsoever in any of the seven books* [**neither was there**

in the eighth book, THE OUTLYING FELLS]. *And of course, every foot of the mountain paths described was trodden by the author himself. As if that were not remarkable enough, Wainwright revealed that, with the exception of a strange number of spoiled sheets at the beginning – rejected by him on a strange whim I'll deal with later – he embarked on his first page, dealing with the ascent of Dove Crag from Ambleside, in a style of line drawing and lettering that remained completely unaltered throughout the whole 13 years of his work on the Guide, from* BOOK ONE *to* BOOK SEVEN. *There were no layout guides, no page plans (he didn't know how many pages any book would take up until he finished it) and no nice visuals to impress the publishers, since to all intents and purposes he was his own publisher. There was virtually no assembly nor any pasting-up of separate items involved in the camera-ready artwork he produced: each page was drawn up – text, map, diagram, bird's eye view or whatever – on one piece of paper, rarely needing any correction of any sort. Whenever a gap occurred some useful sketch, note or exhortation was found to fill it, so skilfully that the reader would never guess which portions of any given page had been inserted in this fashion, so well integrated did they appear to be.*

Next, Ken discusses the PRODUCTION PROCESS. Bear in mind, he is talking about a process that existed in the 1950s and 1960s – well before photocomposition in the early 1970s and, at the end of the 1980s, the advent of desktop publishing.

Can an almost complete ignorance of printing technique and orthodox book production be the starting point of an exercise in which the author decides to execute all the camera-ready artwork including the text, thus by-passing all copy-editing and reading of galley proofs? Is it anything other than foolish caprice when that same author proposes to finance the printing and publication at his own risk? And when all the apparent shortcomings are compounded by a passionate devotion to his subject which must surely affect the proper detachment needed for such a work, how could the result be anything but embarrassing? Yet this was not the case. From a modest beginning the Guide grew in popularity until it became, by the time of the last book, the *walker's guide to the Lakeland fells; and even now, when some of the information is obsolete because of changes in land use or ownership* [**this was written before the guides were revised by Chris Jesty**] *– and after successive attempts to supplant it by other publications, it still retains that unique attraction to fresh readers which first endeared it to their elders 40 years ago. Why?*

He now spells out the KEY FACTORS that were working to AW's advantage at the time he began his guides.

Wainwright brought to his task a number of advantages. Firstly, the fine, sure manuscript skill of an old-style accountant trained in

IT STARTED HERE: On the evening of Saturday, 9 November 1952 AW drew his first page of the PICTORIAL GUIDES – the ascent of Dow Crag from Ambleside.

Dove Crag 5

ASCENT FROM AMBLESIDE
2500 feet of ascent : 5 miles

The natural approach lies along the south ridge, over Low Pike and High Pike: this is incomparably the finest route from Ambleside. It is even better, however, as a way down and should be reserved for descent if the return is to be made to Ambleside.

The best alternative ascent is by way of Scandale Pass (the 'short cut' here is a time-saver only when descending).

The variation by High Bakestones is on steep grass. Its merits are an accompanying beck to 2000' and a visit to a very fine cairn.

looking north

Dove Crag cannot be seen from Ambleside, but rising from the fields north of the town is its clearly-defined south ridge, offering an obvious staircase to the summit.

ledger-keeping. In his youth he had been taught that mistakes in book-keeping were just not permissible; there could be no fudging and covering up of errors. Secondly, a delicate, painstaking ability with topographical drawing. Thirdly, a reasonable proficiency with a camera, essential to the gathering of information that could be later analysed at leisure. Fourthly, an inimitable, endearing writing style. To these was added a piece of good fortune in the shape of the recently republished two-and-a-half-inch-to-the-mile Ordnance Survey maps of the Lake District. His passion for the fells was equalled by his passion for the maps, so much so that he would happily settle down for an evening studying a less-familiar portion of a recently-bought map, as others would the next chapter of a book by their favourite thriller writer.

Next, Ken looks at the single most innovative aspect of the guides – what AW describes as his views from 'an imaginary space station'.

*These were the factors present when, on 9 November 1952, Wainwright began on the first page of BOOK ONE: THE EASTERN FELLS. The subject of that page was the ascent of Dove Crag from Ambleside, illustrated by a diagram [**facing page**] devised by him especially for the purpose of clarifying features of the route which would not be apparent from a conventional map.*

Ken looks in detail at how this diagram was created.

THE 'MOVING' BIRD'S EYE VIEW

Figure 2
Graphic showing conventional bird's eye view.

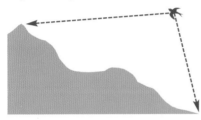

Figure 3
Graphic showing Wainwright's hybrid form.

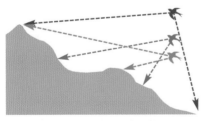

*It would be useful at this point to go into some detail about the form of this diagram, since it was one he consistently adhered to throughout all seven books of the Guide; of all the visual devices he employed this was the most significant. Though it could be superficially classified as a bird's eye view, it is rather more complicated than that. If we examine the diagram closely we see that at the foot it is virtually a map, with the paths, walls and other such features laid out as though we were looking down at them from directly above; but as the path ascends the viewpoint changes, becoming progressively more oblique, until by the time we are looking at the summit it has become the outline we observe on the ground at the beginning of the climb. This transition, described as a theoretical possibility, might have appeared unconvincing, liable to be misinterpreted; yet in practice it works extremely well. Figure 2 [**above left**] shows a conventional bird's eye view for comparison with Figure 3 [**immediately below Figure 2**], (my) attempt at a representation of Wainwright's hybrid form (though it has to*

be said that, in an interview conducted on 20 September 1982, Wainwright disclaimed any theoretical approach to this form of diagram on his part; his solution was, he said, 'just plain common sense').

NOTE: In my opinion, the 'moving bird's eye' was even more sophisticated than this – I'll give examples of the ascents of Bowfell and Haystacks later.

There is a feature of the ascent diagrams which looks simple enough on the page and is taken for granted by the user, but which involved a great deal of painstaking drawing: it is the inclusion of contour lines at 100ft intervals. These were, of course, taken from the Ordnance Survey maps; but their conversion to Wainwright's hybrid form of bird's eye view required a very rare dedication. This was justified, not only for the obvious reason that the walker is made aware of the relative steepness of ascent or descent on any part of the route, but also because the contour lines themselves model the shape of the land most effectively, especially on the upper levels where the angle of view becomes more oblique. There was no place for woolly approximations. The author had set himself a target from the outset, when he stated in his notes in conclusion to BOOK ONE, '. . . this book is full of imperfections. But let me also dare to say that . . . it is free from inaccuracies'. Wainwright confessed to me that the transferral of the Ordnance Survey contours to his diagrammatic views presented him with the most demanding challenge in the Guide. It is, I believe, no coincidence that none of his subsequent emulators in the field of hand-drawn walkers' guides has felt able to attempt this particular feat, undeniably useful though it clearly is.

Next, Ken discusses the bugbear that caused AW to scrap nearly a hundred pages and re-draw them.

In the concluding notes . . . already mentioned, the author stated: 'I started the book determined that everything in it should be perfect, with the consequence that I spent the first six months filling wastepaper baskets', referring in part to the rejection of the first 90 pages he'd so laboriously drawn, solely on the basis that he had failed to align the text on the right-hand side as well as on the left-hand side [**known as 'justification**].

NOTE: A little digression. This is text looks when it is 'justified':

Some mountains are obviously named by reference to their physical characteristics. Crinkle Crags is one of these, and it was probably first so called by the dalesfolk of the valleys of the valleys to the east and around Windermere, whence its lofted serrated ridge, a succession of knobs and depressions, is aptly described by the name.

And this is how it looks when it is 'unjustified':

> Some mountains are obviously named by reference to
> their physical characteristics. Crinkle Crags is one of
> these, and it was probably first so called by the
> dalesfolk of the valleys of the valleys to the east and
> around Windermere, whence its lofted serrated ridge, a
> succession of knobs and depressions, is aptly described
> by the name.

In unjustified text (sometimes known as 'ragged right' when it
is aligned left) there is a uniform space between each word in
a line. In justified text, these spaces between the words can
widen, but when the gap between each word gets past a certain
a point it starts to look ridiculous, like this rather extreme
example:

> Some   mountains   are   obviously   named
> by   reference   to   their   physical
> characteristics.

Now, back to Ken's talk:

*This particular piece of nit-picking flew in the face of the long-
established custom in manuscript work, where a free, or
'unjustified' edge on the right was considered entirely appropriate.
When I asked Wainwright about this, he said: 'Yes, this was
something I was very keen on. I felt that, because of the involved
maps, diagrams and other material, I should keep as neat and
orderly an arrangement of text as possible, even though it meant
a lot of finicky work to get it. I've never seen anyone else do this
in manuscript, so I had to work out my own technique. This is how
I did it: I placed a sheet of paper over the page artwork sheet so
that the top edge was just below where the line of text was to
be drawn, then I wrote out the next line, making it as near as
possible the right length; of course, except for the rare chance it
would turn out to be either too short or too long, all I needed to
do was to expand or contract the character widths and spaces
between words accordingly when writing out the line again on the
actual artwork page. If, however, the line came out too short or
too long to be adjusted in this way, I could change a word –
another advantage of being my own author, designer, client and, in
this case typesetter.'*

*As to his overall design approach, Wainwright, when asked if he
laid out each book in general, then each chapter and then each
page or double-page spread, said: 'No, I just began with a map or
diagram relating to the ascent, then added some text to fill in the*

COMPLEX: (Right) An ascent of Great Gable featuring a delicate placement of text and diagrams.

NOW THAT REALLY IS A BIRD'S EYE VIEW: The Hanging Stone on the steep slopes of Base Brown is the perfect place to look down on the start of the walk described on Great Gable 15. 15/6/09.

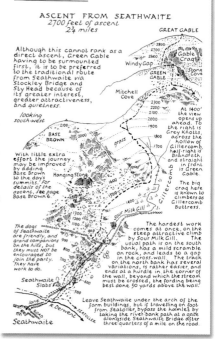

Great Gable 15

ASCENT FROM SEATHWAITE
2700 feet of ascent
2¼ miles

GREAT GABLE

Although this cannot rank as a direct ascent, Green Gable having to be surmounted first, it is to be preferred to the traditional route from Seathwaite via Stockley Bridge and Sty Head because of its greater interest, greater attractiveness, and quietness.

looking south-west

BASE BROWN

With little extra effort the journey may be improved by adding Base Brown to the day's summits. For details of the ascent, see page Base Brown 6.

Hanging Stone

The dogs of Seathwaite are friendly, and grand companions on the hills, but they must NOT be encouraged to join the party. They have work to do.

Seathwaite Slabs

lane

R. Derwent

Seathwaite

Leave Seathwaite under the arch of the farm buildings, but if travelling on foot from Seatoller, bypass the hamlet by taking the river bank path at a gate alongside Seathwaite Bridge after three quarters of a mile on the road.

Windy Gap

Gable Crag

Stone Cove

GREEN GABLE

Mitchell Cove

At 1400' the view opens up ahead. To the right is Grey Knotts, across the hollow of Gillercomb, half-right is Brandreth and straight in front is Green Gable.

The big crag here is known to climbers as Gillercomb Buttress.

grass

Sour Milk Gill

The hardest work comes at once, on the steep attractive climb by Sour Milk Gill. The usual path is on the south bank, has a mild scramble on rock, and leads to a gap in the cross wall. The track on the north bank has several variations, is rather easier, and ends at a hurdle in the corner of the wall, beyond which the stream must be crossed, the fording being best done 50 yards above the wall.

spaces around the drawing and so build up a first page, then gradually accumulate a chapter, each chapter dealing with a separate fell. When I'd done all the fells in one of my seven divisions of Lakeland – in THE EASTERN FELLS, for example, there were 35 – that became a book . . . it didn't occur to me that I needed more than just common sense to build up a chapter, and then a book, as I went along. Some elements were clearly more essential than others and seemed to have their own natural place within the chapter. It was fairly obvious, for example, that there should be a general view of the subject right at the beginning of each chapter and so I placed it consistently on the first left-hand page. Detail views were, though, mostly inserted where I found space available.'

This conveys a notion of minimal planning, perhaps an impatience with the elaborations and divisions of responsibility normal in publishing. The phrase 'common sense' occurs frequently in his accounts of his work on the Guide; but a look at one of the more *complex pages – Great Gable 15, for example* [**see diagram on facing page**] *– suggests that a most <u>un</u>common sense was at work here. It seems that Wainwright was being somewhat disingenuous in claiming such a relatively casual, 'common sense' view of planning.*

The delicate fitting of diagrams and text, the subtle change of letter size and use of italic, the feeling that nothing here is superfluous, and above all the unforced yet unmistakable consistency between similar diagrams within the chapter, within each book and within the whole Guide, are marks of great forethought: no happenstance here. The fact, therefore, that Wainwright was a one-man band did not mean he dispensed with copy-editing, cross-checking, space-planning and many of the strategems common to more orthodox publishing.

Finally, Ken assesses the legacy of AW's publishing achievement, in a more modern context (remember, this talk was given in 1996).

Alfred Wainwright's A PICTORIAL GUIDE TO THE LAKELAND FELLS *has been recognised as an outstanding publishing achievement; but is it unique and inimitable or does it offer us a useful model for works of this kind? And if it does, is that model available only to single-handed author-designer publishers like him, or has it some relevance also to the more normal condition of making illustrated books in this genre? I believe the latter is the case. True, much of Wainwright's approach to book design arose from the mix of production ignorance and unique skills he brought to it, and it would be neither feasible nor desirable to replicate these conditions in commending the Guide as a general, not merely a specific, model. But there is much in the conventional publishing of guidebooks, and of other kinds of illustrated works, that is hide-bound and production-led, rather than concept-led. We should not rely merely on the new potentialities of technical advances such as CD-ROM, useful though they may be.*

There is much to be gained from attempting to look though the innocent eye of Alfred Wainwright, whose vision of the kind of book he had in mind was untrammeled by existing practice. Is it too fanciful to envisage a fruitful combination of his hand-wrought model with the liberating techniques of electronic publishing?

To these very perceptive remarks I would like to add some visual analysis (over the next four pages), and to say to Ken: many thanks for your help with this – much appreciated.

Bowfell VIA **The Band** ... how
the diagram differs from the real view

next page

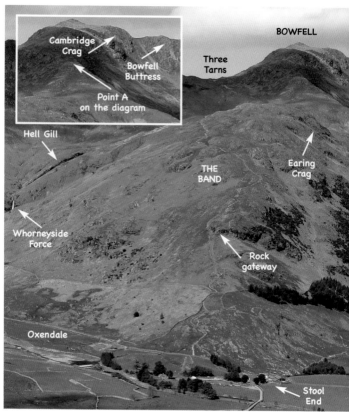

Labels on the image: BOWFELL; Cambridge Crag; Bowfell Buttress; Point A on the diagram; Three Tarns; Hell Gill; THE BAND; Earing Crag; Whorneyside Force; Rock gateway; Oxendale; Stool End

HOW THE MOVING BIRD'S EYE WORKS ITS MAGIC...

A FELL IN ALL ITS GLORY: Bowfell as seen from little Side Pike. 25/5/07

The picture of Bowfell from Side Pike (above) and the summit close-up illustrates perfectly how AW used a moving bird's eye perspective to create his diagrams of ascent. In the photo, the summit of Bowfell appears much smaller than in the diagram. The INSET photo is proportionally closer to the size it appears in the

diagram. Also, notice how wide The Band looks (because it is that much closer to the viewpoint, Side Pike). And Hell Gill and Whorneyside Force are way out to the left in the photo; in the diagram, the moving viewpoint makes them look much closer to The Band.

But the most compelling evidence in the photo that AW used moving viewpoints

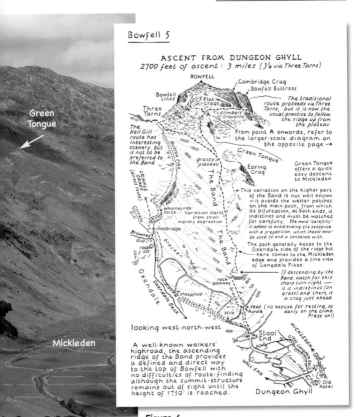

Bowfell 5

ASCENT FROM DUNGEON GHYLL
2700 feet of ascent : 3 miles (3¼ via Three Tarns)

BOWFELL

Cambridge Crag
Bowfell Buttress

Bowfell
Links

Flat
Crags

Three
Tarns

climbers
traverse

The traditional
route proceeds via Three
Tarns, but it is now the
usual practice to follow
the ridge up from
the plateau

The Hell Gill
route has
interesting
scenery, but
is not to be
preferred to
the Band

From point A onwards, refer to
the larger-scale diagram on
the opposite page →

grassy
plateau

Green Tongue

Earing
Crag

Green Tongue
offers a quick
easy descent
to Mickleden

CRINKLE CRAGS (direct route)

Whorneyside
Force

Variation starts
from small
marshy depression

footbridge

Browney
Gill
rock on
top

Crinkle
Gill

bracken

The Band

This variation on the higher part
of the Band is not well known
— it avoids the wetter patches
on the main path, from which
its bifurcation, at both ends, is
indistinct and must be watched
for carefully. The word 'carefully'
is added to avoid ending the sentence
with a preposition, which should never
be used to end a sentence with

The path generally keeps to the
Oxendale side of the ridge but
here comes to the Mickleden
edge and provides a fine view
of Langdale Pikes.

Oxendale

Oxendale Beck

sheepfold

rock
gateway

stile

If descending by the
Band, watch for this
sharp turn right
— it is indistinct (on
grass) and there is
a crag just ahead

seat (no excuse for resting, so
early on the climb.
Press on!)

hurdle

looking west-north-west

400

Stool
End

MICKLEDEN

Gt. Langdale Beck

A well-known walkers'
highroad, the ascending
ridge of the Band provides
a defined and direct way
to the top of Bowfell with
no difficulties of route-finding
although the summit-structure
remains out of sight until the
height of 1750' is reached.

WALL END

farm road

Old
Hotel

Dungeon Ghyll

to create the diagram is
the area just beyond
Earing Crag, flagged on
the diagram as grassy
plateau. Because the
viewpoint (Side Pike) is
lower than the highest
point of The Band, in the
photo the plateau is
completely hidden.

Classic Haystacks

next page

Figure 4
*Graphic showing the moving bird over The Band
as it views the ascent of Bowfell*

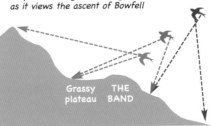

Grassy
plateau

THE
BAND

Warnscale Bothy

Green Crag

Green Crag Gully

Toreador Gully

Quarry road

Warnscale Beck

Haystacks 6

ASCENT FROM GATESGARTH
via WARNSCALE
1600 feet of ascent : 2¼ miles   HAYSTACKS

A : Slack Gill
B : Warn Gill
C : The Y Gully
D : Toreador Gully
E : Green Crag Gully
F : Little Round How
G : Great Round How
H : Blackbeck Tarn
I : Innominate Tarn

× circular sheepfold

BIRD'S EYE VIEW: The bird is resting on the main ridge of Fleetwith Pike and is looking towards the classic ascent of Haystacks. 12/7/11

28

Blackbeck
Tarn

The Y
Gully

Warn
Gill

Black
Beck

Path from
Gatesgarth

Big zigzag
(750ft)

Big zigzag
(just above
600ft
contour)

THE BIG
CLOSE-UP
DIAGRAM
IN ACTION

Unlike the ascent of Bowfell, there is a lot more detail shown in the latter stages of this classic climb of Haystacks, via Warnscale Bottom. Once again, the fixed-point photo cannot capture the whole climb, whereas the 'flying bird' can.

In the photograph, the plateau of Haystacks beyond the rim of crags cannot be seen (except for a tiny part of Blackbeck Tarn). In the diagram (facing page) AW is able to show a mass of detail beyond Green Crag – up to Blackbeck Tarn and beyond.

The word **typography** derives from the Greek τύπος (*typos*), meaning **form**, and γραφή (*graphe*), meaning **writing**. It is the technique of arranging type in order to make written language legible and readable – and is achieved by selecting the correct* typeface for the task in question, the size of the type, the length of the line, and various other sophisticated techniques, principally: **leading** (the amount of spacing between each line of type); **tracking** (the amount of space between multiple letters); and **kerning** (the space between pairs of letters). I know that AW wasn't trained in this; I doubt he knew these terms; nevertheless, that didn't stop him being . . .

HANDY WITH TYPE

HIGH RAISE   Low White Stones

2400.

ruined fence

path dodges from one side of the fence to the other to avoid wet ground

SERGEANT MAN

The first fence reached marks the head of Far Easedale, NOT Greenup. Go straight on here. This is a confusing place in mist.

Ferngill Crag

Recent generations of walkers have blazed a new trail to the head of Far Easedale. Originally, the bridle-path crossed the beck half-a-mile lower down, but it cannot now be traced on the ground although still shown on some maps in current use to the exclusion of the new track.

path crosses slab above fall, and needs care

Deer Bield Crag (vertical grey rock)

If the return is to be made to Grasmere, and the weather is clear, the alternative route via Sergeant Man (and then preferably Blea Rigg) is strongly recommended for the descent.

This is an interesting route besides being direct, practicable in mist, and avoiding other summits; as far as Greenup Edge use is made of the path along Far Easedale to Borrowdale.

NATURAL FEATURES

is usual to regard High Raise as Lakeland's centrally situated fell. An area without definite boundaries cannot have a determinable centre, and the 'most central fell' must remain a matter of individual opinion. A study of the o of the district suggests that High Raise decided bias to the south, however, and Ullscarf better fits the description, while,

TWO EXTRACTS: From THE CENTRAL FELLS; High Raise 2 (above) and the left-hand edge of High Raise 5 (the ascent from Grasmere).

These two extracts from the High Raise chapter (BOOK THREE) show how the size of a typeface and the way it is used are rather an art form. Both are at 75 per cent original size, so the proportion between them is constant; the 'natural features' section (above) is set at the full width of the page and there is a lot more text in one block than anywhere in the ascent diagram (left). Consequently, AW makes the text larger to compensate for the wider lines the reader had to scan. On the ascent diagram, notice the subtle changes in font size and style. The 'normal' hand-written font is upright – like this – and to stand out elsewhere AW occasionally writes in italic – *like this*. Notice, too, that longer sections of type are slightly bigger, especially the summary of the ascent (at the foot of the page), which was common throughout ascent diagrams in the guidebooks.

30

Typeface that helped create the SECOND EDITIONS

Serif Sans-Serif

Lakeland font

ABCDEFGHIJKLMNOPQRSTUVWXYZ
abcdefghijklmnopqrstuvwxyz
0123456789!@£%&*()?+-=<>|"""'';:,.:-)

The extraordinary efforts of Chris Jesty in revising all AW's original guidebooks to Lakeland would not have been possible without a little technical assistance. The decision by publisher Frances Lincoln to create a new typeface (also known as a font) based on AW's hand-written notes from the original guidebooks truly was a masterstroke. Imagine how strange the revised guidebooks would have been if all the new text that it was necessary to insert had NOT been in AW's hand-written style (or at least an amazing resemblance to it). The new typeface that was created is called Lakeland, and it is a *sans-serif* typeface. Sans, of course, is French for *without,* and the distinction between a typeface with a serif and without is easy to understand by looking at the words Serif Sans-Serif (above). The serif-style typeface is so named because of curvy bits at the end of letters such as 's' and 'f' and the way letters such as 'e' have subtle changes of thickness. The sans-serif font has letters of a uniform thickness.

The close-up of the Lakeland typeface shows that it is based on hand-drawn letters. Note the lower-case 'e' which has a straight diagonal crosspiece. This is the most noticeable feature of the new font.

*WHAT IS THE 'CORRECT' TYPEFACE?

'Normal' books are usually set in a serif font such as this (Caslon) and the text is invariably justified, so that the ends of lines (to the right and left) align with the line above and below – except when a paragraph ends, like this.

AW's hand-written font is a sans serif, and is considerably 'wider' than the font used for the preceeding paragraph. Here's what I mean . . .

'Normal' books are usually set in a serif font such as this (Caslon) and the text is invariably justified, so that the ends

. . . the hand-written font takes up more space, meaning fewer words in each line compared to the kind of font used in a traditional book.

WHY DID HE DO IT THIS WAY?

Why did AW head East at the start? Why those very odd BOOK ONE views? What did he change in the later guidebooks? And why were THE OUTLYING FELLS done in such a different style?

A few days before writing this chapter I just happened to tune in to the 'Blighty' TV channel and watch the second episode (a repeat that I hadn't seen before) of Julia Bradbury's *Coast To Coast* in which she followed AW's footsteps from St Bees Head to Robin Hood's Bay. The section she was walking was from Rosthwaite to Shap and included a stopover in Patterdale, where she went into the local shop and the cameras showed a sign that announced this was the first place where AW began selling BOOK ONE of A PICTORIAL GUIDE TO THE LAKELAND FELLS. And it struck me that, for lovers of the Lake District, this moment in 1955 was as exciting as the latest iPhone, PlayStation or Facebook launch is for technophiles and cyberfreaks in the 21st century.

This was the moment when traditional guidebooks (Baddeley and the rest), with their maps and long, written descriptions of the walk concerned, practically became irrelevant overnight. This was the moment when instant graphics, bite-sized pieces of useful information, detailed maps, beautifully crafted drawings and a chatty, witty and informative writing style all

combined in a guidebook like no other. Well, not for long!
Within two years along came another, a year later a
third, and then four more over the next eight years. So
were born the seven books that made up A PICTORIAL
GUIDE TO THE LAKELAND FELLS. And eight years later,
along came another one – THE OUTLYING FELLS OF
LAKELAND – to add to the originals and complete a set of
guidebooks that covered pretty well every substantial
height within the Lake District National Park and its
immediate vicinity.

What was your first book? BOOK ONE, or perhaps
THREE, maybe FOUR? Mine was BOOK SIX (for reasons
that are outlined in *Some personal notes in conclusion* – see
page 347). AW's guide to The North Western fells was a
beauty – in my opinion up there with the best of his
guidebooks, and . . . Hey, hey, hey, I hear you say, the 'best'?

*GOLDEN
GATEWAY:
A stunning
rainbow over
Ullswater,
Glenridding
and Patterdale
(as seen from
Arnison Crag)
seems like a
21st-century
metaphor for
the success of
AW's Lakeland
guidebooks.*
13/9/11

Aren't they all wonderful? Of course they are, but some are better than others (again, my opinion). But it's an opinion I would like to back up with facts; hence this chapter.

All inventions develop. Early Dyson cleaners were big and clunky and had annoyingly fiddly filters you had to empty by tapping them on the side of a waste bucket; now they're sleek and designer-friendly. Early Apple Mac computers had the aesthetic appeal of a wind farm, were excruciatingly slow and crashed a lot. Now they have a stable operating system, they whizz along at goodness-knows-how-many megahertz per second and their design is state-of-the-art. Why should we expect AW's guidebooks to be any different? In my opinion, they're not. In my opinion they didn't reach peak performance until BOOK FOUR, and many would argue that The Southern Fells was never bettered. But before we get that far, let's start at the very beginning . . .

BOOK ONE: THE EASTERN FELLS

Why did AW choose The Eastern Fells to be the 'guinea pig' as it were? Perhaps we can go back to that episode of *Coast To Coast* for an answer, in which it was revealed that he was a regular visitor to a B&B in Patterdale then called Ullswater View (indeed, there are framed signatures of his stays there, including one trip in 1944 with his first wife Ruth and son Peter). It's pretty clear too, from things he has written, that Ullswater and Patterdale were among his favourite places in Lakeland. I wouldn't mind betting that in 1952 he was so much better acquainted with this group of fells than any of the others that it made perfect sense to start there. And then there's The Far Eastern Fells to consider. Much of the area of BOOK TWO was less well known than its immediate neighbour one step to the west; certainly less 'sexy' – no Striding Edge over here, just striding-out territory. AW may not have been a marketing man but he was clearly shrewd enough to know that the launch area had to be one that was well known. And how much more well known could one get than Helvellyn, the single-most ascended mountain in the whole of Lakeland? Starting with The Eastern Fells and then moving on to the east was entirely logical.

So let's look at BOOK ONE – as it was then when AW wrote and illustrated it – with the benefit of some hindsight. The first thing to note was that AW didn't even design a dust jacket for it. He simply overlooked it. When the second book in the series was published (with a dust jacket) people who bought it could get a free dust jacket for the first book.

BOOK ONE, of course, was designed to be just one-seventh of one pictorial guidebook, so it has one unique feature: a two-page INTRODUCTION to the series (facing page), nicely designed with a partial border, two trees and two outlines of fells (they look like Blencathra and Skiddaw to me). And it features writing very much from the heart:

Surely there is no other place in this whole wonderful world quite like Lakeland . . . No other so exquisitely lovely, no other so charming, no other that

INTRODUCTION

INTRODUCTION

Surely there is no other place in this whole wonderful world quite like Lakeland ...no other so exquisitely lovely, no other so charming, no other that calls so insistently across a gulf of distance. All who truly love Lakeland are exiles when away from it.

Here, in small space, is the wonderland of childhood's dreams, lingering far beyond childhood through the span of a man's life: its enchantment grows with passing years and quiet eventide is enriched by the haunting sweetness of dear memories, memories that remain evergreen through the flight of time, that refresh and sustain in the darker days. How many, these memories .... the moment of wakening, and the sudden joyful realisation that this is to be another day of freedom on the hills .... the dawn chorus of bird-song ...... the delicate lacework of birches against the sky ..... morning sun drawing aside the veils of mist; black-stockinged lambs, in springtime, amongst the daffodils ...... silver cascades dancing and leaping down bracken steeps ..... autumn colours ....a red fox running over snow ..... the silence of lonely hills .... storm and tempest in the high places, and the unexpected glimpses of valleys dappled in sunlight far beneath the swirling clouds ....rain, and the intimate shelter of lichened walls ...... fierce winds on the heights and soft breezes that are no more than gentle caresses ....a sheepdog watching its master

.... the snow and ice and freezing stillnesses of midwinter: a while world, rosy-pink as the sun goes down........ the supreme moment when the top cairn comes into sight at last, only minutes away, after the long climb........ the small ragged sheep that brave the blizzards..... the symphonies of murmuring streams, unending, with never a discord ....curling smoke from the chimneys of the farm down below amongst the trees, where the day shall end .....oil lamps in flagged kitchens, huge fires in huge fireplaces, huge suppers.......... glittering moonlight on placid waters ..... stars above dark peaks ..... the tranquillity that comes before sleep, when thoughts are of the day that is gone and the day that is to come ..... All these memories, and so many more, breathing anew the rare quality and magical atmosphere of Lakeland ....memories that belong to Lakeland, and could not belong in the same way to any other place............ memories that enslave the mind forever.

Many are they who have fallen under the spell of Lakeland, and many are they who have been moved to tell of their affection, in story and verse and picture and song.

This book is one man's way of expressing his devotion to Lakeland's friendly hills. It was conceived, and is born, after many years of inarticulate worshipping at their shrines. It is, in very truth, a love-letter.

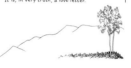

calls so insistently across a gulf of distance. All who truly love Lakeland are exiles when away from it.

Here, in small space, is the wonderland of childhood dreams, lingering far beyond childhood through the span of a man's life: its enchantment grows with passing years and quiet eventide is enriched by the haunting sweetness of dear memories, memories that remain evergreen through the flight of time, that refresh and sustain in the darker days ... Many are they who have fallen under the spell of Lakeland, and many are they who have been moved to tell of their affection, in story and verse and picture and song.

This book is one man's way of expressing his devotion to Lakeland's friendly hills. It was conceived, and is born, after many years of inarticulate worshipping at their shrines. It is, in truth, a love letter.

After such a poetic start and with such an innovatory approach (which other guidebook writers have since tried but failed to emulate) BOOK ONE was always going to be a publishing phenomenon even if initial sales were slow because industrial action on the nation's railways hit distribution. At the time, it must have seemed amazing to its first purchasers. However, with the benefit of hindsight we can see that AW was feeling his way in this initial publication. Some things clearly didn't work. First, the VIEWS. In three chapters – **Catstycam**, **Dollywaggon Pike** and **Nethermost Pike** – silhouettes of selected fells were drawn (barely the size of a pinkie fingernail) which required the reader to spin the guidebook to see tiny drawings that hardly seemed to differ. It didn't work and such views were never seen again. Likewise, the more common 'bicycle wheel'-style view that he used through all the guidebooks was not as detailed and developed in the first book. For example, the view from the summit of **Stybarrow Dodd** is fine around the edges but includes only one summit from BOOK THREE – Harrison Stickle – missing out a whole swathe of middle-distance fells entirely. From BOOK TWO onwards AW became much more adept at squeezing closer fells into such views.

Now on to **Helvellyn**, the daddy of the eastern fells. Because of the sheer number of ascents (from east and west) AW chose a way of presenting them that he didn't use again for any similar fell with multiple ascents. From each side (east and west) he allocated one page to summarise each route of ascent in a single paragraph each; on the opposite page was a cross-section of each ascent. The 'bird's eye'-style diagrams were on separate pages, some of which had scant or no notes. And 'five-star' ascents – and I'm thinking in particular of **Helvellyn** via Striding Edge – were given none of the special treatment given to similar ascents in later books such as Pillar via the High Level Route, Bowfell via Climbers Traverse and Great Slab, and even the upper slopes of a relatively minor fell such as Eagle Crag. I'm absolutely convinced that if The Eastern Fells had been, say, the third book in the series there would have been a detailed, full-page, almost step-by-step diagram for Striding Edge. On the ascent diagram all that's written about Striding Edge is this 13-word sentence: *A rock-chimney at the end of the Edge is a little awkward.*

In general, there is a lot less detail in BOOK ONE than in later books. The diagrams are less detailed (with fewer rocks, boulders and scree) and the spaces around the maps are mainly white, in sharp contrast to later books where every inch is crammed with little asides, historical titbits and local legends. There is also some repetition (the repeated lament about Keppel Cove Tarn) and a complete absence of what I will call 'special features' – more of that later.

This sounds like criticism; it isn't. Considering AW tossed away nearly 100 pages (and several months' work) while undertaking his first book in the series, it really is a staggering achievement. An achievement that became even more significant with the publication of

BOOK TWO: THE FAR EASTERN FELLS

The first thing to notice: no **Catstycam**-like views, and better bicycle-wheel views, with more detail. Next, more rocks, boulders and scree in the diagrams of ascent – just look at the ruggedness of Mardale Ill Bell 5 from BOOK TWO for an example, and compare that to Nethermost Pike 6 from BOOK ONE (facing page). Do you see the difference?

BOOK TWO gives the impression of being far 'busier', of more happening on the pages, especially the maps where AW filled up white space rather more successfully than in BOOK ONE. It still hadn't reached the heights of later books in that respect, but it was a considerable (and noticeable) improvement. The irony, of course, is that the far eastern fells are generally smoother and less rugged than the eastern fells – yet the books tell a different story!

Finally, on to the single most important innovation in BOOK TWO – and you will find this on page three of the **Loadpot Hill** chapter. This was a full-page feature with the heading *The antiquities and oddities of Moor Divock*. It was a page all about the stone circles, boundary stones, the influence of the Romans, the Druids and goodness knows who else, and it was significant because this was the first time AW had digressed – in a full-page format – from the basics of climbing a fell, checking the view and then descending safely. Such an approach was to be a theme of his later books.

There was one other interesting aspect, and that was the cover drawing of BOOK TWO. In all the other six PICTORIAL GUIDES the front-cover drawing featured some significant landmark or fell that was, without exception, rocky and rugged: BOOK ONE – Striding Edge on **Helvellyn**; BOOK THREE – The Howitzer (the summit rocks of **Helm Crag**); BOOK FOUR – **Scafell's** greatest feature and one of the grandest sights in Lakeland, Scafell Crag; BOOK FIVE – Sharp Edge on **Blencathra**; BOOK SIX – The Notch on **Hopegill Head**; and BOOK SEVEN – the summit of **Steeple**. The front-cover drawing of BOOK TWO was of a cairn (on the top of Artlecrag Pike, a shoulder of **Branstree**). Yes, it's a nice cairn, but it's a cairn. Couldn't AW have found a stunning mountain landmark to have illustrated this book? Well, probably not, because I can't think of one. The Long Stile ridge of **High Street** is arguably the most exciting situation in the far eastern fells, but fine though it is it's hardly a Striding Edge.

RUGGED: Mardale Ill Bell ascent diagram.

SMOOTHER: Much less Nethermost 'noise'.

BOOK THREE: THE CENTRAL FELLS

The first question that needs to be answered is why was BOOK THREE the third in the series when it could easily have been the seventh? Think about this: we know AW was a very logical man; a trained accountant; a patient, diligent type – he had to be to plan the 13-year undertaking that was A PICTORIAL GUIDE TO THE LAKELAND FELLS. He was logical when he worked out the structure of his eighth Lakeland guidebook. The chapters of the fells featured in THE OUTLYING FELLS OF LAKELAND started in the south-eastern corner of the perimeter and then went round the edge clockwise. The first seven guidebooks, following such a pattern, would then have been in this order: **The Eastern Fells**, **The Far Eastern Fells**, The Southern Fells, The Western Fells, The North Western Fells, **The Northern Fells**, and then, only then, The Central Fells. Perfectly logical – but not perfect marketing, because it would have meant the two books featuring such grand fells as Scafell Pike, Bowfell, Crinkle Crags, Great Gable, High Stile, Pillar and the rest would have been numbers three and four in the list. I'm pretty convinced that AW had enough commercial savvy to know he had to keep one of these two for the final book, and it simply had to be The Western Fells of course, because of Haystacks (keeping the best – in his opinion – to last). My guess is that's why The Central Fells are where they are chronologically. They're not the biggest (the lowest group of all seven with the highest fell being High Raise at just 2500ft), but what they lack in inches they make up for in the astonishing number of very popular fells: Harrison Stickle, Pike o'Stickle, Pavey Ark, Silver How, Loughrigg Fell, Helm Crag, Walla Crag, Grange Fell . . . all delectable in their own right and, crucially, all within easy striking distance of tourist centres such as Great Langdale, Ambleside, Grasmere, Keswick and Borrowdale. It made a perfect third book – packed with interest after the relative quiet of the fells way out east.

There really is no feeling that the pages somehow go blank, and, like BOOK TWO, it includes a full-page feature – the Stone Age axe factory on Pike o'Stickle. And there were three more firsts: the first big close-up diagrams to deal with particularly intricate or exciting parts of the climb – these were Eagle Crag from Stonethwaite and Jack's Rake (Pavey Ark chapter); the first large-scale maps (six inches to a mile instead of the usual two inches to a mile) which were in evidence in the Harrison Stickle, Pavey Ark and Loft Crag chapters; and the first super-detailed summit map – the Helm Crag chapter; its top surely warranted one. This was a book that moved up another notch in terms of detail and interest, perhaps helped by there being fewer drawings of lakes (see page 182)! It was a perfect hors d'oeuvre ahead of the main course, which was of course . . .

BOOK FOUR: THE SOUTHERN FELLS

The book that has it all: three of AW's 'best six' fells – Scafell Pike, Bowfell and Crinkle Crags; the first mention that a best half-dozen was in the offing (with a nice 'tease' to BOOK SEVEN in the process); two fantastic mountain massifs – Scafell-Bowfell and Coniston Old Man and its satellites; more super-detailed summits (Scafell Pike and Great End); and a seemingly never-ending list of special features:

Two-page special on **Coppermines Valley** (Coniston Old Man); one-page special on **Boulder Valley** (Coniston Old Man); one-page special on **the names of fells** (Coniston Old Man); four-page ridge plan of **Bowfell-Crinkle Crags** (Crinkle Crags); two-page special on

Esk Hause (Esk Pike); one-page special on **The Valley Route** (Great End); one-page special on **Cust's Gully** (Great End); one-page special on **Sty Head** (Great End); one-page special on **The Valley of Tarn Beck** (Grey Friar); one-page special on the **Roman Fort** (Hard Knott); three-page special on **Rossett Gill** (Rossett Pike); one-page special on **Dove's Nest Caves/Caves in Lakeland** (Rosthwaite Fell); one-page special on **Broad Stand** (Scafell); one-page special on **Lord's Rake** (Scafell); one-page special on **The West Wall Traverse** (Scafell); and a two-page special on Wetherlam's **Hundred Holes**.

No wonder, then, that it was the biggest (pagination) of the PICTORIAL GUIDES; no wonder that it set new standards for the remaining books to follow; no wonder that whenever I've lost my copy (fell out of my pocket on Brown Tongue; 'borrowed' by a friend; left in the USA) I've always forked out for a replacement. Counting the second edition, by my reckoning I've acquired this particular guidebook five times! It's about time the publishers gave me a break . . .

There was another detailed close-up of an intricate part of an ascent (**Climbers Traverse** on Bowfell), and yet more firsts: the first double-page drawing (**Great Slab** on Bowfell). AW really did love this most majestic of all fells – and he's not the only one. There soon followed the second double-page drawing (**Wastwater Screes** below Whin Rigg); a detailed drawing outlining the many buttresses and gullies of Dow Crag (compare this with the rather less impressive analysis of **Dove Crag** in BOOK ONE); the first 'key to a drawing', a device he clearly liked because subsequently he used it on a number of occasions – this was on Great End 2, showing geographical aspects of the mountain's page-one drawing on the facing page; the first complete two-page ascent diagrams: *Scafell Pike 15-16, 17-18* and *21-22* (*Pavey Ark 5* did not include a diagram; *Eagle Crag 3-4* included a ridge walk); the first, and only, soliloquy (Scafell Pike); the first *Some personal notes in conclusion* to include a self-portrait; and the first cross-reference to *Some Personal notes in conclusion*, from the Pike o'Blisco chapter. Finally, there was more humour, which might be because he was really getting in to the swing of this guidebook thing by then. And then, after the Lord Mayor's Show . . .

BOOK FIVE: THE NORTHERN FELLS

Which is a little unfair considering two of Lakeland's mightiest mountains grace its pages in some style, but I think AW summed it up in his final observations when he stated that *Caldbeck Fells are NOT 'worth all England else'*. Like the fells in BOOK TWO, he pointed out that much of the area is unspoiled and free from the crowds toiling up to Rossett Pass or Sty Head Pass; he likened the terrain of Skiddaw Forest (the 'back o'beyond') to Scotland. Perhaps this lonely area will get more attention now that Skiddaw House has been taken over by the Youth Hostel Association.

I wouldn't mind betting that when AW mapped out the order of the guidebooks he thought to himself: 'Boy, I'll need a breather after BOOK FOUR.' Well, he might have got it on the gentler gradients of the Uldale Fells and the Caldbeck Fells, but on the southern fringes are two fells which are among the best loved and most impressive in Lakeland, one of which has a touch of the Wild West about it. They are, of course, **Skiddaw** and **Blencathra**: the former, one of the district's 3000-footers, being a massive structure made from a different, softer rock than the volcanic rock giants further south; the latter, one of the most spectacular mountains in Lakeland with a bewildering choice of routes to the summit. The chapter on **Blencathra**, occupying 36 pages, is a mighty tribute to a mighty mountain. It features no fewer than 12 ascents and four full-page drawings, and includes the classic climb up its central ridge (Halls Fell), the other spectacular ascent via the serrated ridge of Sharp Edge, plus that 'Wild West' route (via Blease Gill). There are four features:

> One-page special on the **River Glenderamackin (Souther Fell)**; one-page special on **Carrock Fell mines**; two-page special on **Dodd Wood (Dodd)**; one-page special on the **Caldbeck Fell mines (High Pike)**. Also, there is an interesting legend about the **spectral army of Soutra Fell (Souther Fell)**.

This is a nicely put-together book for the walker seeking gentler things than further south (with the exception of **Blencathra** of course), and it does have one first: the first chapter to have an odd number of pages (**Ullock Pike**). But in his closing notes, it's clear that AW had other things on his mind – The North Western Fells, *which I have long considered the most delectable of all.*

BOOK SIX: THE NORTH WESTERN FELLS

After two quiet years 'oop north' this is the book that, I suspect, AW had been longing to do. At the end of BOOK FIVE he summed it up nicely: *All my walks during the past few years have ended at Keswick Bus Station, where there is a splendid open view of the mountains between Borrowdale and Bassenthwaite, a tremendously exciting array of sharp peaks and lofty ridges.* This is a book that is positively jam-packed with special features:

> One-page special on the **caves and quarries** of Castle Crag; two-page special on **Force Crag** (Grisedale Pike); one-page special on **the hinterland of Goat Crag** (High Spy); one-page special on **Goldscope Mine** (Hindscarth); one-page special on **Hobcarton Crag** (Hopegill Head); and a four-page special on **Wythop Valley and Wythop Wood** (Sale Fell) – this latter feature is particularly fascinating (*see* Strange geography, pages 260-261).

And it's oozing with lovely writing: the road to Scale Hill (Hopegill Head), the thick black line (Castle Crag 4), the eulogy about Dale Head's summit cairn, and the introductions to Catbells, Rannerdale Knotts and Castle Crag immediately spring to mind. There's more humour (the abominable snowman, Outerside 1, is a classic); and there are two outline drawings detailing views that work very effectively (Causey Pike 9 and 10).

BOOK SIX is a wonderful guidebook. It's not the biggest, it doesn't have the 'best' mountains – though it does have some of the best ridge walks you'll find anywhere in Lakeland – and it's not a trailblazer in terms of the development of the series. What it is, however, is the book that exudes the most enthusiasm: *In other areas I have sometimes tired a little of repeatedly tramping the same tracks, but not here.*

BOOK SEVEN: THE WESTERN FELLS

This is the book of the chapter: by that, I mean that it may not have as many special features as BOOK FOUR, but it makes up for that with a consistently high standard of great chapters about great fells: Haystacks (of course); Great Gable (rivalling Blencathra as the best chapter of all 214 in the PICTORIAL GUIDES for sheer depth and interest in the mountain itself); Pillar (a wonderful chapter, a wonderful mountain); Base Brown (a fantastic opener about a medium-size fell that wouldn't normally attract lots of attention even though it overlooks the sacred Seathwaite); Yewbarrow (the perfect closing page); Fleetwith Pike (page 6 is simply a beautiful piece of layout); Red Pike Wasdale (an enthusiastic appreciation of an underrated fell with another great piece of design – page 6). The final PICTORIAL GUIDE is like this, I believe, for two reasons: The Western Fells are an extraordinarily strong set of great mountains (only rivalled by The Southern Fells in that respect, IMO), so AW just let them do their own talking; and he didn't have any more tricks in his locker to unveil – although some of the old ones were never done as well as in this book, in particular the close-up details of the Gable Girdle (two pages devoted to the walk around Great Gable) and the topography of its magnificent Great Napes (four pages). There are, however, the usual clutch of interesting features:

One-page special on **Stockdale Moor** (Caw Fell); two-page special on the high cross-country route **Moses' Trod** (Great Gable); three-page special on the **Pillar Rock portfolio** (Pillar).

All this . . . plus treasure on Lank Rigg . . . Yewbarrow becomes the second fell to have an odd number of pages . . . and *Some personal notes in conclusion* that everybody had been waiting for listed not only his 'best six' but a whole lot of other bests. I'm sure many people would rate this as AW's best guidebook; if not, it surely pushes BOOK FOUR very hard.

THE OUTLYING FELLS OF LAKELAND

On the penultimate page of BOOK SEVEN, AW writes: *Regretfully, I reject suggestions of a Book Eight: 'The Outlying Fells'.* He rejected the idea for only six years before beginning work on his final Lakeland guidebook, the first edition of which was published in 1974.

To many of his fans, it must have come as something of a shock (although perhaps not to those who had seen A COAST TO COAST WALK a year earlier, which had the same 'feel' as this guidebook). It was packed with tops to be sure (116 at the latest count – there has always been some confusion about this number but that is put to rest on page 55), but instead of every fell getting its own chapter as in the PICTORIAL GUIDES, many were lumped together with others, making a total of 56 chapters. And instead of ascents, AW devised walks. The idiosyncrasies of THE OUTLYING FELLS are explained in some detail on page 60.

Personally, I think AW succeeds magnificently with this book. To have based it on the PICTORIAL GUIDES would have only invited comparison with its illustrious predecessors, which I am not sure he would have wanted. By approaching the subject in a different fashion – no less interesting and informative – to suit a different market (older, less active walkers) he gave his final Lakeland guidebook a unique identity. Rather like its author, in fact.

Upper Kentmere, as seen on the descent

1 : Rainsborrow Crag
2 : Ill Bell
3 : Froswick
4 : Thornthwaite Crag
5 : High Street
6 : Mardale Ill Bell
7 : Nan Bield Pass
8 : slopes of Harter Fell

16

LOOKING GOOD: *Some of AW's finest drawings are to be found in* THE OUTLYING FELLS. *This is a view in the chapter on Green Quarter Fell. Look at the subtle way he picks out the light and shadow of the valley bottom in a sketch that is as delightful as the vista itself.*

The Outlying Fells in detail – see pages 54-61

TAKE A BOUGH

Some of the trees that lit up (well, not quite!) the PICTORIAL GUIDES

AW has a love-hate relationship with the trees of Lakeland. He loves the naturally occurring trees that softened the mountainous landscapes, the trees that cloaked the valleys in shimmering green and golden reds, the brave survivors that clung on in places where a rock-climber would have had trouble making a belay.

He hates the planted, regimented evergreens that obliterated once-beautiful places such as Ennerdale (*ten thousand saw I at a glance* – and he wasn't referring to daffodils), Thirlmere and others. This is what he writes in the Grange Fell chapter, beside the illustration of the delightful wooded ascent from Grange: *Every one of these trees has been drawn with affection: they make a wonderful display. Witness here how Nature arranges her plantings, and* compare with Whinlatter and Thirlmere and Ennerdale!

> 1500
> .1400 A young rowan has secured a precarious roothold on this crag. Can it survive? Will some kind reader write to the author in 1970 and say it is still alive and well?

ROBINSON'S ROWAN: First edition.

He had his favourite single trees or clusters, too; such as The Mosedale Tree (the only named tree in the Lakeland OS maps), illustrated right in the Mellbreak chapter and pictured below; the young rowan tree on Robinson (see the first edition flashback, above). As Chris Jesty reported in the second edition of BOOK SIX, this tree is still flourishing. And then there was the solitary Scots pine near Holme Fell (now gone, but replaced by a younger version), and the similar species on Castle Crag – *There are magnificent Scots pines near the wall at the top of the wood* (pictured top right).

AW loved these, and many more around the district that he drew either singly or in groups – always with an adoring pen.

FINE PINES: From the Castle Crag **chapter.**
5/11/10

TAKE CARE
DO NOT START FIRE

and so waste the effort spent in drawing all the little trees on this map. The Forestry Commission, too, will be annoyed.

PLEA FROM THE HART(ER): From the Harter Fell **chapter.**

YEW TUBE: The only tree to be given a name on an Ordnance Survey map – The Mosedale Tree, beside Mellbreak.
26/4/05

THE HIGH LIFE

All the 'Wainwrights', all in one place, at a glance

HIGHEST IN ENGLAND: The frozen summit rocks of Scafell Pike.   23/11/07

Here they are . . . all 214 'Wainwrights' – the individual fells – from A PICTORIAL GUIDE TO THE LAKELAND FELLS in one place – actually, spread over seven (eight if you count the facing page) jam-packed pages, but let's not be pedantic, shall we?

Well, some pedantry is in order, because we're sticking with the quaint concept of measuring the height of Lakeland's fells in feet. There's something distinctly underwhelming about proclaiming in a Keswick pub that there are only four 914.4-metre summits in the Lake District, isn't there?

And we're sticking to the heights given in the guidebooks (the second edition revisions) - so that means no 3209ft Scafell Pike, no 3117ft Helvellyn, no 2959ft Bowfell (sounds of loud hoorays from the Dog and Gun...)

Now sit back and enjoy a stats fest.

EXTRA FEET: The dramatic 14ft summit cairn on Thornthwaite Crag would move the fell up two places in the rankings (44= to 42) if the cairn counted as part of the fell (it doesn't!).

5/3/09

RANK	NAME	HEIGHT (feet)	BOOK	HEIGHT LOWER THAN PREVIOUS
1	**Scafell Pike**	**3210**	S	n/a
2	Scafell	3162	S	48
3	**Helvellyn**	**3118**	E	**44**
4	Skiddaw	3053	N	65
5	**Great End**	**2984**	S	69
6	Bowfell	2960	S	24
7	**Great Gable**	**2949**	W	**11**
8	Pillar	2927	W	22
9	**Nethermost Pike**	**2920**	E	**7**
10	Catstycam	2917	E	3
11	**Esk Pike**	**2903**	S	**14**
12	Raise	2897	E	6
13	**Fairfield**	**2863**	E	**34**
14	Blencathra	2847	N	16
15	**Skiddaw Little Man**	**2837**	N	**10**
16	White Side	2832	E	5
17	**Crinkle Crags**	**2816**	S	**16**
18	Dollywaggon Pike	2815	E	1
19	**Great Dodd**	**2812**	E	**3**
20	Grasmoor	2791	NW	21

THE 214 FELLS

EASTERN
35 fells: 80,143ft
Ave. per fell: 2290ft

FAR EASTERN
36 fells: 75,923ft
Ave. per fell: 2109ft

CENTRAL
27 fells: 48,605ft
Ave. per fell: 1800ft

SOUTHERN
30 fells: 68,182ft
Ave. per fell: 2273ft

NORTHERN
24 fells: 51,115ft
Ave. per fell: 2130ft

NORTH WESTERN
29 fells: 55,860ft
Ave. per fell: 1926ft

WESTERN
33 fells: 70,649ft
Ave. per fell: 2141ft

21	**Stybarrow Dodd**	**2770**	E	**19**
22	Scoat Fell	2760	W	10
23	**St Sunday Crag**	**2756**	E	**4**
24	Eel Crag	2749	NW	7
25	**High Street**	**2718**	FE	**31**
26	Red Pike	2707	W	11
27	**Hart Crag**	**2698**	E	**9**
28	Steeple	2687	W	9
29	**Lingmell**	**2649**	S	**38**
30	High Stile	2644	W	5
31	**High Raise**	**2634**	FE	**10**
32	Coniston Old Man	2633	S	1
33=	**Kirk Fell**	**2630**	W	**3**
33=	Swirl How	2630	S	0
35	**Green Gable**	**2628**	W	**2**
36	Haycock	2618	W	10
37	**Brim Fell**	**2611**	S	**7**
38=	Dove Crag	2598	E	13
38=	**Rampsgill Head**	**2598**	FE	**0**
40	Grisedale Pike	2593	NW	5
41	**Watson's Dodd**	**2589**	E	**4**
42	Great Carrs	2575	S	14
43	**Allen Crags**	**2572**	S	**3**
44=	Glaramara	2569	S	9
44=	**Thornthwaite Crag**	**2569**	FE	**3**
46	Kidsty Pike	2560	FE	0
47	**Dow Crag**	**2555**	S	**4**
48	Harter Fell	2552	FE	3
49	**Red Screes**	**2546**	E	**6**
50=	Grey Friar	2536	S	10
50=	**Sail**	**2536**	NW	**0**
52	Wandope	2533	NW	3
53	**Hopegill Head**	**2525**	NW	**12**
54	Great Rigg	2513	E	12
55=	**Caudale Moor**	**2502**	FE	**11**

THE 'LOW' LANGDALES

From Windermere, the Langdale Pikes look like mighty mountains (they are, of course, but not in height terms - at 2415ft Harrison Stickle only clocks in at 68= on the 214 list). Incidentally, in the first edition of BOOK THREE Harrison Stickle's height was given as 2403ft; it has grown by 12ft since, which has moved it up from 71st to equal 68th.

MIGHTY MOUNTAINS: *The Langdale Pikes from Black Fell.*   13/12/10

SNOW UP ABOVE: Froswick, the distinctive summit of Ill Bell, and little Troutbeck Tongue (foreground) from Kirkstone Pass.
13/2/12

55=	Wetherlam	2502	S	0
57	**High Raise**	**2500**	C	2
58	Slight Side	2499	S	1
59	**Mardale Ill Bell**	**2496**	FE	3
60	Ill Bell	2484	FE	12
61	**Hart Side**	**2481**	E	3
62	Red Pike	2479	W	2
63	**Dale Head**	**2473**	NW	6
64	Carl Side	2447	N	28
65	**High Crag**	**2443**	W	4
66	The Knott	2423	FE	20
67	**Robinson**	**2417**	NW	6
68=	Harrison Stickle	2415	C	2
68=	**Seat Sandal**	**2415**	E	2
70	Sergeant Man	2414	C	1
71	**Long Side**	**2405**	N	9
72	Kentmere Pike	2397	FE	4
73	**Hindscarth**	**2385**	NW	12
74	Clough Head	2381	E	4
75	**Ullscarf**	**2370**	C	11
76	Froswick	2359	FE	11
77	**Birkhouse Moor**	**2356**	E	3
78	Thunacar Knott	2351	C	5
79=	**Brandreth**	**2344**	W	7
79=	Lonscale Fell	2344	N	0
81	**Branstree**	**2339**	FE	5
82	Knott	2329	N	10
83	**Pike o'Stickle**	**2323**	C	6
84	Whiteside	2317	NW	6
85	**Yoke**	**2316**	FE	1

STATS & TRIVIA

Lakeland's pair of 'Ill Bells' (Mardale Ill Bell and Ill Bell) are in consecutive places (59 and 60) with just 12ft between them. Which perhaps isn't such an amazing coincidence: both Lakeland's High Pikes (**High Pike**, 2157ft; **High Pike**, 2155ft), also in consecutive places (107 and 108), have just 2ft between them. The four other 'pairs' are somewhat further apart (in places and feet):

High Raise (2634ft) and High Raise (2500ft) are 26 places apart (31 and 57 respectively);

Harter Fell (2552ft) and Harter Fell (2140ft) are 65 places apart (48 and 113 respectively);

Red Pike (W) (2707ft) and Red Pike (B) (2479ft) are 36 places apart (26 and 62 respectively);

Tarn Crag (2176ft) and Tarn Crag (1801ft) are 47 places apart (104 and 151 respectively).

DISTINCTIVE TOP: The serpentine summit ridge of Causey Pike, from Scar Crags.   2/6/11

86	Bowscale Fell	2306	N	10
87	Pike o'Blisco	2304	S	2
88=	Caw Fell	2288	W	16
88=	Pavey Ark	2288	C	0
90	Grey Knotts	2287	W	1
91	Gray Crag	2286	FE	1
92	Rest Dodd	2283	FE	3
93	Loft Crag	2270	C	13
94	Seatallan	2266	W	4
95	Great Calva	2265	N	1
96	Cold Pike	2259	S	6
97	Bannerdale Crags	2241	N	18
98	Ullock Pike	2230	N	11
99	Sheffield Pike	2215	E	15
100	Wether Hill	2210	FE	5
101	Bakestall	2208	N	2
102	Scar Crags	2205	NW	3
103	Loadpot Hill	2201	FE	4
104	Tarn Crag	2176	FE	25
105	Carrock Fell	2169	N	7
106	Whiteless Pike	2165	NW	4
107	High Pike	2157	N	8
108	High Pike	2155	E	2
109	Place Fell	2154	FE	1
110	Selside Pike	2149	FE	5
111	Middle Dodd	2146	E	3
112	High Spy	2143	NW	3
113	Harter Fell	2140	S	3
114	Great Sca Fell	2136	N	4
115	Fleetwith Pike	2126	W	10
116	Base Brown	2120	W	6
117	Rossett Pike	2106	S	14
118	Grey Crag	2093	FE	13
119	Little Hart Crag	2091	E	2
120	Causey Pike	2090	NW	1
121=	Starling Dodd	2077	W	13
121=	Mungrisdale Common	2077	N	0
123	Yewbarrow	2058	W	19
124	Birks	2040	E	18
125	Hartsop Dodd	2028	FE	12

HIGHS & LOWS

EASTERN
HIGHEST:
Helvellyn – 3118ft
LOWEST:
Arnison Crag – 1424ft
DIFFERENCE: 1694ft

FAR EASTERN
HIGHEST:
High Street – 2718ft
LOWEST:
Troutbeck Tongue – 1191ft
DIFFERENCE: 1527ft

CENTRAL
HIGHEST:
High Raise – 2500ft
LOWEST:
Loughrigg Fell – 1101ft
DIFFERENCE: 1399ft

SOUTHERN
HIGHEST:
Scafell Pike – 3210ft
LOWEST:
Holme Fell – 1040ft
DIFFERENCE: 2170ft

NORTHERN
HIGHEST:
Skiddaw – 3053ft
LOWEST:
Latrigg – 1203ft
DIFFERENCE: 1850ft

NORTH WESTERN
HIGHEST:
Grasmoor – 2791ft
LOWEST:
Castle Crag – 951ft
DIFFERENCE: 1840ft

WESTERN
HIGHEST:
Great Gable – 2949ft
LOWEST:
Low Fell – 1352ft
DIFFERENCE: 1597ft

THREE-FIGURE FELL: Castle Crag is 951ft high.   7/3/07

126	Great Borne	2019	W	9
127	**Heron Pike**	**2008**	**E**	**9**
128	High Seat	1995	C	13
129	**Illgill Head**	**1983**	**S**	**12**
130	Seathwaite Fell	1970	S	13
131	**Haystacks**	**1959**	**W**	**11**
132	Bleaberry Fell	1932	C	27
133	**Shipman Knotts**	**1926**	**FE**	**6**
134	Brae Fell	1920	N	6
135	**Middle Fell**	**1908**	**W**	**12**
136	Ard Crags	1906	NW	2
137=	**Maiden Moor**	**1887**	**NW**	**19**
137=	The Nab	1887	FE	0
139	**Blake Fell**	**1878**	**W**	**9**
140	Sergeant's Crag	1873	C	5
141	**Hartsop Above How**	**1870**	**E**	**3**
142	Outerside	1863	NW	7
143	**Angletarn Pikes**	**1857**	**FE**	**6**
144	Brock Crags	1842	FE	15
145	**Knott Rigg**	**1824**	**NW**	**18**
146=	Lord's Seat	1811	NW	13
146=	**Steel Fell**	**1811**	**C**	**0**
148	Rosthwaite Fell	1807	S	4
149	**Meal Fell**	**1804**	**N**	**3**
150	Hard Knott	1803	S	1
151	**Tarn Crag**	**1801**	**C**	**2**
152	Blea Rigg	1776	C	25
153	**Lank Rigg**	**1775**	**W**	**1**
154	Calf Crag	1762	C	13
155	**Great Mell Fell**	**1760**	**E**	**2**
156	Whinn Rigg	1755	S	5
157	**Arthur's Pike**	**1747**	**FE**	**8**
158=	Gavel Fell	1726	W	21
158=	**Great Cockup**	**1726**	**N**	**0**
160	Bonscale Pike	1718	FE	8
161	**Crag Fell**	**1716**	**W**	**2**
162	Souther Fell	1713	N	3
163	**High Hartsop Dodd**	**1702**	**E**	**11**
164	Whinlatter	1696	NW	4
165	**Sallows**	**1691**	**FE**	**5**
166	Mellbreak	1676	W	15
167=	**Beda Fell**	**1670**	**FE**	**6**
167=	Broom Fell	1670	NW	0
167=	**Hen Comb**	**1670**	**W**	**0**
170	Low Pike	1667	E	3
171	**High Tove**	**1665**	**C**	**2**
172	Little Mell Fell	1657	E	8
173	**Stone Arthur**	**1652**	**E**	**5**

STATS & TRIVIA

LIVES UP TO ITS NAME: Red Pike (Buttermere) gets its name from the soil in the area. 7/6/06

The Lake District is a colourful place – but how colourful are its fells? Well, surprisingly, not that much . . . On the 214 list there are only SEVEN colours (eight if you include American spelling!).

Here are the 14 (or 16) fells that have a colo(u)r in their title:

RED: **Screes**, two **Pikes** (Wasdale and **Buttermere**).

WHITE: **Side**, **Whiteside** and **Whiteless Pike** (perhaps this latter fell is – literally – colour<u>less</u>!).

GREEN: **Gable, Crag**.

GREY: **Friar, Knotts, Crag**.

GRAY: **Crag, . . . stones**.

Base **BROWN**.

SILVER: **How**.

BLACK: **Fell**.

174	Eagle Crag	1650	C	2
175	**Dodd**	**1647**	**N**	**3**
176	Green Crag	1602	S	45
177	**Grike**	**1601**	**W**	**1**
178	Wansfell	1597	FE	4
179=	**Longlands Fell**	**1585**	**N**	**8**
179=	Sour Howes	1585	FE	0
181	**Gowbarrow Fell**	**1579**	**E**	**6**
182	Armboth Fell	1570	C	9
183	**Burnbank Fell**	**1558**	**W**	**12**
184	Barf	1536	NW	22
185	**Lingmoor Fell**	**1530**	**S**	**6**
186	Raven Crag	1520	C	10
187	**Great Crag**	**1500**	**C**	**20**
188	Barrow	1494	NW	6
189	**Catbells**	**1481**	**NW**	**13**
190	Graystones	1476	NW	5
191	**Binsey**	**1466**	**N**	**10**
192=	Glenridding Dodd	1450	E	16
192=	**Nab Scar**	**1450**	**E**	**0**
194	Arnison Crag	1424	E	26
195	**Steel Knotts**	**1414**	**FE**	**10**
196	Buckbarrow	1410	W	4
197	**Gibson Knott**	**1379**	**C**	**31**
198=	Fellbarrow	1363	W	16
198=	**Grange Fell**	**1363**	**C**	**0**
200	Low Fell	1352	W	11
201	**Helm Crag**	**1299**	**C**	**53**
202	Silver How	1292	C	7
203	**Hallin Fell**	**1271**	**FE**	**21**
204	Walla Crag	1234	C	37
205	**Ling Fell**	**1224**	**NW**	**10**
206	Latrigg	1203	N	21
207	**Troutbeck Tongue**	**1191**	**FE**	**12**
208	Sale Fell	1178	NW	13
209	**Rannerdale Knotts**	**1165**	**NW**	**13**
210	High Rigg	1163	C	2
211	**Loughrigg Fell**	**1101**	**C**	**62**
212	Black Fell	1056	S	45
213	**Holme Fell**	**1040**	**S**	**14**
214	Castle Crag	951	NW	89

FROM THE 'BACK': A not-so-often-seen view of the popular Helm Crag from the Greenburn Valley. 18/10/10

Of **Castle Crag**, the only one of the 214 fells below 1000ft, AW says . . . *Castle Crag is so magnificently independent, so ruggedly individual, so aggressively unashamed of its lack of inches, that less than justice would be done by relegating it to a paragraph in the High Spy chapter.*

WHAT'S IN A NAME?

214 individual fells are featured in AW's PICTORIAL GUIDES. There are:

42 named 'Fell' or '...fell': Scafell, Bowfell, Scoat, Kirk, Brim, Harter (x2), Lonscale, Bowscale, Caw, Carrock, Place, Great Sca, Brae, Seathwaite, Bleaberry, Middle, Blake, Steel, Rosthwaite, Meal, Great Mell, Gavel, Crag, Souther, Breda, Broom, Little Mell, Longlands, Wansfell, Grange, Gowbarrow, Armboth, Burnbanks, Low, Lingmoor, Hallin, Ling, Sale, Loughrigg, Black, Holme.

33 single words: Helvellyn, Skiddaw, Pillar, Catstycam, Fairfield, Steeple, Blencathra, Lingmell, Haycock, Glaramara, Sail, Wandope, Wetherlam, Robinson, Hindscarth, Ullscarf, Froswick, Brandreth, Branstree, Yoke, Seatallan, Bakestall, Birks, Haystacks, (The) Nab, Whinlatter, Sallows, Mellbreak, Grike, Barf, Catbells, Binsey, Graystones.

29 'Crag' or 'Crags': St Sunday, Eel, Hart, Dove, Dow, High, Gray, Loft, Tarn (x2), Grey, Little Hart, Calf, Eagle, Sergeant's, Green, Raven, Great, Arnison, Helm, Walla, Castle, Thornthwaite, Crinkle, Allen, Bannerdale, Scar, Ard, Brock.

24 'Pike' or 'Pikes': Scafell, Esk, Nethermost, Dollywaggon, Red (x2), Kidsty, Kentmere, Cold, Ullock, Sheffield, High (x2), Selside, Fleetwith, Rossett, Low, Causey, Heron, Arthur's, Bonscale, Whiteless, Angletarn.

14 two words: High Street, High Stile, Red Screes, Grey Friar, Pike o'Blisco, Pavey Ark, High Spy, Base Brown, Mungrisdale Common, Hen Comb, High Tove, Stone Arthur, Nab Scar, Troutbeck Tongue.

10 'Dodd': Great, Stybarrow, Rest, Watson's, Middle, Starling, Hartsop, High Hartsop, Dodd, Glenridding.

TWO STICKLES AND ONE CRAG:
Pike o'Stickle (dark sugarloaf, far left), Loft Crag and Harrison Stickle from Lingmoor Fell. 19/8/10

9 'Knott' or 'Knotts': The, Thunacar, Knott, Hard, Gibson, Grey, Shipman, Steel, Rannerdale.

7 'Rigg' or '...rigg': Great, Knott, Blea, Lank, Whin, High, Latrigg.

7 'Side' or '...side': White, Slight, Carl, Hart, Long, Whiteside, Outerside.

5 'Great': End, Carrs, Calva, Borne, Cockup.

5 'Head': Rampsgill, Hopegill, Dale, Clough, Illgill.

4 'Barrow' or '...barrow': Barrow, Yewbarrow, Buckbarrow, Fellbarrow.

4 'How/Howe/Howes': Swirl, Hartsop Above, Sour, Silver.

4 'Moor' or '...moor': Grasmoor, Caudale, Birkhouse, Maiden.

3 'Man': Skiddaw Little, Coniston Old, Sergeant.

3 'Raise': High (x2), Raise.

2 'Bell': Mardale Ill, Ill.

2 'Gable': Great, Green.

2 'Hill': Wether, Loadpot.

2 'Stickle': Harrison, Pike o'.

1 'Stone': Arthur.

NOTE: Or, two **Arthurs** (which would mean no **Stone** and one fewer **Pike**)

LEVEL PLAYING FIELD

There are an amazing* fourteen pairs of equal-height fells among the 214 fells in the PICTORIAL GUIDES:

- Kirk Fell & Swirl How	2630ft
- **Dove Crag & Rampsgill Head**	2598ft
- Glaramara & Thornthwaite Crag	2569ft
- Grey Friar & Sail	2536ft
- **Caudale Moor & Wetherlam**	2502ft
- Harrison Stickle & **Seat Sandal**	2415ft
- Brandreth & **Lonscale Fell**	2344ft
- Caw Fell & Pavey Ark	2288ft
- Starling Dodd & **Mungrisdale Common**	2077ft
- Maiden Moor & **The Nab**	1887ft
- Lord's Seat & Steel Fell	1811ft
- **Longlands Fell** & Sour Howes	1585ft
- Glenridding Dodd & Nab Scar	1450ft
- Fellbarrow & Grange Fell	1363ft

The only triplets are:

- **Beda Fell**, Broom Fell & Hen Comb	all 1670ft

If you add the twins and the triplets, then 31 of AW's 214 fells share a height with at least one other fell. That's 14.5%.

Incidentally, Glaramara and Kidsty Pike (2560ft) and not Thornthwaite Crag would have made an 'equals' list from the first edition. Back in those days, Glaramara was deemed to be 2560ft high (equal with Kidsty Pike). Glaramara has grown by 9ft since (according to the second edition), so moves up a place from 45= (first edition) to 44= now . . . and is now only 3ft (and one place) behind its ridge-neighbour Allen Crags.

* Statisticians among you may well object that this adjective should be 'predictable'. I don't know, I'm not a statistician.

EQUAL BUT DIFFERENT: Gentle Caw Fell (left) and rugged Pavey Ark (right).

28/6/11 & 4/3/08

WHAT'S IN A LETTER?

According to *Wikipedia*, the relative frequencies of the **first letter** of a word in the English language are: **T** (16.7%), **A** (11.6%), **S** (7.7%), **H** (7.2%) and **W** (6.6%). The relative frequencies of **any letter** in a word in the English language are: **E** (12.7%), **T** (9.0%), **A** (8.2%), **I** (7.0%) and **S** (6.3%).

When it comes to the names of the **214 fells**, however, there is a different first-letter pattern, with **H** leading the way on 30 (14%, helped by 12 'Highs'), **S** on 28 (13%), then **G** on 27 (12.6%, with 11 'Greats'). Fourth and fifth on the list are **B** with 25 (11.7%) and **L** with 16 (7.5%).

INITIAL LETTERS OF NAMES OF FELLS:
A = 6, B = 25, C = 14, D = 5, E = 3, F = 4, G = 27, H = 30, I = 2, J = 0, K = 5, L = 16, M = 7, N = 3, O = 1, P = 5, Q = 0 R = 10, S = 28, T = 5, U = 2, V = 0, W = 11, X = 0, Y = 2, Z = 0.

In the **alphabetical list**, there are some interesting groupings of fells that are particular favourites of AW:

34-7: Carrock Fell, Castle Crag, Catbells, Catstycam; **95-7: Haystacks, Helm Crag, Helvellyn; 150-54: Pavey Ark, Pike o'Blisco, Pike o'Stickle, Pillar, Place Fell** (all the 'P' fells get high praise from the AW); **159-61: Red Pike (B), Red Pike (W), Red Screes.**

PPPPPRECIPITOUS: The awesome Pillar Rock from the climb up from the Memorial Bridge in Ennerdale. 28/6/11

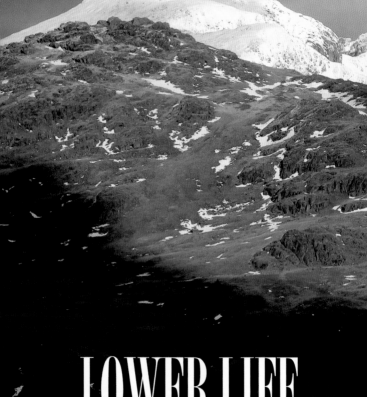

LOWER LIFE

All the Outliers, all in one place, at a glance

OUTSIDE, LOOKING IN: One of the benefits of climbing an Outlier is a
different perspective of Lakeland favourites. From Caw, the snow-covered
giants of Lakeland (Scafell and Scafell Pike) soar beyond Harter Fell. 29/01/10

AW doesn't beat about the bush when describing THE OUTLYING FELLS OF LAKELAND, which was first published in 1974 and then revised by Chris Jesty for a second edition. On the first-edition cover page, he describes the book as follows:

> being a Pictorial Guide
> to the lesser fells
> around the perimeter of Lakeland
> written primarily for
> old age pensioners and others
> who can no longer climb high fells
> but can still, within reason, potter
> about on the short and easy slopes
> and summits of the foothills.

But throughout its near-300 pages, he goes to great pains to point out that among the low-level outlying fells there are plenty of rocky, pointy and rugged tops he considers wouldn't be out of place alongside the giants of Lakeland.

Unlike the initial seven guidebooks, THE OUTLYING FELLS OF LAKELAND does not feature separate chapters for each fell (apart from some exceptions – among them favourites such as Black Combe, Caw and Stickle Pike). Instead, the chapters comprise suggested walks, and there are relatively few of the 'viewed-from-a-space-station'-type routes of ascents used in BOOKS ONE to SEVEN.

Instead, there is a far more traditional

THE OUTLYING FELLS

116 (or is it 110?)

There is some confusion about the number of fells featured in AW's eighth guidebook to Lakeland's fells. At the end of the book, he lists 110 named fells and summits, but according to *Wikipedia* (and they are right) of the 110, seven refer to others in the list and Newton Fell has two summits.

Therefore, the first equation to consider is: 110−7+1=104.

When you add the 12 unnamed fells featured in the book you come up with the definitive number: 116.

RANK	FELL NAME	CHAPTER NAME	HEIGHT (feet)
1	**Walna Scar**	WALNA SCAR	2035
2	Great Yarlside	THE WASDALE HORSESHOE	1986
3	**Black Combe**	BLACK COMBE	1970
4	Howes	HOWES	1930
5	**Whit Fell**	WHIT FELL	1881
6	Wasdale Pike	THE WASDALE HORSESHOE	1852
7	**Great Saddle Crag**	THE WET SLEDDALE HORSESHOE	1850
8	Nameless	THE BANNISDALE HORSESHOE	1819
9	**Buck Barrow**	WHIT FELL	1799
10	Burn Moor	WHIT FELL	1780
11	**Nameless**	THE BANNISDALE HORSESHOE	1771
12	Kinmont Buck Barrow	WHIT FELL	1754
13	**White Howe**	THE BANNISDALE HORSESHOE	1737
14	Nameless	THE BANNISDALE HORSESHOE	1736
15	**Caw**	CAW	1735
16	Lord's Seat	THE CROOKDALE HORSESHOE	1719
17	**High Wether Howe**	SEAT ROBERT	1705
18	Little Yarlside	THE WASDALE HORSESHOE	1691
19	**Seat Robert**	SEAT ROBERT	1688
20	Capplebarrow	THE BANNISDALE HORSESHOE	1683
21	**Fewling Stones**	SEAT ROBERT	1667
22	Sleddale Pike	THE WET SLEDDALE HORSESHOE	1659
23	**Ulthwaite Rigg**	THE WET SLEDDALE HORSESHOE	1648
24	Hare Shaw	THE NADDLE HORSESHOE	1639
25	**Stainton Pike**	STAINTON PIKE	1632
26	High House Bank	THE CROOKDALE HORSESHOE	1627

guidebook approach, with lively and detailed descriptions of the routes and relatively few ascent diagrams. However, there is one feature that readers won't find in the seven predecessors: a time guide to the walk . . . with each hour marked on the maps (which stand out particularly well in red in the Chris Jesty-revised second edition).

As usual, the last of AW's Lakeland guidebooks is full of wonderful drawings, interesting historical facts and figures, and his dry wit and captivating turn of phrase. Eagle-eyed readers will note the number of interesting buildings featured among the drawings and some surprisingly

LOW-LEVEL LOVE: Gummer's How is a favourite fell of many who visit south Lakeland. 15/6/10

rugged situations – a number of dramatic waterfalls really do look as if they should be in Borrowdale or Wasdale or Dovedale, rather than in less obvious locations around the periphery of Lakeland.

RANK	FELL NAME	CHAPTER NAME	HEIGHT (feet)
27=	**Nabs Moor**	**HOWES**	**1613**
27=	Robin Hood	THE CROOKDALE HORSESHOE	1613
29	**Yoadcastle**	**THE CIRCUIT OF DEVOKE WATER**	**1610**
30	Long Crag	THE BANNISDALE HORSESHOE	1602
31	**Woodend Height**	**THE CIRCUIT OF DEVOKE WATER**	**1597**
32	Whatshaw Common	THE WASDALE HORSESHOE	1593
33	**Hesk Fell**	**HESK FELL**	**1566**
34	Stoupdale Head	BLACK COMBE	1548
35	**Pikes**	**CAW**	**1520**
36	Great Ladstones	SEAT ROBERT	1439
37	**Nameless**	**THE NADDLE HORSESHOE**	**1427**
38=	Brunt Knott	POTTER FELL	1400
38=	**Great Worm Crag**	**GREAT WORM CRAG**	**1400**
40	Hollow Moor	GREEN QUARTER FELL	1394
41	**Hugh's Laithes Pike**	**THE NADDLE HORSESHOE**	**1390**
42	Nameless	THE NADDLE HORSESHOE	1380
43=	**Nameless**	**GREEN QUARTER FELL**	**1370**
43=	White Pike	THE CIRCUIT OF DEVOKE WATER	1370
45	**White Combe**	**BLACK COMBE**	**1361**
46	Harper Hills	THE NADDLE HORSESHOE	1358
47	**Green Pikes**	**CAW**	**1350**
48	Nameless	THE NADDLE HORSESHOE	1320
49=	**Langhowe Pike**	**SEAT ROBERT**	**1313**
49=	Todd Fell	THE BANNISDALE HORSESHOE	1313
51	**Whiteside Pike**	**THE BANNISDALE HORSESHOE**	**1302**
52	Nameless	POTTER FELL	1266

JUST LIKE THE ALPS: Well, if multiplied by ten! Stickle Pike may be just 1231ft high, but when snow-covered it looks like a Bernese Oberland giant. 15/3/06

RANK	FELL NAME	CHAPTER NAME	HEIGHT (feet)
53	**Nameless**	POTTER FELL	**1262**
54=	Heughscar Hill	HEUGHSCAR HILL	1231
54=	**Stickle Pike**	STICKLE PIKE	**1231**
56	The Pike	HESK FELL	1214
57	**Lamb Pasture**	THE BANNISDALE HORSESHOE	**1205**
58	Nameless	STICKLE PIKE	1183
59	**Dent**	FLAT FELL AND DENT	**1131**
60	Faulds Brow	FAULDS BROW	1125
61	**Knipescar Common**	KNIPESCAR COMMON	**1118**
62	Scalebarrow Knott	THE NADDLE HORSESHOE	1109
63	**Boat How**	BOAT HOW	**1105**
64	Top o'Selside	TOP O'SELSIDE	1091
65	**Ulgraves**	POTTER FELL	**1090**
66	The Knott	STAINTON PIKE	1071
67	**Gummer's How**	GUMMER'S HOW	**1054**
68	Rough Crag	THE CIRCUIT OF DEVOKE WATER	1049
69	**Carron Crag**	CARRON CRAG	**1025**
70	Ponsonby Fell	PONSONBY FELL	1020
71=	**Seat How**	THE CIRCUIT OF DEVOKE WATER	**1020**
71=	Tarn Hill	STICKLE PIKE	1020
73	**Water Crag**	THE CIRCUIT OF DEVOKE WATER	**997**
74	Great Stickle	STICKLE PIKE	990
75	**Burney**	BURNEY	**979**
76	Cold Fell	COLD FELL	955
77	**Dunnerdale Fells**	DUNNERDALE FELLS	**920**
78	The Knott	STICKLE PIKE	925
79=	**Caermote Hill**	CAERMOTE HILL	**920**
79=	St John's Hill	CAERMOTE HILL	*920
81	**High Knott (a.k.a. Williamson's Monument)**	HIGH KNOTT	**901**
82	Claife Heights	CLAIFE HEIGHTS	900
83	**Flat Fell**	FLAT FELL AND DENT	**871**
84	Staveley Fell	STAVELEY FELL	870
85	**High Light Haw**	TOP O'SELSIDE	**860**
86	Hugill Fell	HUGILL FELL	840
87	**Beacon Fell**	BEACON FELL	**836**
88	Reston Scar	RESTON SCAR	834
89	**Setmurthy Common**	WATCH HILL	**833**
90	Grandsire	SCHOOL KNOTT	818
91	**Low Light Haw**	TOP O'SELSIDE	**810**
92=	Blawith Knott	BLAWITH KNOTT	806
92=	**Nameless**	SCHOOL KNOTT	**806**
94	Clints Crags	CLINTS CRAGS	804
95	**Latterbarrow**	LATTERBARROW	**803**
96	Orrest Head	ORREST HEAD	783
97	**Newton Fell (North)**	NEWTON FELL	**780**
98=	Dunmallet	DUNMALLET	775

RANK	FELL NAME	CHAPTER NAME	HEIGHT (feet)
98=	Tottlebank Height	BLAWITH KNOTT	775
100	Watch Hill	WATCH HILL	770
101	Scout Scar	SCOUT SCAR	764
102	School Knott	SCHOOL KNOTT	760
103	Hooker Crag	MUNCASTER FELL	757
104	Irton Pike	IRTON PIKE	751
105	Nameless	TOP O'SELSIDE	748
106	Wool Knott	WOODLAND FELL	730
107	Hampsfell	HAMPSFELL	727
108	Lord's Seat	WHITBARROW	706
109	Cunswick Scar	SCOUT SCAR	679
110	Yew Bank	WOODLAND FELL	678
111	Bigland Barrow	BIGLAND BARROW	630
112	Brant Fell	BRANT FELL	629
113	Finsthwaite Heights	FINSTHWAITE HEIGHTS	600
114	Newton Fell (South)	NEWTON FELL	585
115	Cartmel Fell (a.k.a. Raven's Barrow)	CARTMEL FELL	500
116	Humphrey Head	HUMPHREY HEAD	172

* St John's Hill is listed as an Outlying Fell in the index at the back of the book, but in the chapter on Caermote Hill it is not mentioned once by name, and only appears on the map. Judging by the contour lines, its height appears to be around the same as that of Caermote Hill, so in this list it appears right beside its 'parent fell'.

THE FELL THAT FELL INTO THE SEA

CLIFF AND SEA: Humphrey Head.   10/3/11

AW says of **Binsey**: [It] *is the odd man out ... detached and solitary ... yet it is much too good to be omitted from these pages.* He feels pretty well the same about 172ft-high Humphrey Head: *Outlying it certainly is ... A fell it is certainly not ... Yet its isolation, far-ranging views, bird life ... rocky reefs and interesting approach combine to make the place unique in the district, giving better reason for its inclusion in this book than its omission. Fellwalkers need an occasional change of scene. Here is one, on Humphrey Head.*

THE OUTLYING FELLS
116 fells : 118,143ft
Ave. per fell : 905ft

HIGH & LOWS
HIGHEST:
Walna Scar - 2035ft
LOWEST:
Humphrey Head - 172ft
DIFFERENCE: 1863ft

STATS & TRIVIA
124 fells in the first seven guidebooks are HIGHER than Walna Scar (2035ft).

39 Outlying Fells are LOWER than the lowest fell in the first seven guidebooks (Castle Crag, 951ft).

The 116 Outliers, if all had a separate chapter, would occupy THREE books of the size of the original guides.

HIGH POINTS AT A LOWER LEVEL . . .

The revisions made to THE OUTLYING FELLS for its second edition (2011) are significant, particularly one: the use of a dotted red line to indicate routes (as in all the revisions) is particularly effective in this book; on maps, the red lines stand out so much more effectively in the second edition, and the one-hour 'time stamps' that AW uses in THE OUTLYING FELLS are much clearer as a result. Some other things that set this book apart from the magnificent seven are:

Cairns: old and new

Whatever the fells themselves lack in inches, the book makes up for them with the plethora of cairns illustrated. They range from ancients cairns such as those found on Yew Bank, Tarn Riggs, Great Worm Crag, Hesk Fell, Stainton Pike, Boat How and Irton Pike. Elsewhere, in the Seat Robert chapter, drawings of five separate cairns appear on one page!

Building and monuments

This book features a large number of drawings of buildings/structures/bridges/monuments/relics in various states of repair. By my count, 47 of them, ranging from a Roman building (Walls Castle, the Muncaster Fell chapter), to a seventh-century Runic cross (Ponsonby Fell), to a 19th-century monument that celebrates Henry VI being looked after by local shepherds before fleeing to France after his defeat at the Battle of Towton in 1461 (Ireton Pike chapter).

KEEPS THE RAIN OFF: The Umbrella – the shelter on the summit of Scout Scar.
17/9/04

Planes, trains and automobiles (and boats)

Planes: Well, at least a plane . . . the remnants of which are scattered on Black Combe's higher western slopes and in the valley of Blackcombe Beck, east of the summit. *Trains:* The Ravenglass and Eskdale Railway has its own page in the Ireton Pike chapter, with two drawings of trains (*Makes a nice change from drawing mountains, though*). *Automobiles:* Two cars, looking more like Postman Pat versions than the real thing, appear on the Kendal Western Bypass in the Scout Scar chapter. *Boats:* Strictly speaking, this should be singular: from Windermere looking towards Gummer's How.

DIFFERENCES

THE OUTLYING FELLS differs from the earlier seven guidebooks:

- There is no geographical overview.
- There is no list of fells in height order.
- There are no ridge walks.
- There are some unique ways of describing views.
- There is a 2-page 'contents' section listing the chapters and their pages.
- The chapters do not have page numbers within them, but the book has a conventional page numbering system.
- The chapters are listed by geographical location, starting in the south-east and moving in a clockwise direction around the circular perimeter of Lakeland.
- An index lists the named fells and summits (it ignores the nameless summits).
- Six pages at the back of the book are reserved for notes.
- There are no 'Personal notes in conclusion'.

TOP OF THE (SOUTH LAKELAND) WORLD: The summit of Black Combe. 5/6/09

BLACK COMBE: THE 'DADDY' OF THE OUTLIERS

It may not be the highest of the Outliers (Walna Scar and Great Yarlside edge it into third place), but Black Combe is the most extensive fell in the book – physically (on the ground) and according to the number of pages assigned to its chapter. In fact, its 16 pages place it well ahead of its nearest rival – The Bannisdale Horseshoe weighs in at a mere 10 pages. AW considers this to be a mountain that commands respect from afar and when one is on its extensive slopes: *It appears aloof, rising on the southern seaboard and overtopping all else like a huge whale stranded on a beach . . .*

Because of this (detachment) he says, *it is rarely included by fellwalking visitors in their itineraries, yet is within the boundary of the National Park . . . and its ascent, in conditions of clear visibility, is one of the most rewarding.* Like **Skiddaw**

Little Man this is because of its position as an outsider looking into the heart of the district, but unlike **Skiddaw**'s subsidiary peak (which is overlapped by its parent) no fell is ever going to dominate Black Combe – with its position on the Cumbrian seaboard offering spectacular views in exactly the opposite direction to Lakeland. *Half of the panorama is the glittering sea, with the Isle of Man seen in stark outline and Wales, Ireland and Scotland as shadowy silhouettes on a high horizon of water.*

AW adds: *Black Combe was made to be climbed, and climbed it should be. It is considerate to the old and infirm: the grass bridleway to its summit from Whicham is amongst the most delectable of Lakeland fell paths.*

Which other can be ascended in carpet slippers?

. . . BUT ONE LOW POINT (a personal view)

The absence of any *personal notes in conclusion* is one aspect of the book that is disappointing. Admittedly, the INTRODUCTION is much more personal than in his earlier guidebooks (which does ease the pain somewhat), but wouldn't it have been nice to have been given one more personal view from the great man. Oh well . . .

LEVEL PEGGING: Pike Howe and Side Pike sit right across Langdale from each other.
23/1/12

SIDE BY SIDE (PIKES)

Halfway-up Langdale cousins have got views to die for

Two subsidiary summits on either side of Great Langdale offer wonderful views totally out of proportion to the effort entailed in reaching them – including views of each other. Rugged little **Side Pike** on Lingmoor Fell and perky **Pike Howe** on Harrison Stickle both get good write-ups from AW. Side Pike, which must have been so close to getting its own chapter in BOOK FOUR (it's like a Langdale version of Castle Crag; there's only one way up for normal walkers and at 1187ft it's over 200ft higher than the Borrowdale fell), gets a lot of attention on Lingmoor Fell 5: *The west ridge of Side Pike, starting from the cattle grid, is an excellent walk, the views of the Langdale Pikes being MAGNIFICENT.* It's not often AW emphasises things with capitals, which

CLOSE PALS: Side Pike and the Langdales. Pike Howe is arrowed, far right.   19/8/10

PARENT FELL: Harrison Stickle from the rocks on the top of Pike Howe.   23/1/12

shows how highly he rated the views from this shapely little pike.

Across the valley, Pike Howe doesn't get as many words, but three are enough to establish its credentials: *A splendid viewpoint.* Pike Howe, indeed, offers superlative intimate views of the most scenic section of Great Langdale, but, surprisingly, the close-up view of 'dad' – that's Harrison Stickle – is also magnificent. This is a place, on a nice summer's day, to settle down and have a piece of Kendal mint cake washed down with a cool drink before resuming the ascent of the Langdale Pikes.

Every summit view is described, starting on page 110

PAGE TURNERS

How the fells add up

TOP OF THE PILE: The always-awesome Sharp Edge on Blencathra, the fell with the most Wainwright pages devoted to it.   *11/9/07*

This may be the most colourful chapter in the whole book — because it features every fell in THE PICTORIAL GUIDES (or chapter in the case of THE OUTLYING FELLS). It reveals how much space AW devoted to each fell. So let's start at the very beginning . . . with the fell that takes the most pages being, of course, the mighty **Blencathra**.

36 pages: Blencathra |

30 pages: Scafell Pike |

28 Pages: Great Gable | **Skiddaw** |

26 pages: Helvellyn |

20 pages: Bowfell | Crinkle Crags |

18 pages: Coniston Old Man | Harrison Stickle | Pillar |

16 pages: Black Combe | Grasmoor | **Great End** | Grisedale Pike | High Stile | Loughrigg Fell | Scafell |

14 pages: Caudale Moor | Dale Head | **Dodd** | Esk Pike | Fairfield | Harter Fell | **High Pike** | High Raise | **High Street** | Hopegill Head | Loadpot Hill | **Skiddaw Little Man** | Ullscarf | Wetherlam |

12 pages: Blea Rigg | **Carrock Fell** | Caw Fell | **Dollywaggon Pike** | Dow Crag | Eel Crag | Glaramara | **Great Dodd** | Haystacks | High Raise | High Spy | **Knott** | Lord's Seat | Red Pike (B) | **Red Screes** | Sale Fell | Sergeant Man | **Thornthwaite Crag** | Wether Hill | Whiteside |

10 pages: **Bakestall** | **Bannerdale Crags** | The Bannisdale Horseshoe | Barf | Bleaberry Fell | **Bowscale Fell** | Brandreth | **Carl Side** | Catbells | Causey Pike | **Dove Crag** | Graystones | **Great Calva** | **Great Sca Fell** | Green Gable | Grey Friar | Grey Knotts | **Hart Crag** | Haycock | Helm Crag | Hindscarth | Ill Bell | Kentmere Pike | **Latrigg** | Lingmell | Lingmoor Fell | **Lonscale Fell** | Mardale Ill Bell | Mellbreak | **Nethermost Pike** | Pavey Ark | Pike o'Blisco | Place Fell | **Raise** | Rampsgill Head | Red Pike (W) | Robinson | **St Sunday Crag** | Scoat Fell | Silver How | Steel Fell | **Stybarrow Dodd** | Swirl How | Tarn Crag | Wandope | **Wansfell** | Whin Rigg | White Side | Yoke |

9 pages: Ullock Pike | Yewbarrow |

8 pages: Allen Crags | Angletarn Pikes | Barrow | Base Brown | **Binsey** | Birkhouse Moor | Blake Fell | **Branstree** | Broom Fell | Calf Crag | Castle Crag | **Catstycam** | **Clough Head** | Fleetwith Pike | **Gowbarrow Fell** | Grange Fell | **Great Carrs** | Grey Crag | Hampsfell | Harter Fell | **Hart Side** | High Crag | High Seat | **Illgill Head** | Kirk Fell | Lank Rigg | Loft Crag | **Long Side** | Maiden Moor | Outerside | Pike o'Stickle | Rossett Pike | **Seat Sandal** | Seatallan | Sheffield Pike | **Souther Fell** | Steeple | Tarn Crag |

6 pages: Ard Crags | Armboth Fell | **Arthur's Pike** | Beda Fell | **Birks** | Bonscale Pike | **Brae Fell** | Brim Fell | Caw | Circuit of Devoke Water | **Crag Fell** | The Crookdale Horseshoe | Eagle Crag | Fellbarrow | Finsthwaite Heights | Gavel Fell | **Gray Crag** |

Great Borne | **Great Cockup** | Great Crag | **Great Rigg** |
Grike | Hard Knott | Hartsop Dodd | **High Pike** | Howes |
Kidsty Pike | Knott Rigg | **Little Hart Crag** | **Longlands Fell** |
Low Fell | **Meal Fell** | Middle Fell | Muncaster Fell |
Mungrisdale Common | The Naddle Horseshoe | Newton Fell |
Potter Fell | **Rest Dodd** | Rosthwaite Fell | Sail | Scout Scar |
Seat Robert | **Selside Pike** | Sergeant's Crag | Stainton Pike |
Starling Dodd | Stickle Pike | Thunacar Knott | Top o'Selside
| Walla Crag | Walna Scar | The Wasdale Horseshoe |
Watson's Dodd | The Wet Sleddale Horseshoe | Whinlatter |
Whitbarrow | Whiteless Pike | Whit Fell | Woodland Fell |

4 pages: Arnison Crag | Beacon Fell | Bigland Barrow | Black Fell |
Blawith Knott | Boat How | **Brock Crags** | Buckbarrow |
Burnbank Fell | Caermote Hill | Carron Crag | Claife Heights |
Cold Pike | Dunnerdale Fells | Faulds Brow | Flat Fell and
Dent | **Froswick** | Gibson Knott | **Glenridding Dodd** | **Great
Mell Fell** | Great Worm Crag | **Green Crag** | Green Quarter
Fell | Gummer's How | **Hallin Fell** | **Hartsop Above How** | Hen
Comb | **Heron Pike** | Hesk Fell | Heughscar Hill | **High Hartsop
Dodd** | High Rigg | High Knott | High Tove | Holme Fell |
Humphrey Head | Irton Pike | Knipescar Common | **The Knott**
| Latterbarrow | **Little Mell Fell** | Ling Fell | **Low Fell** |
Middle Dodd | The Nab | Nab Scar | Orrest Head |
Ponsonby Fell | Rannerdale Knotts | Raven Crag | Sallows |
Scar Crags | School Knott | Seathwaite Fell | Shipman Knotts
| Slight Side | **Sour Howes** | Staveley Fell | **Steel Knotts** |
Stone Arthur | Troutbeck Tongue |

2 pages: Brant Fell | Burney | Cartmel Fell | Clints Crag | Cold Fell |
Dunmallet | Hugill Fell | Reston Scar | Watch Hill |

How did AW decide on the allocation of space in his guidebooks? Before I started researching this book, it was a question that hadn't really occurred to me. It seemed perfectly natural that the biggest, the grandest, the highest mountains were allocated more space, and that the lesser fells – lower, less rugged, grassier, etc. – were given their appropriate allocation.

A glance at the 'page allocation chart' above would appear to confirm this view, with the 'page grabbers' in the top places being lofty, considerable mountains. Indeed, of the top 16 fells that are allocated 16 pages or more, 11 are from the the highest 20: These are: **Blencathra**, Scafell Pike, Great Gable, **Skiddaw**, Helvellyn, Bowfell, Crinkle Crags, Pillar, Grasmoor, Great End and Scafell. Two others are also of a good height – Coniston Old Man and High Stile – and are both the 'parent fell' of a range of mountains, while two further fells – Harrison Stickle and Grisedale Pike – are among the most climbed of Lakeland mountains because of their ease of access from Ambleside/Keswick respectively.

And that leaves Loughrigg Fell. It really is a case of 'playing with the big boys'. At 1102ft, it comes in at 211 on the list of 214 with only Black Fell, Holme Fell and Castle Crag below it. Yet AW used 16 pages to describe its myriad charms, more than other favourites such as **Carrock Fell** (12 pages),

LOUGHRIGG VIEW: Looking north to Grasmere, Helm Crag (in shadow, centre) from Loughrigg Fell. 28/1/11

LOUGHRIGG TARN: One of the most photogenic tarns in Lakeland. 28/9/11

RYDAL CAVE: Another Loughrigg Fell attraction. 24/5/11

Place Fell (10 pages) and, of course, his absolute favourite, Haystacks (12 pages). Why is this? Well, here are some theories: BOOK THREE features 27 fells, far fewer than BOOK TWO (36 fells) and BOOK SIX (33 fells), so there was a little more space available for lower fells (and let's not forget, the central fells are the lowest in the area, with its number one mountain High Raise tipping the scales at 2500ft exactly). This doesn't account for BOOK FIVE though (24 fells) – or does it? The northern fells are home to two giants (vertically and geographically) of Lakeland, **Blencathra** and **Skiddaw**, which were allocated 64 pages between them, so maybe that's not the answer. Maybe there's just a lot going on in and around this little fell nestled in a glorious position overlooking Grasmere, Rydal and Ambleside and right at the start of Great Langdale. Maybe it's just a question of it being in the right place at the right time. I wasn't quite satisfied with that answer, and one wet and miserable afternoon when I had nothing better to do I got out the pocket calculator and started tapping in a few numbers – and LO AND BEHOLD, I came up with some very interesting answers.

First, I looked at the *highest* and *lowest* fells in the page allocations from 10 to 16. Then, I divided their heights by the number of pages to get the feet-per-page calculation (*fpp*). I was thus able to determine . . . goodness, that makes me sound like a scientist, or even a policeman! Let's try again . . . I *found* the following:

HIGHEST	PAGES	LOWEST
Scafell (3162ft) fpp = 198ft	16	Loughrigg Fell (1101ft) fpp = 69ft
Esk Pike (2903ft) fpp = 207ft	14	Dodd (1647ft) fpp = 118ft
Dollywaggon Pike (2815ft) fpp = 235ft	12	Sale Fell (1178ft) fpp = 98ft
Nethermost Pike (2920ft) fpp = 292ft	10	Latrigg (1203ft) fpp = 120ft

It's not exactly rocket science, of course, but the clear pattern is that some fells over perform (in terms of pages per height), and there certainly is some correlation between the two, as we have already seen.

Loughrigg Fell has just an amazing *fpp* figure of 69ft (1102 divided by 16). Which, on the face of it, makes it the 'best' fell statistically. Looking at all of the fells reveals it is run close by **Blencathra** (2847 divided by 36 = *fpp* of 79ft). Blencathra, by any reckoning, is one of the gems of Lakeland (AW thought so), so maybe this theory does have some validity. If it does, then for the higher-rated fells (those with a low *fpp*, if you see what I mean), there must be some fells that seriously underperform. My eye was drawn to Catstycam. AW gives it fulsome praise – *If Catstycam stood alone, remote from its fellows, it would be one of the finest fells in Lakeland* – but he goes on to lament that it is dominated by **Helvellyn**, and is really the termination of an eastern spur linked by Swirral Edge. In this respect, Catstycam and Steeple (which is another fell with a neat, pointed top but which is likewise dominated by Scoat Fell) are eerily similar. Steeple was also given eight pages in its relevant book. But Catstycam is over 200ft higher, and it is this height (2917ft) that made me think it was the biggest under-achiever (its *fpp* is 365ft).

HIGH FELL, LOW PAGINATION: Catstycam, with Ullswater beyond, as seen from the descent to Swirral Edge. 1/6/09

I looked some more, and in the six-pages category my eye went to Brim Fell (2611ft). Sure enough, its *fpp* was 435ft. Had I, at last, found the 'worst' fell in Lakeland? Not so fast! In the four-page section, standing out like a sore thumb, was Slight Side at a height of 2499ft and with an *fpp* of 625ft. Here we have it. Uhuh, no we don't, because a quick flick through the Slight Side chapter finds no map of its extensive hinterland leading down towards Eskdale. AW asks the reader to refer to the map in the Scafell chapter, which covers the same area. So it's hardly Slight Side's fault it's not six pages, is it? And besides, its lovely pointed summit warrants inclusion in AW's list of the six best summits in his concluding notes to BOOK SEVEN . . . which proves one thing: there are lies, damned lies and statistics.

NOTE: The eagle-eyed among you will spot that tiny little Humphrey Head (a 172ft headland that sticks out into Morecambe Bay) has four pages allocated to it. A quick burst with the calculator produces: 172 divided by 4 = an fpp of 42ft. So this, then, is the finest of all AW's fells? Well, it's certainly the finest surrounded by water at high tide, but it surely doesn't count as a fell – AW certainly doesn't think so (see page 59 for his assessment of its low-level charms).

CLOUDS OVER BLENCATHRA: From the summit of Clough Head.   7/9/09

PHOTOGRAPHIC HITCH

Just 33 pages into BOOK ONE, the first readers of A PICTORIAL GUIDE TO THE LAKELAND FELLS got their first view of its author – on page 7 of the **Clough Head** chapter, seated on the edge of the summit cairn, pipe in hand, left leg (characteristically, as it subsequently turned out) stretched right out. A knapsack was by his side and socks were rolled over his trousers (as they used to be worn back then). AW didn't want to use photographs in his

Blencathra from Clough Head

guidebooks, but in those days he couldn't even take a time-release picture, so had to draw himself without reference.

The year BOOK ONE came out (1955) another Englishman named Alfred (who liked to appear in his own creations) filmed the movie *To Catch a Thief*. The English-born Hollywood director Alfred Hitchcock and AW had much in common – a desire to create something wonderful and the expertise to do it.

STRANGE GROOVES

It's not just two sets of wacky rocks that make the summit of Helm Crag one of the most interesting places in Lakeland

DEPRESSION WARNING: *The Howitzer (top left) looks out over a valley.*   31/7/08

From the ground, whether it's from Grasmere or Dunmail Raise, it's obvious that Helm Crag has a pretty interesting summit. Two sets of distinctive rocks – **The Lion and The Lamb** at the Grasmere end and **The Howitzer** (the summit of the fell) – adorn the ends of a 250-yards-long summit ridge.

AW explains the other strange phenomenon – three parallel rocky ridges and two depressions – with help from a nifty summit diagram (below) but, surprisingly, with no accompanying drawing. Which is where this book comes in, of course; above is a view of the summit ridge (far left), and the first (widest) depression leading to the secondary ridge (far right). Helm Crag's summit is unique in Lakeland.

Group of rocks
The Howitzer

main cairn

GIBSON KNOTT

secondary ridge
depression
summit ridge

crags perched boulder

The Lamb
The Lion
cleft

dangerous × fissure

GRASMERE

cave ×

MAP:
How AW
drew it: these
pictures show
the depression
from both ends of the ridge.

ABOVE: *The Howitzer as seen from The Lion and The Lamb.*

ABOVE: *Vice versa.*

All the fells of Lakeland
are lovely in their own way,
but some are lovelier than others . . .

CLIMBS TO THE

We've already touched on how AW viewed his beloved A PICTORIAL GUIDE TO THE LAKELAND FELLS . . . *It was conceived, and is born, after many years of inarticulate worshipping at their shrines.*

But before he put pen to paper he didn't worship from afar; he took a pay cut and moved from his home town (Blackburn) to live and work in Kendal, the Gateway to Lakeland. He didn't worship from a little closer, either – from Grasmere or Grange, from Coniston or Buttermere village; he worshipped right up close, on old mine roads and shepherds' tracks and tourist trails and zigzag paths that led only in one direction: upwards.

He worshipped beside the tarns twinkling like gems in the high hollows and the hanging valleys; he worshipped alongside the dark crags and even darker gullies; he walked on scree, over boulders, through bracken and heather and across flooded becks and sodden bogs, with the shrines in his sights: first the high ridges; then the summits. He loved every fell (even Armboth Fell, just a little) but he loved others more than most. And, like all of us, he loved some ascents more than others.

This chapter examines AW's favourites. He never graded them, but he sprinkled them with adjectives. Here 88 of the 214 fells from the PICTORIAL GUIDES are featured, and 11 of the 56 chapters from THE OUTLYING FELLS, and I've tried to get into AW's mindset in order to grade them, from one to five stars (I know, that's going to be controversial!). They say football is all about opinions (personally, I think goals are more important, but there you are); so are the ascents of the Lakeland fells. These are my opinions, based on AW's eloquent articulations. I'm sure you have yours, too.

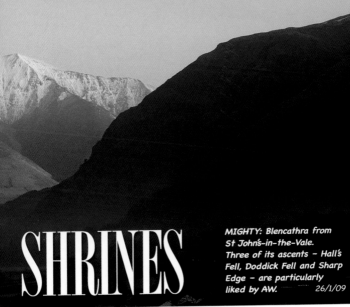

SHRINES

MIGHTY: *Blencathra from St John's-in-the-Vale. Three of its ascents – Hall's Fell, Doddick Fell and Sharp Edge – are particularly liked by AW.* 26/1/09

Angletarn Pikes | from Patterdale
The ascent: Angletarn Pikes 5
This delightful walk should be in the itinerary of all who stay at Patterdale; the climb is pleasant and the views excellent.
Rating: ★★

Ard Crags | from Rigg Beck
The ascent: Ard Crags 3
Especially in August, a climb up to a personal heaven of one's very own.
Rating: ★★★

Arnison Crag | from Patterdale
The ascent: Arnison Crag 2
A short and easy walk.
Rating: ★★★

Bannerdale Crags | from Mungrisdale
The ascent: Bannerdale Crags 6
The most direct route [the east ridge] . . . Towards the end this becomes a grand scramble in an impressive situation – a bit of real mountaineering.
Rating: ★★

Barf | from Thornthwaite
The ascent: Barf 4
It is one of the very best of the shorter Lakeland climbs.
Rating: ★★★

Barrow | from Braithwaite
The ascent: Barrow 5
. . . a favourite Sunday afternoon ramble, in the category of Latrigg and Catbells and Loughrigg Fell, and every step of the way is a joy.
Rating: ★★

Beacon Fell | from Brown Howe
The ascent: page 99
It is the summit, abrupt and rocky, and the far-reaching view that make the ascent so worth while.
Rating: ★★★

Binsey | from Bewaldeth
The ascent: Binsey 4
On a warm clear day in August the purple heather and glorious panoramic view together make Binsey one of the best places for spending an hour of undisturbed peace and enjoyment. Or take the family.
Rating: ★★

Black Combe | from Whicham
The ascent: page 166

71

Without complications . . . and much the best . . . the splendid path and the unparalleled views make it a classic.

Rating: ★★★

Blake Fell | from Loweswater

The ascent: Blake Fell 5
A route of interesting detail and lovely views.

Rating: ★

Blake Fell | from Lamplugh

The ascent: Blake Fell 6
From the west, the approach by Cogra Moss has always been the best.

Rating: ★

Bleaberry Fell | from the Borrowdale road

The ascent: Bleaberry Fell 4
This is a beautiful climb.

Rating: ★★

Blawith Knott | from Woodland Fell Road

The ascent: page 109
The view . . . is best lingered over by a leisurely perambulation of the top of the fell.

Rating: ★★

Blencathra | from Threlkeld
via Hall's Fell

The ascent: Blencathra 17
For active walkers and scramblers, this route is positively the finest way to any mountain-top in the district. It is direct, exhilarating, has glorious views, and (especially satisfying) scores a bull's eye by leading unerringly to the summit-cairn.

Rating: ★★★★★

Blencathra | from Scales
via Doddick Fell

The ascent: Blencathra 21
A grand climb . . . with striking views of the objective.

Rating: ★★★

Blencathra | from Scales
via Sharp Edge

The ascent: Blencathra 25
Sharp Edge is the highlight of this walk, shining like a beacon on what is otherwise a rather dreary . . . approach.

Rating: ★★★

Bowfell | from Dungeon Ghyll
via The Band

The ascent: Bowfell 5
A well-known walkers' highroad. [If the climbers' traverse is used – instead of the usual route via Three Tarns – the scenery of Flat Crags, Cambridge Crag,

FINAL DESTINATION: The shapely outline of Bowfell, from the River Esk.   25/6/09

Bowfell Buttress and Great Slab surely
adds another star to the ascent.]
Rating: ★★★★

Bowfell | from Eskdale
   The ascent: Bowfell 8
   *A very beautiful and a most interesting
   walk – one of the best.*
   Rating: ★★★★

Bowscale Fell | from Mungrisdale
   The ascent: Bowscale Fell 5
   Best [route] of all is the east ridge.
   Rating: ★★

Bowscale Fell | from Bowscale
   The ascent: Bowscale Fell 7
   *Bowscale Tarn remains one of the best
   scenes of its kind in the district.*
   Rating: ★★★

Carrock Fell | from Stone Ends
   The ascent: Carrock Fell 8
   *This route, 'Rake Trod', is the one used
   and recommended by local people.*
   Rating: ★★

Cartmel Fell | from Cartmel
Fell Church
   The ascent: page 43
   Short, but too good to be omitted.
   Rating: ★

Catbells | from Hawse End
   The ascent: Catbells 5
   *One of the very best of the shorter
   climbs. A truly lovely walk.*
   Rating: ★★★★★

Causey Pike | from Stair
   The ascent: Causey Pike 4
   *The route [is] charming, the views
   superlative, the finish a bit of real
   mountaineering, and the summit a place
   of distinctive character.*
   Rating: ★★★★

Caw | from Seathwaite
   The ascent: page 122
   *The view to the Scafells . . . will win
   most hearts.*
   Rating: ★★

Coniston Old Man | from Coniston
   The ascent: Coniston Old Man 8
   *The day trippers' route . . . but
   let's be fair – the scenery of Low Water
   is very good.*
   Rating: ★★

Crinkle Crags | from Dungeon Ghyll

**BIRD'S EYE VIEW: Looking down on Low
Water (Levers Water in the background)
and the tourist path to the summit of
Coniston Old Man.**   30/4/07

via Red Tarn, and via Three Tarns
   The ascent: Crinkle Crags 5 & 6
   *A full traverse of the ridge . . . splendid
   mountain excursion.*
   Rating: ★★★★

Dale Head | from Little Town
   The ascent: Dale Head 6
   Via the old copper mine: *This is a
   mountaineering 'must'.*
   Rating: ★★★

Dollywaggon Pike | from Grisedale
   The ascent: Dollywaggon Pike 7
   Via The Tongue, a narrow ridge that
   makes a bee-line to the summit.
   Interesting and exhilarating.
   Rating: ★★★

Dove Crag | from Patterdale
   The ascent: Dove Crag 4
   *The climb from Dovedale . . . gives . . . a
   much more interesting and intimate
   approach; the sharp transition from the
   soft loveliness of the valley to the
   desolation above being very impressive.*
   Rating: ★★★

Dow Crag | from Coniston
   The ascent: Dow Crag 8
   *The most impressive and rewarding
   mountain walk available from Coniston.*
   Rating: ★★★★

Eagle Crag | from Stonethwaite

73

The ascent: Eagle Crag 3 & 4
An ingenious route through crags and scree - the ascent reveals all of the beauty of the Stonethwaite landscape.
Rating: ★★

Esk Pike | from Eskdale
The ascent: Esk Pike 7
A walk of exceptional beauty and interest, but [at 8.5 miles from Boot, 7 miles from Wha House] a very long one.
Rating: ★★★★

Fairfield | from Patterdale
The ascent: Fairfield 7
The gradual revelation of the savage northern face of Fairfield as the view up Deepdale unfolds gives a high quality to this route.
Rating: ★★★

Fleetwith Pike | from Gatescarth
The ascent: Fleetwith Pike 6
The view in retrospect is superb. There are no problems of route selection and no risk of going astray. A beautiful climb. Do it!
Rating: ★★★★★

Glaramara | from Rosthwaite
The ascent: Glaramara 5
This is a typical Lakeland climb, and although the final mile hardly maintains the interest of the early part of the walk there is recompense in the glorious views, that to the north being of unsurpassed beauty.
Rating: ★★★

Glenridding Dodd | from Glenridding
The ascent: Glenridding Dodd 2
The Dodd is so conveniently situated and offers so delightful a view that it might be expected that walkers would have blazed a wide path to the top. Such is not the case, however . . .
Rating: ★

Grange Fell | from Grange
The ascent: Grange Fell 3
A most beautiful short climb . . . sacrifice any other walk, if need be, but not this!
Rating: ★★★★★

Grange Fell | from Rosthwaite
The ascent: Grange Fell 4
This is an excellent little expedition, with splendid views . . .
Rating: ★★★

Great Crag | from Stonethwaite
The ascent: Great Crag 3
This is a most beautiful short climb, best done on a sunny day in August, for then the upper slopes are ablaze with heather.
Rating: ★★★

Great Crag | from Watendlath
The ascent: Great Crag 4
All walks from Watendlath are pleasant, and this one is particularly attractive where it crosses an area of bog myrtle and jointed rushes.
Rating: ★

Great End | from Sty Head
The ascent: Great End 6
Subject to the qualification that the last section is a very rough climb, this is an excellent ascent, giving a satisfying sense of achievement.
Rating: ★★

Great End | from Seathwaite
The ascent: Great End 9
. . . nobody will regret a day that includes Great End in its itenary: it is a magnificent mountain, scarcely inferior to the [Scafell] Pike, and, in some respects, to be preferred.
Rating: ★★★

Great Gable | from Seathwaite
The ascent: Great Gable 15
It is to be prferred to the traditional route . . . via Stockley Bridge and Sty Head because of its greater interest, greater attractiveness, and quietness.
Rating: ★★

Great Gable | from Honister Pass
The ascent: Great Gable 17
This is an excellent route for motorists, who may abandon their cars on the pass with a height of 1190ft already achieved, and experience the wind on the heath, brother; for the next five hours with no thought of gears and brakes and clutches and things, and feel all the better for exercising their limbs as nature intended.
Rating: ★★

Great Gable | from Gatesgarth
The ascent: Great Gable 18

ALL IN VIEW: *From the ridge of Kinn, the climb from Braithwaite to Grisedale Pike continues on to the higher ridge of Sleet How before the final steep haul to the summit.* 6/11/06

There is sustained interest all the way, the scenery being unusually varied and the route ingenious and a delight to follow. This is the finest of the many approaches to Great Gable: a splendid mountain walk.
Rating: ★★★★

Green Crag | from Eskdale
The ascent: Green Crag 3
A wet morning in Eskdale need not necessarily mean a day's fellwalking lost, for if the sky clears up by the early afternoon here is a short expedition well worth trying.
Rating: ★

Grisedale Pike | from Braithwaite
The ascent: Grisedale Pike 8
Excepting Catbells only, Grisedale Pike is probably the most-climbed fell in the north-western area and invariably the ascent is made by the route here depicted. Now that the start has been improved the whole walk is delightful.
Rating: ★★

Grisedale Pike | from Thornthwaite
The ascent: Grisedale Pike 9
Ascents by two little-known ridges . . . coupled with an unusual line of approach calling for interesting route-finding. A

splendid expedition of charm and variety.
Rating: ★★★

Gummer's How | from Newby Bridge
The ascent: page 45
Here is a fellwalk in miniature, a little beauty, with heather, a few rocks to scramble on, soft couches for repose, a classic view and a rustic Ordnance column.
Rating: ★★

Hallin Fell | from The Hause
The ascent: Hallin Fell 2
There is one royal road to the top: this is the wide grass path leaving the Hause opposite the church, and it can be ascended comfortably in bare feet . . .
Rating: ★★

Hampsfell | from Grange-over-Sands
The ascent: page 64
Of Grange's many attractions, Hampsfell is the one most likely to appeal to a semi-retired fellwalker. It is a hill small and unpretentious yet endowed with an air of freedom and grace . . .
Rating: ★

Harrison Stickle | from Dungeon Ghyll via Pike Howe
The ascent: Harrison Stickle 9
It is not only the quickest and easiest way to the top but has two other distinct virtues: it is pleasant underfoot . . . and . . . is the 'purest' route . . .
Rating: ★★★

Harrison Stickle | from Dungeon Ghyll via Stickle Tarn
The ascent: Harrison Stickle 10
The highlight of this walk is the impressive view of Pavey Ark, one of the finest scenes in Lakeland.
Rating: ★★★

Hart Crag | from Patterdale
The ascent: Hart Crag 6
The Link Cove route especially is an interesting climb through the inner sanctuary of Hart Crag, the scene being impressive.
Rating: ★★

Harter Fell | from Mardale
The ascent: Harter Fell 8
This is an excellent expedition, richly rewarding in intimate scenes of Harter

Fell's grand northern cliffs and in the views of Haweswater.
Rating: ★★★★

Harter Fell | from Eskdale
The ascent: Harter Fell 6
There is not a more charming ascent than this, which is a delight from start to finish. Harter Fell's grand rocky pyramid gives an air of real mountaineering to the climb, the views of Eskdale are glorious and the immediate surroundings richly colourful.
Rating: ★★★★★

Hart Side | from Dockray
The ascent: Hart Side 5
The joy of this walk is . . . in the splendid high-level route to it from Dockray, which excels in views of Ullswater.
Rating: ★

Haystacks | from Gatesgarth
via Scarth Gap
The ascent: Haystacks 5
The ascent of Haystacks via the pass of Scarth Gap is a prelude of much merit and beauty . . .
Rating: ★★★★

Haystacks | from Gatesgarth
via Warnscale
The ascent: Haystacks 6
For sustained interest, impressive crag scenery, beautiful views, and a most delightful arrangement of tarns and rocky peaks, this short mountain excursion ranks with the very best.
Rating: ★★★★★

Helm Crag | from Grasmere
The ascent: Helm Crag 4
This is a splendid little climb; if it has a fault it is that it is too short. But for the evening of the day of arrival in Grasmere on a walking holiday it is just the thing: an epitome of Lakeland concentrated in the space of two hours . . .
Rating: ★★★★

Helvellyn | from Patterdale
and Glenridding
The ascent: Helvellyn 13 & 15
The best [way] of all, well known, popular and often densely populated in summer. The big attraction is an airy rock ridge

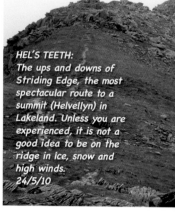

HEL'S TEETH:
The ups and downs of Striding Edge, the most spectacular route to a summit (Helvellyn) in Lakeland. Unless you are experienced, it is not a good idea to be on the ridge in ice, snow and high winds.
24/5/10

[Striding Edge], very fine indeed.
Rating: ★★★★★

Heughscar Hill | from Askham
The ascent: page 219
It is clothed in patches of bracken and a velvet turf on which carpet slippers would be more appropriate than boots, but its greatest joy is the spine of limestone outcropping in rocky pavement along the top.
Rating: ★

High Raise | from Mardale
The ascent: High Raise 7
All [the routes] are interesting, and the [ascent via the] south-east ridge especially is an attractive climb.
Rating: ★★★

High Street | from Mardale
The ascent: High Street 6
The connoisseur's route up High Street, the only route that discloses the finer characteristics of the fell. The ascent is a classic, leading directly along the crest of a long, straight ridge . . . The views are excellent throughout.
Rating: ★★★★

High Spy | from Seatoller or
Rosthwaite.
The ascent: High Spy 7
A variety of scenery, starting with sylvan

beauty and ending in moorland bleakness.
Rating: ★

Hindscarth | from Newlands Church.
The ascent: Hindscarth 6
*Make a special note of the Scope End
ridge: this route, on an enchanting track
along the heathery crest, is really
splendid . . . In descent, the route earns
full marks for the lovely views of
Newlands directly ahead.*
Rating: ★★★★

Hopegill Head | from Whinlatter Pass
The ascent: Hopegill Head 9
*The climb to the ridge by the fence is
the one dull section in a walk otherwise
full of interest and, towards the end,
quite exhilarating.*
Rating: ★★

Hopegill Head | from High Lorton
The ascent: Hopegill Head 10
*A grand high-level walk (the best
mountain climb available from Lorton)
with splendid views and an
exhilarating finish.*
Rating: ★★★

Illgill Head | from Wasdale Head
The ascent: Illgill Head 6
*On a day when the sojourner at Wasdale
Head doesn't feel quite up to Scafell or
Gable or Pillar, here is a very simple*

*climb . . . that he may find no less
rewarding, especially if he continues
beyond the summit for a long easy mile
to Whin Rigg, during which traverse he
will enjoy scenery that not even Scafell
or Gable or Pillar can match.*
Rating: ★★★

Irton Pike | from Irton Road
Railway Station
The ascent: page 184
*The gem of a wide panorama is Great
Gable - a noble sight . . . Climb Irton
Pike while ye may!*
Rating: ★★

Latrigg | from Keswick
The ascent: Latrigg 5
*There is a bewildering choice of paths,
that by Mallen Dodd being the best. The
descent by the east ridge and return to
Keswick by Brundholme Woods completes
a very beautiful short walk.*
Rating: ★★★

Long Side | from Ravenstone
The ascent: Long Side 5
*This delightful climb deserves a high,
even urgent priority from fellwalkers
who know it not. The undulating Edge
. . . is an inspiring ladder . . .*
Rating: ★★★

Lord's Seat | from Thornthwaite

The ascent: Lord's Seat 7
*An enjoyable climb, full of interest all
the way.*
Rating: ★★

Loughrigg Fell | from Grasmere
The ascent: Loughrigg Fell 5
*This walk is a succession of delights
when free of traffic, the scenery and
views being unsurpassed.*
Rating: ★★★★

Loughrigg Fell | from Ambleside
The ascent: Loughrigg Fell 6
A beautiful walk, to be done leisurely.
Rating: ★★★★

Loughrigg Fell | from Rydal
The ascent: Loughrigg Fell 7
*There is no better introduction to the
manifold attractions of Loughrigg Fell
than this easy and delightful approach.*
Rating: ★★★

Loughrigg Fell | from Skelwith Bridge
The ascent: Loughrigg Fell 10
*Splendid views and contrasting scenery,
consistent only in its loveliness, make this
the most rewarding short climb available
from Skelwith Bridge.*
Rating: ★★★

Low Fell | from Loweswater
The ascent: Low Fell 3
*Wait for a bright clear day. Don't forget
the camera.*
Rating: ★

Low Fell | from Thackthwaite
The ascent: Low Fell 4
*For elderly walkers . . . a very lovely
epitome of the best of the days gone by.*
Rating: ★

Low Pike | from Ambleside
The ascent: Low Pike 2
*The approach by any of the variations,
from the pleasant woods and pastures to
the bleak craggy ridge is very attractive.*
Rating: ★

Mardale Ill Bell | from Mardale
The ascent: Mardale Ill Bell 5
*Of the many excellent climbs available
from Mardale Head the direct ascent of
Mardale Ill Bell ranks high, the walk
being favoured by striking views of two
of the finest tarns in Lakeland, each set
amongst crags in wild and romantic*
surroundings.
Rating: ★★★★

Meal Fell | from Orthwaite
The ascent: Meal Fell 3
*Pleasant walking and interesting scenery
make this short journey into the Uldale
Fells very enjoyable.*
Rating: ★

Mellbreak | from Loweswater
The ascent: Mellbreak 5
*Highly recommended. This short climb
. . . is a grand way to the top – except
for the initial scree. It is especially
beautiful when the heather is in bloom.
The upper part of the path is a joy
to follow. Steep but no difficulties.*
Rating: ★★★

Muncaster Fell | from Muncaster
Castle car park
The ascent: page 189
*The supreme joy . . . is the delectable
traverse of its ridge . . . Here is
enchantment.*
Rating: ★★

Nethermost Pike | from Grisedale
The ascent: Nethermost Pike 6
*This is a first-class route for scramblers.
The east ridge is steep and exciting,
finishing with an arête like a miniature
Striding Edge.*
Rating: ★★★

Orrest Head | from Windermere
railway station
The ascent: page 27
*It is a popular walk, deservedly, for here
the promised land is seen in all its glory.*
Rating: ★★

Outerside | from Braithwaite
The ascent: Outerside 5
*. . . a rewarding introduction to a grand
circle of hills around Coledale.*
Rating: ★

Pavey Ark | via Easy Gully
and North Rake
The ascent: Pavey Ark 7
*This is a surprisingly easy way to the
summit, without difficulties of any sort
[I think AW is referring to Jack's Rake
here!]. It deserves to be far better
known. Try it some time!*
Rating: ★★

Pillar | from Wasdale Head via
High Level Route

The ascent: Pillar 9

*The usual route (via Black Sail Pass and
the ridge) is an excellent walk and the
easiest way to any of the Wasdale
summits [but better to join the High
Level Route, giving an extra star].*

Rating: ★★★[★]

Pillar | from Black Sail Youth Hostel
via High Level Route

The ascent: Pillar 10

*Sojourners at the hostel are fortunate in
having Pillar on their doorstep, and can
enjoy one of the best days of their
young lives by climbing it.*

Rating: ★★★★

Pillar | from Ennerdale via
the Memorial Footbridge

The ascent: Pillar 13

*A steep and rough, but romantic and
adventurous climb in magnificent
surroundings: the finest way up the
mountain. Pillar Rock grips the
attention throughout.*

Rating: ★★★★★

Place Fell | from Patterdale

The ascent: Place Fell 5

*One cannot sojourn at Patterdale
without looking at Place Fell and one
cannot look long at Place Fell without
duly setting forth to climb it. The time is
very well spent.*

Rating: ★★

Rampsgill Head | from Patterdale
and Hartsop

The ascent: Rampsgill Head 5

*This is a most enjoyable excursion with a
succession of widely different views, all
excellent; and the route itself . . . is an
interesting puzzle to unravel.*

Rating: ★★

Rannerdale Knotts | from Buttermere

The ascent: Rannerdale Knotts 3

*This is a short but very rewarding
climb in the same category as
Loughrigg Fell from Ambleside, Latrigg
from Keswick, and Helm Crag from
Grasmere.*

Rating: ★★★

Red Pike (B) | from Buttermere

The ascent: Red Pike (B) 6

*[If the direct route via Bleaberry Tarn is
overpopulated] . . . Perfect peace and
quiet will be found by Far Ruddy Beck
and in the heathery hollow of Ling Comb,*

*FIVE-STAR CLIMB: Pillar
Rock on the approach
from the Memorial
Footbridge.
22/8/07*

a place of solitude.
Rating: ★

Red Pike (W) | from Wasdale Head
   The ascent: Red Pike (W) 6
This route serves to prove that the Scafells and Great Gable have not a monopoly of the best walks around Wasdale Head. The ridge of Red Pike is excellent, lovely turf alternating with a few simple scrambles on pleasant rock.
   Rating: ★★★

Robinson | from Newlands Church
   The ascent: Robinson 5
Newlands has many good things to offer the walker and the ascent of Robinson by the ridge is amongst the best. There is a great diversity of scene during the climb, and the views in retrospect are very beautiful . . .
   Rating: ★★★★

Robinson | from Buttermere
   The ascent: Robinson 7
It's a pity about the [Buttermere] Moss: it rather spoils a splendid ascent.
   Rating: ★

Sale Fell | from Wythop Mill
   The ascent: Sale Fell 10
A sylvan approach gives added pleasure to this simple climb. As an introduction to the Wythop Valley (an introduction warmly to be commended) this route is excellent and instructive.
   Rating: ★

Scafell | from Wasdale Head
   The ascent: Scafell 10
The Brown Tongue-Lord's Rake route . . . much the finest way to the summit . . . was [in 2008] unstable as a result of rockfalls and usable only with great care.
   Rating: ★★★

Scafell Pike | from Borrowdale
via Esk Hause
   The ascent: Scafell Pike 17-18
Of the many routes of approach to Scafell Pike, this . . . is the finest. The transition from the quiet beauty of the valley pastures and woods to the rugged wildness of the mountain-top is complete, but comes gradually as height is gained and after passing through much varied scenery, both nearby and distant, that

sustains interest throughout . . .
Rating: ★★★★★

Scafell Pike | from Great Langdale
via Rossett Gill and Esk Hause
   The ascent: Scafell Pike 19
This is a splendid walk, depending for its appeal on a wide variety of scene, and of the elusiveness of the Pike . . . The route suffers from the disadvantage that it cannot be varied, by the average walker, if the return is to be made to Langdale [returning via Esk Pike, Bowfell and The Band, if strength permits, would remove the aforementioned disadvantage and would add one extra star].
   Rating: ★★★[★]

Scoat Fell | from Wasdale Head
   The ascent: Scoat Fell 6
[An] unfrequented [way] that climbs out of Mosedale through the magnificent rock scenery of Blackem Head.
   Rating: ★★

Scout Scar | from Kendal Town Hall
   The ascent: page 6
This is a walk above others: a pleasure every step of the way.
   Rating: ★★★★

Sergeant Man | from Dungeon Ghyll
   The ascent: Sergeant Man 4
A popular walk, with gill, tarn and rock scenery of the highest order and good views all the way.
   Rating: ★★★

Silver How | from Grasmere
   The ascent: Silver How 4
Two routes . . . both supremely beautiful walks. The views are charming.
   Rating: ★★★★

Skiddaw | from Keswick
   The ascent: Skiddaw 11 & 12
A time-honoured route . . . probably the first path to a Lakeland mountain-top to be trodden out distinctly . . . It is not so much a climb as a mountain-walk – to a grand, airy summit.
   Rating: ★★

Steel Fell | from Grasmere
   The ascent: Steel Fell 4
The approach is pleasant . . . climbing along the mile of ascending ridge is very enjoyable.

RETROSPECT: The beautiful view down Cat Gill from the four-star ascent of Walla Crag from the Borrowdale road.   22/10/09

Rating: ★
Steeple | from Ennerdale
The ascent: Steeple 5
A fine climb, even yet! [AW's remark was a coded message: he didn't like the conifers in Ennerdale – although things are improving with a 'softening' of the edges between the plantations and the open fell to create a more natural look.]
Rating: ★★★

Stickle Pike | from Broughton Mills
The ascent: page 128
Lovely tarns . . . soft carpets of turf and bracken, innumerable, pleasant couches where one can lie in comfort and think of real fells like Scafell and Great Gable. But do not voice these thoughts: Stickle Pike is proud and easily hurt.
Rating: ★★

Swirl How | from Coniston
The ascent: Swirl How 4
There is interest all the way, even though, in places, the interest is in things desolate and derelict. A most excellent expedition.
Rating: ★★★

Thornthwaite Crag | from Hartsop
The ascent: Thornthwaite Crag 4
This is a very interesting and enjoyable expedition.
Rating: ★★

Thornthwaite Crag | from Kentmere Reservoir
The ascent: Thornthwaite Crag 6
This approach leads into the unfrequented dalehead of Kentmere and abounds in interest and variety all the way from the village.
Rating: ★★

Ullock Pike | from Bassenthwaite Village
The ascent: Ullock Pike 5
A short, enjoyable climb, with superb views from the small peaked summit.
Rating: ★★

Ullock Pike | from Ravenstone
The ascent: Ullock Pike 6
This enjoyable little climb gets full marks. The Edge is a mile in length and everywhere pleasant, particularly so at its culmination in the small heathery top, a most delightful place with lovely views. This route may be adapted as a way (in fact, the most beautiful and interesting way) to the top of Skiddaw.
Rating: ★★★

Walla Crag | from Keswick
The ascent: Walla Crag 3
No excuse is good enough for missing this easy half-day's walk, which is delightful throughout.
Rating: ★★★

Walla Crag | from the Borrowdale road
The ascent: Walla Crag 4
A beautiful short climb up steep colourful slopes overlooking Derwent Water. If the starting point on the road

is reached via Friar's Crag and Calfclose Bay, and if the return is made via Rakefoot and Brockle Beck [Walla Crag 3], this becomes the best walk easily attainable in a half-day from Keswick.

Rating: ★★★★

Wandope | from Buttermere

The ascent: Wandope 7

No other way up Wandope can compare even remotely with this for beauty and grandeur of views and sustained interest.

Rating: ★★★

Wetherlam | from Tilberthwaite

The ascent: Wetherlam 10

This splendid climb in attractive and contrasting scenery is given added interest by short detours of inspection to the many old copper workings . . .

Rating: ★★

Whin Rigg | from Nether Wasdale

The ascent: Whin Rigg 5

The reward for this climb comes not from the doing of it but from the unique, beautiful and inspiring situation to which it leads: the top of the towering crags and gullies of the Screes, a scene without counterpart elsewhere.

Rating: ★★

Whitbarrow | from Mill Side

The ascent: page 40

The walk described is the most beautiful in this book; beautiful it is every step of the way . . . All is fair to the eye on Whitbarrow.

Rating: ★★★★★

Whiteless Pike | from Buttermere

The ascent: Whiteless Pike 3

This is a popular climb on a good path, and is very pleasant throughout . . . The views are superb.

Rating: ★★

Whiteside | from Lanthwaite Green

The ascent: Whiteside 8

This ascent, which promises nothing but a hard grind, turns out instead to be a delightful and interesting climb. It is incomparably the best route up the fell.

Rating: ★★★

Woodland Fell | from Woodland

The ascent: page 106

The walk here described is a connoisseur's piece, every step an unhibited joy, every corner a delight.

Rating: ★★★★

Yewbarrow | from Overbeck Bridge

The ascent: Yewbarrow 5

The best route to the top of Yewbarrow, a beautiful and interesting climb highlighted by the moment of arrival at the huge cleft of Great Door.

Rating: ★★★★

ON THE WAY UP: Whin Rigg, with the path to its summit from the top of the huge slice of Greathall Gill prominent. Far left is Yewbarrow. 2/2/07

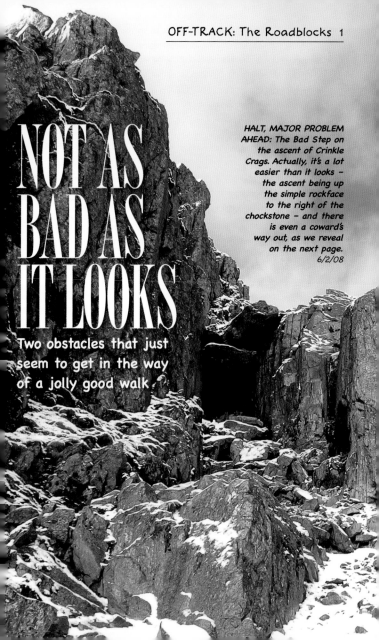

NOT AS BAD AS IT LOOKS

Two obstacles that just seem to get in the way of a jolly good walk.

HALT, MAJOR PROBLEM AHEAD: The Bad Step on the ascent of Crinkle Crags. Actually, it's a lot easier than it looks – the ascent being up the simple rockface to the right of the chockstone – and there is even a coward's way out, as we reveal on the next page.
6/2/08

The picture on the previous page makes the Bad Step on Crinkle Crags look more like something on Everest's north-east ridge than on the best ridge walk in Lakeland. In fact, as AW reveals on Crinkle Crags 17, if you're not up to climbing or descending the easy 10ft rockface (and it is not difficult if you have the remotest little bit of agility), then there is an easy way up around to the left of the main buttress via a grassy rake. Of the Bad Step, AW writes:

THAT'S NOT SO BAD: The Bad Step looks less daunting in the summer months. The much-used detour is round to the left.   29/8/07

> *This is the sort of place that everybody would get down in a flash if a £20 note was waiting to be picked up on the scree below, but, without such an inducement, there is much wavering on the brink. Chicken-hearted walkers, muttering something about discretion being the better part of valour, will sneak away and circumvent the difficulty by following the author's footsteps . . . The Bad Step is the most difficult obstacle met on any of the regular walkers' paths in Lakeland.*

Ahhh, but what about Jack's Rake on Pavey Ark, you might ask? Well, AW makes the perfectly valid point (and I can vouch for this, having made the ascent of Jack's Rake myself, something I don't like to think about if I can help it) that this is not a path for walkers. It's for scramblers only. And only those with as much bottle as a brewery. (See The Two Rakes, pages 94-95).

And then there's **Broad Stand** on Scafell, at the end of the **Mickledore** ridge between Scafell Pike and Scafell, where the vertical meets the horizontal in the most spectacular way in Lakeland. Now, this is where AW contradicts himself in the space of 154 pages (Crinkle Crags 15 to Scafell 3) and little over two-and-a-half miles (the distance a crow would fly across Eskdale between the two mountains). Of Broad Stand, which stands right in the way of the direct ridge route between England's two highest mountains, he writes:

NO ENTRY: At the end of Mickledore, Broad Stand blocks the way to Scafell. The alternatives are a descent to Lord's Rake (far right) or an even greater loss of height (left) to Foxes Tarn.   25/6/09

> *The greatest single obstacle confronting ridge walkers on the hills of Lakeland is the notorious Broad Stand . . . Obstacles met on other ridges can be overcome or easily bypassed; not so Broad Stand . . . The platform is shut in by smooth walls, the route of exit (for experts only) being up the scratched corner on the left. But for mere pedestrians the platform is the limit of their*

exploration and they should return through the cleft, resolving, as is customary, to do the climb next time. The author first made this resolve in 1930 and he repeated it a score of times after that; his continued disappointment was amply compensated by the pleasure of going on living.

Nevertheless, AW advises walkers to visit Broad Stand because of its long history. Going back, in fact, to Thursday, 5 August 1802, when the poet **Samuel Taylor Coleridge** made a historic and unplanned descent of this obstacle (which is generally thought to be even more dangerous than trying to climb it). Memorably, Coleridge wrote in a letter:

I began to suspect that I ought not to go on, but then unfortunately though I could with ease drop down a smooth rock 7ft high, I could not climb it, so go on I must and on I went . . . The next three drops were not half a foot, at least not a foot more than my own height, but every increase increased the palsy of my limbs — I shook all over, Heaven knows without the least influence of fear; and now I had only two more to drop down. To return was impossible — but of these two the first was tremendous, it was twice my own height, and the ledge at the bottom was so exceedingly narrow, that if

I dropped down upon it I must of necessity have fallen backwards and of course killed myself. My limbs were all in a tremble — I lay upon my back to rest myself, and was beginning according to my custom to laugh at myself for a madman, when the sight of the crags above me on each side, and the impetuous clouds just over them, posting so luridly and so rapidly northward, overawed me. I lay in a state of almost prophetic trance and delight — and blessed God aloud, for the powers of reason and the will, which remaining no danger can overpower us!

Coleridge survived, but would have placed himself in a lot less danger if he had taken either of the alternative routes, via **Foxes Tarn** or via **Lord's Rake**. In the first edition of BOOK FOUR, AW recommends the latter route between the two mountains; the second edition, revised by Chris Jesty, recommends the former – probably because of a rockfall on Lord's Rake that left a chockstone perched at the top of the first steep section.

A paragraph in *Scafell 4* states: *In 2008 Lord's Rake was deemed passable with care.* BE WARNED!

The Foxes Tarn route is rough and has a greater descent from Mickledore and therefore an extra 150ft of ascent. You pays your money and you takes your choice.

LORD'S RAKE: *The chockstone at the top of the first section is twice the size of a man.*
1/2/12 & 30/1/06 (inset)

HOW WELL DO YOU KNOW YOUR FELLS?

Quiz time: test your knowledge of the guidebooks

A1: NAME THIS FELL: Quite often known by another name; the second highest in its guidebook; it has a long eastern ridge that passes over three other '214' fells.

A2: NAME THIS FELL: Within its boundary is one of Lakeland's most-famous tourist attractions; a subsidiary peak, Green Hill, has a great view over a popular lake.

A3: NAME THIS TARN: A former reservoir that used to supply water to a now-closed gunpowder works.

A4: NAME THIS FELL: It has ridge routes to Thornthwaite Crag and Ill Bell.

A5: PICTURE QUESTION (right): Sean McMahon's dog is named Casper, but what is the cairn known as?

A6: NAME THIS RIDGE (where the blank is): *Once the ridge is gained from the Pass (a matter of 15 minutes simple climbing over rough grass and mosses) the remainder of this walk, with views improving the whole way, is merely a stroll. .... is one of the easiest ridges in the district . . .*

19/3/08

A7: NAME THIS ROCK FORMATION: *Below the crag west of the summit are many mammoth boulders and one grotesque 12-foot fanged splinter.*

A8: NAME THIS OUTLYING FELL: Three tarns are featured in its chapter: Moss Eccles Tarn, Wise Een Tarn and Three Dubs Tarn.

A9: NAME THIS FELL: Aughertree Fell is a low hill that gets a whole page in AW's chapter on this fell.

A10: NAME THIS FELL: AW's drawing of the ascent route is the only such drawing to include both Borrowdale and Wasdale.

THE ANSWERS are on page 344, but before you go there, there are OTHER QUIZZES: on pages 108, 137, 159, 205, 216, 239 and 259.

HOW MANY DO YOU SEE? Three Tarns, looking towards Crinkle Crags. 26/7/11

THREE VIEWS

Now you see one, now you don't. The tarns that just don't seem to add up

From Bowfell 15, **first edition**

From Bowfell 15, **second edition**

In the first edition of BOOK FOUR, describing an ascent of Crinkle Crags via Three Tarns, AW writes: *Turn left just short of the three tarns but beyond a smaller fourth one (missed in the original count).* In the second edition revision, Chris Jesty amends this to: *Turn left just short of the three tarns (one of which is now very small).* So what happened to the other tarn? Well, presumably it must have dried up; tarns do that. And the same drought conditions must have caused tarn number three to have shrunk.

In the second edition, the view of Three Tarns from Bowfell (Bowfell 15) describing the ridge walk to Crinkle Crags has been modified. OUT has gone the fourth tarn (compare the two images, above), and the third tarn has indeed shrunk considerably. But the second edition of BOOK FOUR was reprinted in 2008, and the main photo on this page (taken in 2011) shows that tarn number three is almost back to the shape it occupied in the first edition (the original image was drawn between 1958 and 1959). Which only proves that tarns that can shrink can also expand – and that, one day, the fourth of the Three Tarns will make a comeback. Three-and-a-half Tarns, perhaps!

Lakes & Tarns chapter starts on page 182

The grandest fell, the finest way up, the highest place in England...

THE DADDY OF THEM ALL

THE BEST SIDE: The Eskdale flank of Scafell Pike, as seen from Bowfell. The ascent from Borrowdale climbs the ridge to the right of the summit.   11/2/10

If you've climbed Scafell Pike once you've probably climbed it several times. Once you've done it there's nothing else left to do, is there? (Not true, but you know what I mean.) Nothing else to do . . . except, of course, to climb it from another direction.

We've probably all got our favourite way up. AW considers the approach from Eskdale shows its grandest and most rugged aspect; but he believes the ascent from Borrowdale (up via Esk Hause, down via the Corridor Route) to be the best Lakeland mountain excursion of the lot. That climb – Scafell Pike from Seathwaite, via Esk Hause – is featured over these six pages in detail. It just happens to be my favourite ascent of Scafell Pike, too.

Seathwaite to Stockley Bridge

The route continues up the valley from the cluster of farm buildings.

At Stockley Bridge

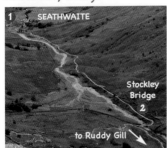

Stockley Bridge to Grains Gill

Cross the bridge and turn left (don't go straight on to Sty Head – that's the return route).

> **from BORROWDALE:**
> The ascent from Borrowdale is pre-eminent, because not only is the scenery excellent throughout but there is the advantage of two interesting and well-contrasted routes, so that one may be used in ascent and the alternative in descent, the whole round, in settled weather, being perhaps the finest mountain-walk in the district. *From Seathwaite – 3½ hours up, 2½ down.*

SUMMARY: How AW assessed, in BOOK FOUR, the route from Seathwaite.

FIRST PART OF THE ROUTE: As shown in the first edition of BOOK FOUR.

Along Grains Gill

ALLEN CRAGS

3

to Ruddy Gill ravine

Scafell Pike 17

ASCENT FROM BORROWDALE
via ESK HAUSE
3,200 feet of ascent   5½ miles from Seatoller

A: A fairly new path cuts off the corner by the wall shelter and is now in common use
B: Path continues behind Great End to Scafell Pike

There is a lengthy dissertation concerning Esk Hause on pages Esk Pike 3 and 4, but not time enough to stop and read it when actively on route for Scafell Pike

The summit here is ALLEN CRAGS

ESK PIKE   Esk Hause   GREAT END
wall shelter
GREAT LANGDALE
D: Central Gully
C: South-east Gully
STY HEAD and WASDALE

Note the strange rocky recess with waterfall on the east bank on the west bank just here

GLARAMARA is the long fell on the left of the valley

The fell bounding the valley on the right is SEATHWAITE FELL

The transition from valley to mountain begins as the path gets higher up Grains Gill, with Allen Crags looming ahead and the climb to the Ruddy Beck ravine just around the shoulder of Seathwaite Fell (the slope to the right).

Grains Gill to Ruddy Gill ravine

An old path (now virtually disappeared) ascends up a tongue to the left, but the new path hugs the left-hand side of Ruddy Gill. Another former path switched to the right of the ravine. That too has gone out of use since the first edition of BOOK FOUR. At point 4 the

GREAT END   LINGMELL

4

to Esk Hause

Ruddy Gill

Sprinkling Tarn

3

scenery has really opened up, with the awesome north face of Great End looming overhead and, to the right, a profile view of Great Gable. The path to Esk Hause makes a 90-degree turn to the left and heads towards the sloping shelf between Allen Crags and the real Esk Hause. AW discusses this confusing landscape on Esk Pike 3 & 4; Esk Hause is also featured in this book on page 281.

Ruddy Gill to Esk Hause

5 GREAT END

4

Sprinkling Tarn

Styhead Tarn

Return path to Stockley Bridge

The view from Great Gable (left) across the Sty Head depression shows how the path crosses a sloping shelf from the corner of Ruddy Gill (4) to Esk Hause (5) which is the pass between Borrowdale and Eskdale that links Great End and Esk Pike (in the clouds). The northern slopes of Bowfell can be seen beyond Esk Pike. It was at this point AW started the second page of his ascent of Scafell Pike from Borrowdale – the chapter about England's highest mountain was the first in the series to use two complete pages for one ascent.

Esk Hause to Ill Crag plateau

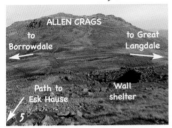

Scafell Pike 18

ASCENT FROM BORROWDALE
via ESK HAUSE

continued

This diagram is on a larger scale than that on the opposite page.

Ill Crag is prominently in view from the section of path between Esk Hause and Calf Cove. It is the highest thing in sight, and wishful thinkers will assume it to be the summit — until the Pike itself is finally revealed, indisputably higher and still far distant across a waste of stones.

Of the many routes of approach to Scafell Pike, this, from Borrowdale via Esk Hause, is the finest. The transition from the quiet beauty of the valley pastures and woods to the rugged wildness of the mountain-top is complete, but comes gradually as height is gained and after passing through varied scenery, both nearby and distant, that sustains interest throughout the long march.

Esk Hause is confusing. Two passes cross a tilted plateau. The key to the ascent of the Pike is the higher pass (above the wall shelter). Many years ago this could have been a problem in a misty ascent from Borrowdale. But now a new path cuts the corner with a beeline straight to the true Esk Hause.

Heading towards Calf Cove

A wide path crosses a gently rising slope with Great End rising away to the right. Ahead is Calf Cove, a stony area that is a foretaste of a 150-yard section of big boulders (7) as the path approaches the gravelly plateau of Ill Crag (8).

Crossing the plateau of Ill Crag towards Ill Crag col

This section (above) is well seen from Great End, and clearly shows the ups and downs that are ahead of the weary walker expecting to be nearing the summit of Scafell Pike. First obstacle is the path through the boulders (7), followed by the easier climb across the plateau of Ill Crag (8). At that point, well before Ill Crag col (9) is reached, there is a shock in store . . . which AW captures in one of his finest ascent drawings.

Ill Crag plateau to Broad Crag col

The next section is best summed up by this wonderful drawing (right) on page 20 of the Scafell Pike chapter, and the caption beneath. The nature of the terrain starts to change at this point. From Ill Crag col (9) the climb becomes more of an ungainly scramble from one boulder to another across the shoulder of Broad Crag (10), down to Broad Crag col (11, hidden from view in the drawing) and then the final haul up to the summit of the Pike (12). There are a few areas of respite, but these are all

(Behind ridge)

Many hearts have sunk into many boots as this scene unfolds. Here, on the shoulder of Ill Crag, the summit comes into sight, at last; not almost within reach as confidently expected by walkers who feel they have already done quite enough to deserve success, but still a rough half-mile distant, with two considerable descents (Ill Crag col and Broad Crag col) and much climbing yet to be faced before the goal is reached.

relative – everywhere the path is slippery, stony or downright rocky. The conditions underfoot are particularly trying in the crossing of Broad Crag.

Crossing Broad Crag

The crossing of Broad Crag from the wide Ill Crag col is torturous. The only relief comes when the narrower Broad Crag col is reached, with paths coming up from Eskdale (left) and the Corridor Route (right).

Broad Crag col, before the final climb to the Pike

Broad Crag col is a good place to look towards Eskdale and Crinkle Crags (above left) and Lingmell, Pillar and Great Gable (right). Now take a deep breath . . .

From Broad Crag col to the summit — more boulders to come!

. . . because the climb from Broad Crag col is initially very steep; it flattens out as a plateau is reached. From here, the summit cairn looks like a squat hotel — but there is still another five minutes of torture ahead, clambering over the final field of boulders that guards the highest point in England.

The summit of England

AW pretty well covers everything you need to know about the summit on pages 23 and 24, and there's a comprehensive guide to the view (if there *is* one!) on the following four pages. If you haven't got to somewhere that looks like the picture below, you're lost. There may not necessarily be snow on the summit, but it can feel as cold as it looks here, even in the height of summer.

The descent: The same way as up, or the Corridor Route

Either way involves returning to Broad Crag col. From here, go straight on for **Esk Hause** and **Seathwaite**; for the **Corridor Route**, turn left, then turn to *Scafell Pike 15* and *16* (second edition) for full details of the descent.

Faced with a choice between the toughest walkers' scramble in Lakeland, and a grassy stroll just around the corner, many mere mortals might opt to take

THE EASY WAY OUT

Pages 5 and 6 of the Pavey Ark chapter are classics: a classic ascent, a classic ascent diagram, some classic writing: *Care should be taken to avoid falling down the precipice or sending stones over the edge. Falling bodies, human or mineral, may constitute a danger to unseen climbers on the rocks or the scree below, or to grazing sheep . . . Jack's Rake is just about the limit that the ordinary common or garden fell walker reasonably may be expected to attempt.*

I would describe myself as an ordinary common-or-garden fellwalker, and I have climbed Jack's Rake. Just like AW, I felt it had to be done, simply because it is there. If it wasn't already an accepted ascent of a Lakeland fell I wouldn't have climbed it if you had paid me. I suspect if that was the case AW would never have contemplated hauling himself up there as one of his 'off-piste' routes (see *Off-piste*, starting on page 270).

JACK'S RAKE

DON'T attempt it in snow or ice; DON'T attempt it if it is dripping with rain-water; DON'T go near it if you haven't got a head for heights.

NORTH RAKE

DO try this delightful approach; DO wallow in the comfort that you're well away from Jack; DO boast of having climbed 'that rake' on Pavey Ark (no one will ever suspect you chickened out of the real deal!).

SEAN McMAHON'S VIEW OF JACK'S RAKE

If you are a lover of scrambles and enjoy the feeling of the 'hands on' rock experience, then Jack's Rake is one of the best ways to reach a fell top. The feeling of exposure is limited to one or two places and the majority of the climb is enclosed in a rocky groove – hard work but a great feeling of fulfilment when you reach the top.

Because of my experience of this route, I would like to offer readers who haven't climbed Jack's Rake my personal advice: don't attempt it in snow or ice; don't attempt it if it is dripping with rain-water; don't go near it if you haven't got a head for heights.

The last point may surprise some people; doesn't AW write that *there is curiously little sense of exposure, for a comforting parapet of rock accompanies all the steeper parts of the ascent.* I would say to that: baloney. There is one place that scared the bejeesus out of me and my climbing companion: the platform at the foot of Gwyne's Chimney and the *slight descent (above steep grass slope – care!).* If this isn't 'exposed' I don't know what is. The few minutes we spent frozen to the spot wondering if we'd ever see the next dawn convinced me of that. If you think you might feel the same kind

94

of high anxiety, content yourself with the other rake on Pavey Ark, the one that (in a not-so-subtle coded message) AW urged his readers to choose instead; content yourself with the ascent described on Pavey Ark 7: *This (North Rake) is a surprisingly easy way to the summit, without difficulties of any sort. It deserves to be far better known. Try it some time!*

If that wasn't a dig at the kind of indignities likely to be suffered on Jack's Rake, I don't know what is!

NOW A NOTE TO TRY TO SALVAGE THE PITIFUL REMNANTS OF MY SELF-RESPECT: With due care and some scrambling agility, Jack's Rake is probably as safe as houses – it just doesn't feel it. Striding Edge has never scared me; Sharp Edge and Shamrock Traverse were a cinch. There was just something about Jack's Rake . . . When I emerged at the top a guy wandered over from the nearby summit and asked me if it was the first time I'd climbed Jack's Rake. I remember to this day how I replied: 'No, it's the last time.' However, I'm willing to give it one more go before I go. How about it, Sean? (on a dry day, please!).

THE ARROW MARKS THE SPOT: The direction of North Rake, mainly on grass with some scree and, two-thirds of the way up, with a view down Easy Gully.   *9/1/07*
INSET: AW's drawing shows exactly how straight the rake is.
BELOW: The rough and steep start of Jack's Rake showing the groove across the rock.   *8/9/08*

A ROCK TO LEAN ON: Sean McMahon's dog Casper strikes an AW pose, nearly fifty years after the BOOK TWO self-portrait. The arrow benchmark in the drawing can still be seen in the photo. 12/11/08

MARK OF AN ARTIST

This BOOK TWO sketch was the first of just two self-portraits that occupy a full page (the other was on the very last page of BOOK SEVEN).

It shows AW reclining against a rock on a shoulder of Harter Fell overlooking Haweswater. And the large arrow on the rock (a benchmark) is still there in Sean's photograph nearly half-a-century later. There's no doubt the location offers a wonderful view – but it's strange that AW chose to draw himself overlooking the lake – make that reservoir – he hated so much, after Manchester Corporation flooded the pretty village of Mardale in 1935 to provide water for the industrial north-west.

NOTE: Once again, as in the BOOK ONE self-portrait, AW is seen smoking a pipe with his left leg extended. And there's that trusty knapsack as well.

Haweswater
from the third cairn

TOP PLACES

AW picked six summits...but he loved a lot more

In the last of his *personal notes in conclusion* (BOOK SEVEN) **AW** names what he considers to be the six best summits in Lakeland:

DOW CRAG, Coniston	HARTER FELL, Eskdale
HELM CRAG, Grasmere	EAGLE CRAG, Langstrath
SLIGHT SIDE, Scafell	STEEPLE, Ennerdale

These were choices based on **AW**'s definition of a splendid summit: *Attributes: a small neat peak of naked rock with a good view.*

Other attributes appear throughout the seven books, typically described by adjectives such as 'interesting', 'delectable', 'glorious', so perhaps a neat peak, naked rock and a good view are not the only criteria to consider when picking favourite summits.

In this chapter, we look at some of his favourite high places . . .

IN THE PICTURE: Among the top six only Steeple (seen here from Black Crag) can be reached without handling rock. 10/11/10

WATER VIEW: Angle Tarn from the summit of Angletarn Pikes.   *5/5/11*

LET THERE BE ROCK

Some of Lakeland's 'lesser' fells make up for their lack of inches with defiant, rocky tops. Here are some of the best:

Angletarn Pikes: *Twin upthrusts of rock . . . give individuality to this unusual summit.*

Arnison Crag: *A rock platform . . . attained . . . only by breaches in a low wall of crag defending it.*

Calf Crag: *Small and rocky . . . a pleasant place for . . . quiet contemplation of the scenery.*

Cold Pike: *The best part of the fell . . . three rocky humps.* [Main cairn on pleasant platform.]

Glaramara: *A rocky platform bearing two cairns . . . a pleasant halting place on the right sort of day.*

Middle Fell: *Crowns a small rocky mound . . . a splendid vantage point.*

Steel Knotts: *May well claim to have the sharpest summit in Lakeland* [and it has its own name - Pikeawassa]. *Only agile walkers will be able to stand upon it.*

Stone Arthur: *The small crags around the summit offer practice for embryo climbers whose main concern is not to drop too far if they fall.*

PLEASANT PLACE: The summit of Calf Crag, looking towards Grasmere. *31/7/08*

PIKEAWASSA: The top of Steel Knotts, looking towards Ullswater. *22/7/08*

BIG PATH: Cold Pike, looking towards Crinkle Crags and Bowfell. *14/7/11*

EXTRA SPECIAL

AW's favourite mountain **Haystacks** fails to make the author's 'best half-dozen' because of its modest height - 1959ft. And its summit doesn't meet all three key criteria (neat peak, naked rock, good view) for one of his top-six tops.

However, anyone who reads the summit description (BOOK SEVEN, Haystacks 10) can have no doubt that the fell also is AW's top top!

Here's what he has to say: *. . . for beauty, variety and interesting detail, for sheer fascination and unique individuality, the summit-area of Haystacks is supreme. This is in fact the best fell-top of all – a place of great charm and fairytale attractiveness . . . the combination of features, of tarn and tor, of cliff and cave, the labyrinth of corners and recesses, the maze of old sheepwalks and paths, form a design, or lack of design, of singular appeal and absorbing interest. One can forget even a raging toothache on Haystacks.*

TOP CAIRN: Looking towards High Crag and the Buttermere Valley. 12/7/11

SUPREME LOCATION: Haystacks and the Buttermere pines. 31/3/08

THE HAYSTACKS FACTOR

. . . applies to summits where there really doesn't seem any hurry to get down. Here are nine recommended tops (5 from BOOK THREE):

Blea Rigg: *The top . . . with its outcrops and tarns, is entirely attractive.*

Glenridding Dodd: *On a sunny day in August . . . a delectable place.*

Grange Fell: Two summits for the price of one: ***Brund Fell*** *. . . steep-sided rock towers;* ***King's How:*** *A steep-sided dome.*

Latrigg: *A grand place . . . especially for fellwalkers on the retired list.*

Pavey Ark: *Environs . . . are delectable . . . beautiful grey rock . . .*

Rannerdale Knotts: *Glorious views . . . for leisurely exploration.*

Tarn Crag: *Beautiful . . . a . . . peak . . . just big enough for a small cairn.*

Ullock Pike: *Upholstered in heather . . . just the sort of place to make one wish it could be parcelled up and taken home for the back garden.*

Walla Crag: *Delectable place for a picnic . . . heathery . . .*

THE FELLS: Super summits 4

SOMETHING FOR A RAINY DAY

. . . or maybe not! Because these fells have interesting summits, you may want to spend more than a few minutes on their tops.

Binsey: *The summit is the best part of the fell . . . surmounted by a great heap of stones (in fact a tumulus).*

Carrock Fell: *Draped like a necklace around the western top (the higher) is a broad band of stones, the ruined wall of the ancient fort: a continuous link except for four breaches corresponding to the main points of the compass.*

Castle Crag: *Circular in plan, about 60 yards in diameter, and a perfect natural stronghold.*

High Pike: *A positive array of objects of interest . . . a cairn, OS column, patch of stones, a ruined house, now a wind shelter, a memorial seat to Mick Lewis 'who loved all these fells'.*

Seatallan: *The summit cairn is a huge tumulus (67 yards in circumference). Without doubt, the biggest cairn in Lakeland.*

ON THE EDGE: Dale Head's imposing cairn and the view towards the Newlands Valley. 1/11/10

PERCHED: Summit of Lingmell, looking towards a snowy Great End. 4/3/10

VIEW OF PATTERDALE: Seen from the summit of Red Screes. 1/2/11

NECKLACE OF STONES: Carrock Fell, looking towards Skiddaw. 25/2/11

EASTERN PROMISE: Kidsty Pike is perched high above Riggindale. 14/6/10

100

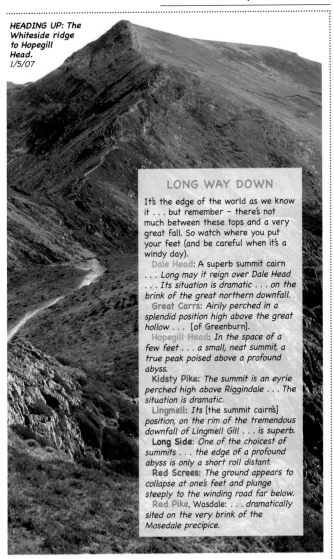

HEADING UP: The Whiteside ridge to Hopegill Head.
1/5/07

LONG WAY DOWN

It's the edge of the world as we know it . . . but remember – there's not much between these tops and a very great fall. So watch where you put your feet (and be careful when it's a windy day).

Dale Head: A superb summit cairn . . . *Long may it reign over Dale Head . . . Its situation is dramatic . . . on the brink of the great northern downfall.*

Great Carrs: *Airily perched in a splendid position high above the great hollow . . . [of Greenburn].*

Hopegill Head: *In the space of a few feet . . . a small, neat summit, a true peak poised above a profound abyss.*

Kidsty Pike: *The summit is an eyrie perched high above Riggindale . . . The situation is dramatic.*

Lingmell: *Its [the summit cairn's] position, on the rim of the tremendous downfall of Lingmell Gill . . . is superb.*

Long Side: *One of the choicest of summits . . . the edge of a profound abyss is only a short roll distant.*

Red Screes: *The ground appears to collapse at one's feet and plunge steeply to the winding road far below.*

Red Pike, Wasdale: *. . . dramatically sited on the very brink of the Mosedale precipice.*

THE POINT OF THE CLIMB

There is no doubt that a mountain with a shapely summit excites the pulses (when one is climbing it) and gives one a supreme air of satisfaction (when perched upon it). It's that 'Yes, I got up here' moment, and although the mountains of Lakeland are pretty low (by world standards), try telling them that! Here are some pointed places that impress AW:

Ard Crags: *Save a visit here for a warm still day in August, and envy not the crowds heading for Great Gable.*

Catbells: *The summit . . . is a small platform of naked rock . . . so popular . . . that often it is difficult to find a vacant perch.*

Catstycam: *Catstycam is a true peak, and its small shapely summit is the finest in the eastern fells; if it were rock and not mainly grass it would be the finest in the district. Here the highest point is not in doubt!*

NICE SHAPE: The pyramid-like outline of Catstycam.   11/3/10

Causey Pike: *Delightful . . . quite unlike any other [top], its narrow crest undulating over five distinct bumps (meticulous visitors will count seven).*

Ill Bell: *A real mountain-top, small in extent and very rough . . . one of the most distinctive summits in Lakeland.*

Loft Crag: *The small, delicately-poised summit makes a splendid halting-place.*

Pike o'Stickle: *The perfect dome, [as] suggested by its appearance from a distance.*

ICING SUGAR: Pike o'Stickle, the second-highest of the Langdale Pikes, especially looks like a 'sugarloaf' in winter
22/2/10

TOP-KNOTT: The summit of Causey Pike as seen from near Little Town. 1/11/10

THE TOP: The distinctive summit cairn of Pike o'Blisco may no longer have its former glories, but it is still visible from a distance. 4/7/06

BLISS O'BLISCO

AW is a great fan of the summit of Pike o'Blisco, the Great Langdale 2300-footer. Here's what he has to say: *This is a beautiful 'top', and a colourful one, with pinky-grey rocks outcropping everywhere from dark heather and green mosses. The main cairn is a shapely edifice,* gloriously situated on a platform of naked rock at the north-western terminus of a summit-ridge 100 yards long.*

* NOTE: Not as shapely now as when AW wrote this: see below.

Personal note...

I first came to Langdale in 1969 and the cairn on Pike o'Blisco was then back to how it looked when AW wrote his chapter on Pike o'Blisco (before he wrote his *personal notes in conclusion* lamenting the cairn's destruction). But the wreckers were not to be deterred, and the summit cairn has since been 'cropped' again, and has yet to return to its former glory.

ROCKY 1481: At less than 1500ft in height, Catbells has a pointed crown that offers great views. 18/12/11

IT'S AN ARD LIFE: But not when you're climbing to the charming summit of Ard Crags. 30/6/09

OLD GLORY: How the summit cairn used to look – a work of art.

SCAFELL PIKE - SUMMIT OF ENGLAND: There is a huge cairn that from afar looks like a hotel. There are also masses of stones. This is the top, looking towards Scafell and Wast Water.
25/6/09

THE GRAND ONES...

These are the summits that everyone wants to climb . . . the high places, the rough places, the grand places. They are the rugged tops to the mountains that are every inch mountains - peaks that dominate their own particular area of Lakeland, whether it is the Vale of Keswick or above Threlkeld; whether it is the head of Great Langdale or Wasdale; or whether it is the rocky side of the Buttermere Valley; or, of course, whether it is just England.

Here are six of AW's best . . .

Blencathra: *The summit is effectively poised above the abyss, precisely at the point where the ridge of Hall's Fell comes up out of the depths to a jutting headland.*

JUTTING HEADLAND: The summit ridge of Blencathra. Hall's Fell top (cairn) looking to Doddick Fell (left) with Skiddaw in the background.
11/9/07

Bowfell: *Bowfell's top is a shattered pyramid, a great heap of stones and boulders and naked rock, a giant cairn in itself . . . The leisurely contemplation of the scene [the view] will not be assailed by doubt as to whether the highest point has in fact been gained for rough slopes tumble away steeply on all sides.*

Great Gable: *The ultimate crest . . . is truly characteristic of the best of mountain Lakeland: a rugged crown of rock and boulders and stones in chaotic profusion, a desert without life, a harsh and desolate peak thrust high in the sky above the profound depths all around.*

High Stile: *A rocky eminence crowned with two cairns immediately above the*

GREAT TOP: Gable is home to the memorial tablet of the Fell and Rock Climbing Club, which holds a Remembrance Day service on the summit every year.   3/2/10

abrupt fall to Chapel Crags ... the more northerly of the two [cairns] is in a magnificent situation with a dramatic view downwards to Bleaberry Tarn.

Skiddaw: *The top ... is rough enough and airy enough to suit all tastes. It takes the form of a stony, undulating ridge exceeding 3000' throughout its length of almost half a mile ... a glorious promenade high in the sky where one can enjoy a rare feeling of freedom and* escape from a world far below, and, for a time, forgotten.

Scafell Pike: The ultimate; the supreme; the one objective above all others ... It is a magnet, not because of its beauty, for this is not a place of beauty, not because of the exhilaration of the climb for there is no exhilaration in toiling upwards over endless stones ... It is a magnet because it is the highest ground in England.

PROMENADE: Skiddaw view, looking towards the Scafells, Esk Pike and Bowfell.   17/12/10

WHAT A VIEW FROM THE SUMMIT: (Right) Er, it's not the summit of Lingmell, it's the view from the northern cairn overlooking Wasdale. The actual summit (left) has a less impressive cairn these days.

Main picture: 1/4/09

Left: 23/11/07

YOU CAIRN'T ALWAYS

THE WAY IT WAS: The 10ft spire on Lingmell's summit.

The level of detail that went into the revisions of all AW's Lakeland guidebooks is nowhere better illustrated than in the Lingmell chapter (on page 7), with the description of the summit. In the first edition, AW writes: *Summit cairns are welcome sights, but they are seldom objects of beauty or admiration. Here, however, on the highest point of Lingmell, is one of singular elegance, a graceful ten-foot spire that quite puts to shame the squat and inartistic edifice crowning the neighbouring very superior Scafell Pike.*

When Chris Jesty came to revise BOOK FOUR, the former summit cairn of Lingmell had long since been replaced . . . but a simple change of tense and a new next sentence did the trick: *Here, however, on the highest point of Lingmell, **was** one of singular elegance . . . The cairn illustrated has been replaced by one much broader, but just as well built, while 250 yards to the north is a column looking much like the one illustrated. Both cairns are poised on the brink of a great precipice.*

GET WHAT YOU WANT

As Sean's stunning picture (above) shows, the secondary column does, indeed, bear a striking resemblance to the original summit cairn, built more than fifty years ago. Here's what I think happened: Someone rebuilt the main cairn which had been destroyed some time before Christmas 1961 (AW's *personal notes* to BOOK FIVE confirm this), and then someone else decided they would replicate the old summit cairn. Naturally, they did not want to tear down the 'new' summit cairn, so instead found a splendid position overlooking Wasdale for their retro-look structure.

That's just a theory. And here's another thought – doesn't the shapely edifice on Lingmell bear a striking resemblance to the Joss Naylor cairn on Buckbarrow? Could they, by any chance, be related?

LOOKALIKE CAIRN: The Buckbarrow structure built by legendary fellrunner Joss Naylor, looking towards the Screes.
26/5/10

HOW WELL DO YOU KNOW YOUR FELLS?

Quiz time: test your knowledge of the guidebooks

B1: NAME THIS FELL: *This short climb is as simple as the diagram suggests. Anybody full of the joy of Spring will do it in 15 minutes (author's time: 35 min.).*

B2: NAME THIS FELL: In which chapter will you see a drawing of a signpost that says: 'No road to the lake' and 'No road to the lake'?

B3: NAME THIS TARN: *. . . tiered crags carved by ice; silent waters embanked by moraines; scattered rocks in the wake of the departed glacier . . .*

B4: NAME THIS FELL: It has ridge routes to Great Rigg and Nab Scar.

B5: PICTURE QUESTION (right): Name the left-hand summit. Clue: It's NOT a 'chapter' fell.

B6: NAME THIS FELL (where the blank is): *Ordinary pedestrians, having already been warned (page 2) that direct access to .... is virtually impossible, are here provided with a route that, if safely accomplished, will establish their right to be classed as better than ordinary.*

1/5/07

B7: NAME THIS ROCK FORMATION: The prominent shattered pillar of rock on the northern side of Lingmoor Fell.

B8: NAME THIS OUTLYING FELL: One of its twin summits features a prominent rock outcrop called White Stone.

B9: NAME THIS FELL: It features a prominent rocky outcrop and viewpoint called Pike Howe that overlooks one of Lakeland's most popular valleys.

B10: NAME THIS FELL: Which ascent features a canyon? *The canyon is Wild West stuff – 'gulch' might be a better word.*

THE ANSWERS are on page 344, but before you go there, there are OTHER QUIZZES: on pages 86, 137, 159, 205, 216, 239 and 259.

HUMPS GALORE: Greenup, from Lining Crag. Check out the moraines to the left of the picture, deposited millions of years ago by a melting glacier. 28/6/05

GLACIAL DEPOSITS

Moraines are all over place – but 24 in one diagram?

The Greenup Valley has an upland hollow below **High Raise**. And in this hollow, AW identified a huge number of moraines – those strange little humpy hills created by glacial deposits – enough to call attention to it on **High Raise 7**, with the words _a strange upland valley of moraines!_

In the diagram to the right we've counted 24 of them; enough, surely, to christen this part of Greenup as Moraines Valley.

The figure of 24 isn't a record – on Great Gable 19 AW drew 29 moraines near Black Sail Youth Hostel!

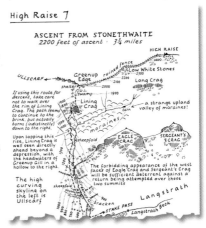

High Raise 7

ASCENT FROM STONETHWAITE
2200 feet of ascent · 3¾ miles

VIEWS OF THE WORLD

(the world of a legendary guidebook writer, that is)

One of the most innovative aspects of the PICTORIAL GUIDES and later THE OUTLYING FELLS was the way the views from summits were presented.

From major heights with far-reaching views a panorama effect was used, with the outline of the fells recorded around all four points of the compass. A second – and the most frequent – way of recording a view was the 'bicycle wheel' method, whereby the summit was at the centre of a diagram and dotted lines led to the fell that could be seen. Again, the four points of the compass were shown, as were concentric circles, usually indicating each 2.5 miles away from the viewpoint. With ascents of the fells, AW was sometimes quite non-committal.

With the views, however, almost without exception, he found something positive to say (although there were some negatives – mainly about flat summits and dull aspects of bigger mountains that blocked more distant views).

In this chapter you will find a short summary of every summit view recorded by AW in his eight guidebooks to Lakeland.

IS THIS LAKELAND'S FINEST VIEW? AW thinks the vista south from the Skiddaw Little Man is superb. Sean McMahon's picture certainly is! The fells on the horizon are, from left: PIKE O'STICKLE, SWIRL HOW, CONISTON OLD MAN, DOW CRAG, GREY FRIAR, BOWFELL, ESK PIKE, (left of centre) GREAT END, (right of centre) SCAFELL PIKE, SCAFELL, GREAT GABLE, DALE HEAD and KIRK FELL. Esk Hause is exactly at the centre fold. 17/12/10

NOTE: All views displayed in one-page 'bicycle wheel' style unless stated.

BOOK ONE: THE EASTERN FELLS

Arnison Crag: Summary: Surrounded by fells, views restricted. **Best features:** To the south-west, the grouping of the hills above Hartsop; Ullswater's upper reach is well displayed.

Birkhouse Moor: Summary: Dull. **Best features:** East face of Helvellyn.

Birks: Summary: Contrasting. **Best feature:** Helvellyn and Nethermost Pike.

Catstycam: Two-page bicycle wheel with silhouettes; **Summary:** Helvellyn gets in the way. **Best features:** Good prospect to the east.

Clough Head: Summary: Good mix of mountain and valley scenery. **Best features:** Very good between south and west.

Dollywaggon Pike: Two-page bicycle wheel with silhouettes. **Summary:** Restricted to north and south-east; good elsewhere. **Best feature:** Western panorama.

Dove Crag: Two-page panorama. **Summary:** Good all-round view except north-west (Fairfield in the way). **Best feature:** Windermere.

Fairfield: Two-page panorama. **Summary:** An excellent all-round view. **Best feature:** St Sunday Crag and Deepdale.

Glenridding Dodd: Summary: Pretty, not extensive. **Best feature:** Ullswater.

Gowbarrow Fell: Summary: Better from Green Hill, half-a-mile south. **Best features:** Fells around Patterdale.

Great Dodd: Two-page panorama; **Summary:** Thirlmere, Derwent Water and Bassenthwaite Lake can be seen a few yards to the west. **Best feature:** View from south to west.

Great Mell Fell: Summary: Uneven. **Best features:** Fine view of Blencathra; Eden Valley eastwards; Grasmoor group.

Great Rigg: Summary: Varied. **Best features:** Ten lakes and tarns; Helvellyn above Grisedale Hause.

Hart Crag: Summary: Unbalanced by bulk of Fairfield. **Best features:** Panorama is extensive in other directions.

Hart Side: Summary: Disappointing; overtopped by main ridge to west. **Best features:** None given.

Hartsop above How: Summary: Outstanding for one reason . . . **Best feature:** . . . which is the ruggedness of the eastern crags of Fairfield, Hart Crag and Dove Crag.

Helvellyn: Four-page panorama, foreground shaded in. **Summary:** Height and location make this one of the most extensive views in Lakeland. **Best features:** Far views to the west, the High Street range, and the bowl of Red Tarn enclosed by the two edges (Striding and Swirral).

Heron Pike: Summary: Neat summit gives good depth to views; seven lakes and tarns in view. **Best features:** Views of Coniston and Langdale fells, overtopped by Scafell Pike.

High Hartsop Dodd: Summary: Moderate view. **Best feature:** Excellent, intimate view of Dovedale.

High Pike: Summary: Restricted view. **Best features:** Views of the central fells and of High Street range.

Little Hart Crag: Summary: Restricted. **Best features:** Charming Hartsop valley; best viewpoint for Scandale.

Little Mell Fell: Summary: Unbalanced – fells to west, Vale of Eden and Pennines to east. **Best feature:** One of best viewpoints for appreciating Martindale.

Low Pike: Summary: Restricted. **Best features:** Coniston fells and

> ### LOW PIKE'S HIGH POINT
> There are several Eastern fells that have views of Windermere, Esthwaite Water and Coniston Water, but only from **Low Pike** can you see these three AND Rydal Water.

mountains around Great Langdale.

Middle Dodd: Summary: Hemmed in, but remarkably good considering. **Best feature:** South-west vista.

Nab Scar: Summary: Half dull, half charming. **Best features:** Eight lakes and tarns and nice views of Coniston and Langdale fells.

Nethermost Pike: Two-page bicycle wheel with silhouettes. **Summary:** Not the best because of bulk of Helvellyn and a summit plateau. Better view from cairn on High Crag to the south. **Best feature:** South-west vista.

Raise: Two-page panorama. **Summary:** Helvellyn blocks southerly views, good elsewhere. **Best features:** Skiddaw and Blencathra.

Red Screes: Four-page panorama. **Summary:** Very fine. **Best feature:** Best view of High Street range.

St Sunday Crag: Summary: Restricted; Ullswater view best from top

of north-east ridge. **Best features:** Helvellyn, Fairfield, High Street range.

Seat Sandal: Summary: Unbalanced because of Fairfield and Helvellyn. **Best features:** Western arc, ten lakes and tarns.

Sheffield Pike: Summary: Restricted. **Best feature:** Ullswater.

Stone Arthur: Summary: Unbalanced by Fairfield, but good nevertheless. **Best features:** View of Easedale Tarn backed by fells, overtopped by Scafell Pike.

Stybarrow Dodd: Two-page bicycle wheel. **Summary:** Dull foreground, but excellent panorama. **Best feature:** Western arc.

Watson's Dodd: Summary: Good west, rest poor. **Best feature:** The west.

White Side: Summary: Unbalanced by the bulk of Helvellyn, but good otherwise. **Best features:** Skiddaw and Bassenthwaite Lake.

BOOK TWO: THE FAR EASTERN FELLS

Angletarn Pikes: Summary: Largely confined to 5-mile radius, but full of interest. **Best features:** Beautiful picture of Brothers Water; fine Deepdale view.

Arthur's Pike: Summary: Lakeland occupies just a quarter of view, but excellently. **Best features:** Full Helvellyn and Fairfield ranges above trench of Ullswater.

Beda Fell: Summary: Upper slopes hide valleys; fells average. **Best feature:** St Sunday Crag, a noble object.

Bonscale Pike: Summary: Its two stone cairns are better viewpoints. **Best features:** Helvellyn and Fairfield.

Branstree: Summary: No views of lakes or tarns, restricted view. **Best feature:** Unexpected view of Scafell and Mickledore.

Brock Crags: Summary: Interesting; fine circle of higher fells. **Best features:** Beautiful and dramatic bird's eye view of Brothers Water and Hartsop.

Caudale Moor: Two-page panorama.

Summary: Extensive. **Best features:** Fine vista towards Morecambe Bay (best 70 yards south of top cairn).

Froswick: Summary: Sandwiched between Thornthwaite Crag and Ill Bell. **Best feature:** Serrated skyline of Scafells and Langdale.

Gray Crag: Summary: Edges of twin escarpments are better viewpoints. **Best feature:** Hayeswater.

Grey Crag: Summary: More Pennine than Lakeland. **Best feature:** Scafell Pike and Scafell over saddle between Yoke and Ill Bell.

Hallin Fell: Summary: Good considering modest elevation. **Best feature:** Classic view of Ullswater; unsurpassed view of the Martindale district.

Harter Fell: Two-page panorama. **Summary:** Good all round. **Best features:** Morecambe Bay, Ingleborough, Coniston fells and Bowfell-Scafell Pike grouping.

Hartsop Dodd: Summary: Edges of

summit give better views. **Best features:** Classic view of Dove Crag and Dovedale; Red Screes rising majestically from Kirkstone.

High Raise: **Summary:** Splendid all round. **Best feature:** South to north arc.

High Street: **Summary:** Splendid all round. **Best features:** Western arc; the Pennines to the east.

Ill Bell: Two-page bicycle wheel. **Summary:** Restricted to north, but elsewhere very good. **Best feature:** Windermere. AW describes Ill Bell as *one of the classic 'stations'* for viewing the lake.

Kentmere Pike: **Summary:** Restricted by higher fells across Kentmere. **Best features:** Windermere, Morecambe Bay and the Pennines.

Kidsty Pike: **Summary:** Restricted by nearby fells. **Best features:** Coniston and Bowfell-Scafell fells.

The Knott: **Summary:** Extensive except for eastward restriction of High Street range. **Best features:** Fairfield and Helvellyn ranges.

Loadpot Hill: **Summary:** Split: Pennines and Lakeland. **Best features:** Cross Fell (Pennines) is prominent.

Mardale Ill Bell: **Summary:** Restricted by nearby fells. **Best feature:** Ridge of Ill Bell, looking magnificent from this angle.

The Nab: **Summary:** Restricted, except to north, by Skiddaw and Blencathra etc. **Best feature:** Scafell Pike over Deepdale Hause.

Place Fell: Four-page panorama, detail in mid-distance **Summary:** A classic, beautiful view of a beautiful corner of Lakeland. **Best features:** Ullswater and Grisedale, but it's all fine.

Rampsgill Head: **Summary:** Extensive and interesting. **Best feature:** Ramps Gill from the larger cairn.

Rest Dodd: **Summary:** Not as good as from The Knott, nearby. **Best features:** Ramps Gill; Great Gable over Deepdale Hause.

Sallows: **Summary:** Mixed; Yoke is unattractive northwards. **Best features:** Pennines round to Morecambe Bay and Black Combe.

Selside Pike: **Summary:** Disappointing towards Lakeland. **Best feature:** The Pennines and Shap village.

Shipman Knotts: **Summary:** Northern half restricted; southern is extensive and pleasing. **Best feature:** The view of Longsleddale.

Sour Howes: **Summary:** Very good, with a crowded western skyline. **Best features:** Pennines, Morecambe Bay around to Black Combe.

Steel Knotts: **Summary:** Varied and interesting. **Best feature:** Best viewpoint for upper Martindale.

Tarn Crag: **Summary:** Very little of Lakeland because of nearby higher fells. **Best feature:** The Pennines and Morecambe Bay.

Thornthwaite Crag: Two-page bicycle wheel. **Summary:** Good, but you need to move around the summit to get best views. **Best feature:** Troutbeck valley leading the eye to Windermere.

Troutbeck Tongue: **Summary:** Overlooked everywhere except to the south. **Best features:** Windermere, and distant peep of Crinkle Crags, Bowfell and Scafell Pike.

Wansfell: **Summary:** Two summits: from Wansfell (the highest) fewer fells can be seen than from the lower Wansfell Pike. **Best feature:** From Wansfell Pike, Windermere and Red Screes to the north.

Wether Hill: **Summary:** Wide prospect of the Pennines, but good views of Lakeland peaks. **Best feature:**

O BROTHER, WHERE ART THOU?

A look on the map would suggest that Hartsop Dodd has a bird's eye view of Brothers Water. Not so. The lake only comes into view (in dramatic fashion) from the descent of the north ridge.

A CLASSIC VIEW: From the modestly elevated Place Fell, looking to Ullswater, Glenridding and the Helvellyn range. 12/3/09

Helvellyn and Fairfield ranges across Martindale.

Yoke: **Summary:** Good combination of fells, lower countryside and sea. **Best feature:** West to high fells of Lakeland (Scafell Pike, Bowfell, Great Gable, etc.)

BOOK THREE: THE CENTRAL FELLS

Armboth Fell: **Summary:** Best view is from Fisher Crag, three-quarters of a mile north-east (Thirlmere and Blencathra). **Best feature:** Westward arc, topping central ridge.

Bleaberry Fell: Three-page panorama. **Summary:** Excellent; best view of Derwent Water from near north-west cairn. **Best feature:** North-west fells, Skiddaw.

Blea Rigg: **Summary:** Good, but none of the Scafell group or western fells. **Best feature:** Easedale Tarn, but must visit top rocks of nearby Blea Crag.

Calf Crag: **Summary:** Restricted and moderate. **Best feature:** Vale of Grasmere and curve of Far Easedale leading to it.

Eagle Crag: **Summary:** Drab eastwards; not as good a view of Stonethwaite Valley as might be expected. **Best features:** West and north.

Gibson Knott: **Summary:** Ridge eastwards is better viewpoint. **Best feature:** Rocky terrain across Far Easedale.

Grange Fell: **Summary:** Two summits, similar views; King's How has better view of Borrowdale than Brund Fell. **Best feature:** Beautiful Borrowdale.

Great Crag: **Summary:** Pleasing, though not extensive. **Best feature:** Upper Borrowdale backed by Great Gable and the Scafells.

Harrison Stickle: Four-page panorama. **Summary:** Only bulk of High Raise robs this marvellous view of top marks. **Best features:** Windermere, and, from the south end of the summit ridge, a striking view down to Stickle Tarn.

Helm Crag: **Summary:** Pretty, though not extensive. **Best feature:** Grasmere from the southern top (the official Lion).

High Raise: Three-page panorama. **Summary:** Very extensive panorama from highest of the central fells. **Best features:** Bowfell-Great End.

High Rigg: **Summary:** Interesting, with Blencathra well displayed. **Best feature:** Clough Head.

High Seat: **Summary:** Excellent, with much of interest in all directions. **Best feature:** The skyline from south to north-west.

High Tove: **Summary:** Excellent westwards, restricted elsewhere. No views of lakes or tarns. **Best feature:** The skyline from south to north-west.

Loft Crag: **Summary:** Not as extensive as from the two nearby Stickles, but has a better prospect of Great Langdale. **Best feature:** Bowfell.

Loughrigg Fell: Four-page panorama. **Summary:** One of the finest views from

DROPLESS GORGEOUS

DRY COUNTRY: Bowscale Fell has a waterless view (but Skiddaw looks great). 8/2/11

one of Lakeland's lower heights. Sparkling mix of water, valleys and fells. **Best features:** They're all good. Visit summits of Todd Crag and Ivy Crag, both excellent viewpoints.

Pavey Ark: **Summary:** Dull middle-distance, everywhere except . . . **Best feature:** . . . the curves of Great Langdale backed by Windermere, enhanced by the steep plunge of the sheer crag overlooking Stickle Tarn.

Pike o'Stickle: **Summary:** Extensive, though interrupted by nearby higher ground. **Best feature:** Bowfell across Mickleden – a magnificent view of a magnificent mountain.

Raven Crag: **Summary:** Patchy, and for that you can thank the Forestry Commission (heavy irony). **Best feature:** Full-length view of Thirlmere (thank Manchester Corporation for that!).

Sergeant Man: Two-page

bicycle wheel. **Summary:** Fine view spoiled by tedious slopes of High Raise. **Best features:** Pavey Ark and Harrison Stickle backed by the Coniston Fells.

Sergeant's Crag: **Summary:** Good, apart from nearby High Raise and Ullscarf. **Best feature:** Langstrath, leading to Bowfell and Esk Pike.

Silver How: **Summary:** Beautiful views with great contrasts between valleys and fells. The vale and village of Grasmere.

Steel Fell: **Summary:** Helm Crag blocks Grasmere view; Coniston fells impressive on the skyline. **Best feature:** Thirlmere backed by Blencathra.

Tarn Crag: **Summary:** Helvellyn range well seen, but little else of interest except for . . . **Best feature:** . . . the splendid prospect of Easedale running down to the Vale of Grasmere.

LEFT–RIGHT LEFT–RIGHT

The northerly position of High Rigg makes it the only central fell with a view of Helvellyn where Helvellyn's summit is seen to the left of its Lower Man. All other central viewpoints have Helvellyn to the right.

The fells where you won't get a view of a lake or tarn

There are a lot of reasons people climb mountains; whatever they are, a benefit of arriving at a summit cairn is a view (cloud-cover permitting), and a view that incorporates lakes and tarns is always worth the climb. That's not to say 'dry' views are necessarily bad – look at the view (left) from the summit of **Bowscale Fell** of Skiddaw; wonderful, isn't it? Bowscale Fell is one fourteen fells in the PICTORIAL GUIDES that has no sight of any *named* tarn or lake. Its own tarn – **Bowscale Tarn** – only comes into the picture with a five-minute walk north-east. The other fells with no views of named lakes or tarns are:

Branstree: Haweswater brought into view by walking a few yards north. **Loadpot Hill:** Flat summit; **Ullswater** view from 150 yards to west. **Armboth Fell:** Just a few nameless puddles. **High Tove:** Small nameless puddles on Armboth Fell don't count! **Illgill Head:** 35-yard walk for the highlight – **Wast Water** – which comes amazingly into the picture. **Bannerdale Crags:** No lakes or tarns are in sight from this neighbour of Bowscale Fell. **Mungrisdale Common: Derwent Water** can be seen after a 100-yard walk across the top. **Graystones:** Walk west to the next prominence for a sight of water. **Whinlatter:** From the east top of the fell **Derwent Water** is visible. **Caw Fell:** None, not even Mockerkin Tarn, due west. **Gavel Fell:** Meadley Reservoir (west-south-west) doesn't count. **Lank Rigg:** Just the small, unnamed summit tarn. **Seatallan:** None from the summit cairn; a short walk north-east brings **Low Tarn** and **Scoat Tarn** into view, and a small portion of **Wast Water**.

Thunacar Knott: **Summary:** Disappointing, with almost complete lack of water. **Best feature:** West, towards Great End and the Scafells.

Ullscarf: Two-page bicycle wheel. **Summary:** Fine panorama from a fell right in the heart of things; just the bulk of Helvellyn spoils it. **Best features:** Beautiful from west to north (Pillar-Skiddaw).

Walla Crag: **Summary:** Not extensive, but full of beauty and charm. **Best features:** Borrowdale and the Vale of Keswick.

BOOK FOUR: THE SOUTHERN FELLS

Allen Crags: **Summary:** Unbalanced, with Great End, Esk Pike and Bowfell closing southern horizon. Much better is a beautiful Borrowdale vista. **Best feature:** Great Gable – look closely to see silhouette of Napes Needle.

Black Fell: **Summary:** Lovely low-level views around head of Windermere and good grouping of mountains north-west. **Best feature:** Area between Ambleside, Wray Castle and Hawkshead.

Bowfell: Four-page panorama, foreground shaded. **Summary:** Stupendous viewpoint; marvellous views enhanced by steep fall from bouldery summit. **Best feature:** Eskdale.

Brim Fell: **Summary:** Extensive, but broad summit restricts foregrounds. **Best features:** Distant skylines.

Cold Pike: **Summary:** Extensive, but restricted by Crinkle Crags. **Best features:** Over Little Langdale to Windermere; down Duddon Valley to estuary and sea beyond.

Coniston Old Man: Two-page bicycle wheel. **Summary:** Wonderful viewpoint, with contrast between Lakeland to north and Sealand (Morecambe Bay) to the south. **Best feature:** Peep over edge to Low Water, Lakeland's best bird's-eye view of an ascent route.

Crinkle Crags: Two-page bicycle

PERFECTION: The view northwards to Borrowdale and Derwent Water, backed by Skiddaw, as seen from Great End. 21/5/07

wheel. **Summary:** Bulky Bowfell and the Scafell group hides nearly all western and north-western fells. **Best feature:** Supremely beautiful views of Eskdale and Duddon Valley; the best viewpoint for both.

Dow Crag: **Summary:** Mountains, okay; foothills, marvellous. **Best features:** Unsurpassed viewpoint for foothills of the Duddon and Esk.

Esk Pike: Two-page bicycle wheel. **Summary:** Scarcely inferior to Bowfell; better northwards (Derwent Water). **Best feature:** The Scafells, rising out of upper Eskdale.

Glaramara: Four-page panorama. **Summary:** Fine viewpoint, only restricted by its second and third summit. **Best feature:** Borrowdale.

Great Carrs: Two-page bicycle wheel. **Summary:** Excellent view, though unbalanced by mass of Swirl How. **Best features:** Scafell and Bowfell groups.

Great End: Two-page bicycle wheel. **Summary:** Very extensive, very beautiful. **Best feature:** Borrowdale and Derwent Water, backed by Skiddaw, is perfection. Best seen from crest of northern cliffs.

Green Crag: **Summary:** Not extensive, but very good blend of high fells and low countryside. **Best features:** Mosedale fells over Burnmoor Tarn.

Grey Friar: Two-page bicycle wheel. **Summary:** Striking views of mountains, lots of them. **Best feature:** Scafell range from the north-west cairn. Best place for appreciating the correct proportions of the range.

Hard Knott: **Summary:** Renowned view of Upper Eskdale. **Best feature:** Scafell range.

Harter Fell: **Summary:** Lovely view enhanced by neat summit peak. Upper Eskdale is excellent. **Best feature:** The wonderful golden sands of the Duddon estuary.

Holme Fell: **Summary:** Modest view, except for . . . **Best feature:** . . . full-length view of Coniston Water; the best place for viewing the lake.

Illgill Head: **Summary:** Unbalanced by dull bulk of Scafell. Nevertheless . . . **Best feature:** . . . the absolute finest view of Wasdale Head. A few steps to the escarpment of the Screes also gives tremendous views down to Wast Water.

Lingmell: **Summary:** Scafell Pike is dull; Scafell is better; western fells round Mosedale the best of all. **Best features:** Astonishing view of Great Gable – it looks almost vertical. Tremendous views down Piers Gill.

Lingmoor Fell: **Summary:** Contrasts: fine mountains and delightful countryside. **Best feature:** Best place to view the fells at the head of Great Langdale (Crinkle Crags round to Harrison Stickle).

Pike o'Blisco: **Summary:** Good prospect of fells and, a few yards in the direction of Great Langdale, a splendid view of the valley. **Best feature:** Bowfell and Crinkle Crags.

Rossett Pike: **Summary:** Overtopped by mountains all round, but . . . **Best feature:** . . . tremendous views of

Bowfell's cliffs and the Great Slab.

Rosthwaite Fell: **Summary:** Disappointing; valleys concealed by wide top. **Best feature:** The Gables.

Scafell: Two-page bicycle wheel. **Summary:** Scafell Pike blocks out Helvellyn, but elsewhere this is a wonderful view. **Best features:** The foothills south-west leading to the sea, and a lovely full-length view of shy Miterdale.

Scafell Pike: Four-page panorama, foreground shaded. **Summary:** Very extensive, with favourites such as Bowfell and Great Gable looking smaller than usual! Valleys not seen as well as from Bowfell, for instance. **Best features:** Looking north to Borrowdale, and south to Scafell and the Isle of Man.

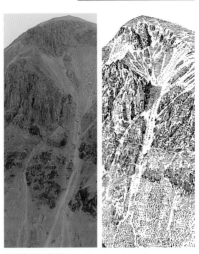

NEARLY VERTICAL: How Great Gable appears from Lingmell. 1/4/09

Seathwaite Fell: **Summary:** Restricted, but with a surprising view of the Helvellyn Dodds. **Best feature:** North: the best place for viewing the Seathwaite valley.

Slight Side: **Summary:** Scafell, Bowfell and Crinkle Crags restrict the view, which is very fine, nevertheless, particularly of the coastal areas of Lakeland. **Best features:** The coastal foothills and seascape behind.

Swirl How: Four-page panorama. **Summary:** Best view of mountains from the Coniston fells; edges Old Man. **Best features:** Bowfell and Scafell groups.

Wetherlam: Two-page bicycle wheel. **Summary:** Extensive. Wetherlam's position thrusting into the Brathay Valley gives it wonderful views of beautiful countryside. **Best feature:** Little Langdale backed by fells.

Whin Rigg: **Summary:** Splendid viewpoint; contrast of sombre hills and soft valleys. **Best features:** The valleys of the Irt and Esk with the sea beyond.

BOOK FIVE: THE NORTHERN FELLS

Bakestall: **Summary:** Skiddaw blocks much of the view, but there is a good prospect of the Helvellyn range. **Best feature:** North-west to the Solway Firth and Scottish hills.

Bannerdale Crags: **Summary:** Interesting rather than attractive. **Best feature:** Faraway and surprising prospect of the Coniston fells.

Binsey: **Summary:** 'Outsider looking in' view that is full of interest. Over 20 miles away the Coniston fells can be seen. **Best feature:** The Solway Firth and Scottish hills.

Blencathra: Eight-page panorama, foreground shaded. **Summary:** One of Lakeland's finest views, enhanced by the steep drop south of the summit. **Best feature:** The wonderful arc between south and west, beyond the subsidiary Gategill Fell top and ridge, giving the contrast of a rugged foreground.

Bowscale Fell: Summary: Interesting to compare with view from nearby Bannerdale Crags, because of Blencathra's bulk. **Best feature:** Blencathra.

Brae Fell: Summary: Limited Lakeland; spectacular elsewhere. **Best feature:** Uninterrupted sweep from Cumbrian coast, round the Solway Firth to the Eden Valley and the Pennines.

Carl Side: Summary: Two-page bicycle wheel. **Summary:** Extensive and beautiful southerly view, though it suffers from a broad foreground. **Best feature:** Derwent Water and Borrowdale.

Carrock Fell: Summary: Good views of western fells and Helvellyn range either side of Blencathra, but . . . **Best feature:** . . . the view east, to the Eden Valley and the Pennines.

Dodd: Summary: Good, since summit pine trees were removed in 2002. **Best feature:** No summit trees!

Great Calva: Summary: Average, apart from view down Lakeland's central trench. **Best feature:** From lower cairn, the best view of Skiddaw Forest – the forest with no trees.

Great Cockup: Summary: View of Solway Firth will get most of attention, except for . . . **Best feature:** . . . Skiddaw rises magnificently in the south.

Great Sca Fell: Summary: Dull, except for unexpected view of Esk Pike, Bowfell and Crinkle Crags. **Best feature:** The coast and Solway Firth.

High Pike: Summary: Glimpses of distant Lakeland favourites. **Best feature:** Supreme viewpoint for coastal plain, Solway Firth, Scottish hills, the Eden Valley and the Pennines.

Knott: Summary: Should be spelled 'Not'; not as good as High Pike for views north; not the best because of a broad top. **Best features:** The cluster of distant favourites due south

> **SEE A TARN FROM A CRAG**
> On page 8 of this chapter **Bowscale Fell** is highlighted as a fell with no views of lakes or tarns – not even its own. To see Bowscale Tarn make a five-minute walk to aptly named Tarn Crags.

(small illustration).

Latrigg: Two-page bicycle wheel and illustration of view south-west. **Summary:** Renowned as one of the most beautiful and charming views in the district. **Best feature:** Derwent Water, in its entirety, beyond the rooftops of Keswick, all backed by a glorious array of fells.

Longlands Fell: Summary: Restricted, apart from fine vista of Grasmoor fells. **Best feature:** Solway Firth and Scottish hills.

Long Side: Two-page bicycle wheel. **Summary:** As for all Skiddaw's satellites, a lovely southern view, but . . . **Best feature:** . . . Solway Firth, Criffel and the hills of Galloway.

Lonscale Fell: Two-page bicycle wheel. **Summary:** A spectacular view, similar to that from Skiddaw Little Man though not with such a sharp drop. **Best feature:** Full-length Thirlmere, Dunmail Raise and Gummer's How, 25 miles away.

Meal Fell: Summary: Plenty of featureless grass slopes nearby. **Best feature:** Seawards.

Mungrisdale Common: Summary: Dull, apart from . . . **Best feature:** . . . Scafell Pike, Great Gable, etc. above the Glenderaterra valley.

Skiddaw: Four-page panorama, foreground shaded. **Summary:** Very extensive. South top is best viewpoint; superb for Keswick, Derwent Water and Borrowdale. **Best feature:** As above.

Skiddaw Little Man: Two-page bicycle wheel, plus one-page southern vista. **Summary:** Quite possibly the best view in Lakeland, certainly the classic view of the heart of Lakeland from the perimeter. All helped by its wonderful situation high above the Vale of Keswick with a steep fall immediately from the summit. **Best feature:** The view south.

Souther Fell: Summary: Dominated

by Blencathra, some glimpses of far Lakeland. **Best feature:** View east to the Eden Valley and the Pennines.

Ullock Pike: Summary: Another

Skiddaw satellite with great views south and to the Solway Firth. **Best feature:** Bassenthwaite Lake, right below, seen in its entirety.

DEEP BLUE: Looking down on Bass Lake from Ullock Pike. The prominent north-western fells are, from left, Grisedale Pike, Hopegill Head and (right) rugged little Barf. 26/8/10

BOOK SIX: THE NORTH WESTERN FELLS

Ard Crags: Summary: Eel Crag, Sail and Wandope restrict the view, but the Helvellyn range is seen from end to end. **Best feature:** Beautiful, pastoral Newlands Valley.

Barf: Summary: Interesting and beautiful view, with Bassenthwaite Lake looking lovely below. **Best feature:** Perfect spot to appreciate the massive build-up of Skiddaw.

Barrow: Summary: Splendid panorama. Contrast between pastoral Vale of Keswick and sombre mountains. **Best feature:** Derwent Water.

Broom Fell: Summary: Fine views of Skiddaw, the Grasmoor group and Solway Firth. **Best feature:** Vale of Lorton, a lovely scene.

Castle Crag: Summary: Restricted by higher fells

(aren't they all?), but excellent because of steep falls from summit, and . . . **Best features:** Skiddaw and Derwent Water; beautiful mid-Borrowdale.

Catbells: Summary: A beautiful viewpoint, one of the best, helped by a) location, and b) the sharp fall from the summit. **Best feature:** Derwent Water and mid-Borrowdale.

Causey Pike: Summary: A splendid view of mountains, softened by the Vale of Keswick and Newlands. **Best feature:** The ridge continuing to Eel Crag.

Dale Head: Four-page panorama, foreground shaded. **Summary:** A superb all-round view, gained with so little effort if climbed from Honister Pass. **Best feature:** The outstanding view of the Newlands Valley, from which

TOGETHER AND APART

The view from Causey Pike, according to AW, is notable for: the Lakeland 'Cats' – '-bells' and '-stycam' – appearing in a straight line; and the three Scafell Pikes appearing as separate fells.

the fell gets its name (head of dale).

Eel Crag: Two-page bicycle wheel. **Summary:** Very extensive view covering the length and breadth of Lakeland. Broad summit prevents views of valleys except . . . **Best feature:** . . . a sharp fall to the Keswick area, seen over the east ridge.

Grasmoor: Three-page panorama. **Summary:** Another very extensive view, but again, a broad top. **Best feature:** The view towards Bowfell-Scafell Pike-Great Gable. AW drew a two-page sketch of this (Grasmoor 9-10).

Graystones: **Summary:** Dreary foreground detracts from view. **Best features:** The coast and Criffel; Skiddaw group; Grasmoor mass across Whinlatter pass; Vale of Lorton.

Grisedale Pike: Four-page panorama, foreground shaded. **Summary:** Very extensive, very beautiful. **Best features:** Vale of Keswick; Hopegill Head and Hobcarton Crag.

High Spy: **Summary:** Extensive, generally good. Good view of Newlands from nearby precipice, but not seen from summit. **Best features:** Scafell group; Helvellyn range.

Hindscarth: **Summary:** Good. Best views of Newlands from northern cairn. Familiar shape of Scafell is hidden by Great Gable. **Best features:** Newlands and the Vale of Keswick.

Hopegill Head: **Summary:** Good, but not as good as the bicycle wheel suggests, says AW. **Best feature:** Quaint glimpse of Pike o-Stickle between Sail and Eel Crags.

Knott Rigg: **Summary:** Unbalanced, because of nearby masses of Robinson and Eel Crag range. **Best feature:** Distant scene of the Helvellyn range.

Ling Fell: **Summary:** Patchy. Skiddaw and Grasmoor groups are good. **Best feature:** Best fell for viewing the town of Cockermouth.

Lord's Seat: **Summary:** Pleasant, but nothing to go crazy about. Good viewpoint for appreciating the

ICY RIDGE: The way to Hopegill Head from the summit of Grisedale Pike. Winter in the Lakes can be this stunning – but you have to know what you're doing (and carry an ice axe and crampons) to get to locations such as these. 4/2/09

strange geography of the Wythop Valley. **Best feature:** Eastwards, Vale of Keswick backed by the distant Pennines.

Maiden Moor: **Summary:** Dreary foreground with limited view of Derwent Water and none of Borrowdale. The cairn on the edge of the plateau to north-east has a more beautiful, though less extensive view. **Best feature:** Looking north to Bassenthwaite Lake, Catbells and the Skiddaw group.

Outerside: **Summary:** Limited view that lacks charm. **Best feature:** Very impressive view of Upper Coledale and the soaring Grisedale Pike opposite.

Rannerdale Knotts: **Summary:** Low fell, limited view, but still very beautiful. **Best feature:** Classic view of Buttermere. Breathtaking.

Robinson: **Summary:** Broad summit spoils things somewhat. Oddities: Scafell Pike exactly covered by Great Gable; rare view of shy Floutern Tarn. **Best feature:** Looking down on Honister Pass.

Sail: **Summary:** Unbalanced by bulk of nearby Eel Crag, but good elsewhere. **Best feature:** The ridge to Causey Pike.

Sale Fell: **Summary:** Good views of Skiddaw and Helvellyn groups, but nearby Lord's Seat hides most of the major southern fells. **Best feature:**

Pastoral Wythop Valley below.

Scar Crags: **Summary:** Good, but nowhere near as beautiful as from nearby Causey Pike. **Best feature:** Peep downwards to Rigg Beck.

Wandope: **Summary:** Eel Crag and Grasmoor unbalance the view, which elsewhere is extensive. Below, the head of Sail Beck is a striking feature. **Best features:** The Scafells, the Helvellyn range on the skyline.

Whinlatter: **Summary:** Generally inferior to views from neighbouring heights, but excels in one direction, south. **Best feature:** Southerly view to Grisedale Pike and Hopegill Head revealing interesting routes above forests.

Whiteless Pike: **Summary:** Neat summit and a fine location, much like Causey Pike, gives a view of mountains and valleys. **Best features:** The Scafell mass across Buttermere; lovely view of Crummock Water and Loweswater.

Whiteside: **Summary:** Patchy; glimpses over Gasgale Crags to the gill below are striking. **Best feature:** The best viewpoint for the coastal plain of West Cumbria, the Solway Firth and the Scottish hills beyond.

BOOK SEVEN: THE WESTERN FELLS

Base Brown: **Summary:** Unbalanced by higher fells, but good views of Borrowdale. **Best feature:** View of the Scafells, flanked by Great End and Lingmell.

Blake Fell: **Summary:** Excellent: splendid array of fells inland; and across West Cumbria to the Scottish hills. **Best features:** Good all round.

Brandreth: Two-page bicycle wheel. **Summary:** Location, not height, makes this a wonderful viewpoint (it looks down Ennerdale and Buttermere). **Best feature:** View of Grasmoor above Crummock Water.

Buckbarrow: **Summary:** Best and most extensive view is from a rocky spur

overlooking Wasdale. **Best features:** Wast Water backed by the Screes; the head of the valley enclosed by the Scafells.

Burnbank Fell: **Summary:** Very restricted. **Best feature:** Coastal view: St Bee's Head round to Criffel.

Caw Fell: **Summary:** Reasonable all-round view, but nothing terribly special. **Best feature:** None in particular.

Crag Fell: **Summary:** Restricted. Nice view up Ennerdale. **Best feature:** Extensive panorama seawards.

Fellbarrow: **Summary:** Wide-ranging view of West Cumbria and the Solway Firth. **Best feature:** Hopegill Head range across Vale of Lorton.

Fleetwith Pike: Summary: Great view of Buttermere is even better 100 yards down north-west ridge. **Best features:** Great Gable and Pillar.

Gavel Fell: Summary: Patchy; seawards, Blake Fell gets in the way. **Best feature:** The Grasmoor group.

Great Borne: Summary: Okay. A few old favourites seen from unusual angles. **Best features:** Pillar, Steeple and Scoat Fell across Ennerdale.

Great Gable: Four-page panorama. **Summary:** Very extensive, very good. Closeness to the Scafells tends to unbalance it a little. Great views from top of Gable Crag north, and, of course, from Westmorland Cairn overlooking Wasdale. **Best feature:** Westmorland Cairn – it probably *is* the finest single view in the Lakes.

Green Gable: Summary: Too close to you-know-what, but that means an outstanding view of Gable Crag. **Best features:** Looking north-west, with a great view of Blackbeck Tarn on Haystacks appearing to spill over into Buttermere (they are a mile apart).

Grey Knotts: Summary: Very good in all directions. **Best feature:** North-west to Buttermere – *superlative beauty* says AW.

Grike: Summary: Not as good as that from Crag Fell, and that's not the best view either. **Best feature:** View west towards the sea.

Haycock: Summary: Good all-round view; curiously, only the top few feet of Pillar and Great Gable can be seen above Scoat Fell and Red Pike. **Best features:** The Scafell range.

Haystacks: Summary: Little to be seen long-range, just the Helvellyn range. Closer-up is very charming. **Best features:** Great Gable and Pillar seen across any of the summit tarns.

Hen Comb: Summary: Better than might be expected. **Best features:** Buttermere in a frame of fells – classic beauty.

High Crag: Summary: Not as extensive as High Stile, but better towards the heart of the district. **Best features:** The best place for viewing the head of Ennerdale, backed by Great Gable and the Scafells.

High Stile: Three-and-a-half-page panorama, foreground shaded. **Summary:** Very good. A few yards from the western cairn is the best view of Bleaberry Tarn. **Best feature:** As above.

Kirk Fell: Summary: Dominated by Great Gable, but still good. **Best feature:** View of the Scafells, which look magnificent.

Lank Rigg: Summary: Little to write home about, except for an unexpected appearance as High Stile. **Best feature:** The villages and towns of West Cumbria, looking like a map.

Low Fell: Summary: A beautiful view south-east (Crummock Water and Buttermere), one of classic beauty. **Best feature:** Grasmoor, a tremendous sight.

Mellbreak: Summary: Attractive views from both summits; the north has, in addition, a fine panorama of the Solway Firth. **Best feature:** Crummock Water backed by the Grasmoor fells.

Middle Fell: Summary: Not extensive, but interesting and beautiful, including Black Combe impressive to the south-east. **Best feature:** Breathtaking view of Wast Water backed by the Screes.

Pillar: Two-page bicycle wheel. **Summary:** Magnificent view, on a par with Great Gable but better in some respects (a wide expanse of shoreline and sea). **Best feature:** Five yards beyond the north wind-shelter is a remarkable view down to Ennerdale and the top of Pillar Rock.

Red Pike (Buttermere):

A GREAT PHOTO

Walk a little way down the western slope from Brandreth for the classic view down the Buttermere valley. AW says it *might well produce the most magnificent picture of the year.*

WESTERN FELLS: *The summit of Pillar, looking towards the Cumbrian coast and St Bees Head, is a splendid viewpoint.*   *22/8/07*

Summary: Very highly rated view, notable for the number of lakes that can be well seen (Loweswater, Crummock Water, Buttermere, Ennerdale Water and Derwent Water – the only other viewpoint for these five lakes is neighbouring High Stile). **Best features:** The Grasmoor group, seen from tip to toe; the Scafells.

Red Pike (Wasdale): Summary: Like the curate's egg – good in parts, with a striking aerial view of Mosedale. **Best feature:** The Scafell group, seen full-length and in true perspective.

Scoat Fell: Summary: Despite being dominated by Pillar there is plenty to occupy interest. **Best feature:** Mosedale, looking to the Scafells.

Seatallan: Summary: Restricted from Haycock round to Scafell. One distant group is the Coniston fells. **Best feature:** West Cumbria coast and Black Combe's hinterland.

Starling Dodd: Summary: Average

RED-HOT VIEW: *The summit of Red Pike (B), with Scafell Pike and Scafell perfectly framed between High Stile (left) and Pillar.*   *28/6/11*

view, but a good place to study Pillar and company. The last summit view recorded by AW among the 214 fells. **Best feature:** Ennerdale Water, seen almost full-length.

Steeple: **Summary:** Hemmed in by Pillar and Scoat Fell, but still a splendid viewpoint. Ennerdale is excellent. **Best**

features: Nearby Mirk and Mirklin Coves.

Yewbarrow: **Summary:** All four of Lakeland's 3000-footers can be seen from its summit. Great view of Wast Water, the deepest lake in England. **Best feature:** The array of mountains around Wasdale Head.

STEEPLE VIEW: Pillar (left), Black Crag (centre) and Great Gable (distance) from the lovely pointed summit of Steeple.
28/6/11

THE OUTLYING FELLS OF LAKELAND

NOTE: Because AW used a wide variety of ways of showing the view here, a short summary of the method of description is included with each chapter where a view is described. All chapters in this section are in order of their appearance in the book – Outliers were listed geographically not alphabetically.

The following chapters feature NO VIEW DESCRIPTION:

Potter Fell, High Knott, Hugill Fell, Reston Scar, Brant Fell, Whitbarrow, Cartmel Fell, Staveley Fell, Newton Fell, Humphrey Head, Finsthwaite Heights, Claife Heights, Carron Crag, Woodland Fell, Burney, Stickle Pike, Dunnerdale Fells, Hesk Fell, Stainton Pike, Whit Fell, Boat How, Muncaster Fell, Ponsonby Fell, Cold Fell, Flat Fell and Dent, Clints Crags, Caermote Hill, Faulds Brow, Dunmallet, Heughscar Hill, Howes, Seat Robert, The Wet Sleddale Horseshoe, The Wasdale Horseshoe.

The following chapters feature PARTIAL VIEW DESCRIPTIONS:

Scout Scar: West to north panorama (outline method); Green Quarter Fell: Drawing of Upper Kentmere as seen from the descent (fells numbered with key); Orrest Head: Two-page panorama, shaded – west to north; School Knott: Langdale skyline; Hampsfell: Two-page panorama, west to north-north-east, plus a list of heights and distances; Bigland Barrow: List of fells (west through to north-north-east) plus a partial panorama (north over Windermere to the far eastern fells; Latterbarrow: Partial panorama, looking north-east; Top o'Selside: Three mini-panoramas – Coniston Fells (from two viewpoints), and Helvellyn-Fairfield-Red Screes; Walna Scar: View of the Scafells; Great

Worm Crag: Eskdale outline; Watch Hill: List of main fells; Circuit of Devoke Water: Three outlines – Pillar group (north), Scafell group (north-north-east), and the Bowfell group (north-east); Irton Pike: Shaded drawing of fells around Wasdale Head; Knipescar Common: South-west outline of the High Street group; The Naddle Horseshoe: Outline of Mardale Head; The Crookdale Horseshoe: Outline of Borrowdale (the eastern one, naturally!); The Bannisdale Horseshoe: Outline of Longsleddale, plus list of the main fells seen from the three main summits (Whiteside Pike, Capplebarrow and White Howe).

The following chapters feature FULL DETAILED VIEW DESCRIPTIONS:

Gummer's How: Two-page bicycle wheel, plus outlines to the north-west (Coniston fells) and to the north (Fairfield, Dove Crag, Red Screes, etc.). **Summary:** Very extensive. Lakeland fells, the Howgills, the Pennines, Morecambe Bay and the estuaries of the Kent and Crake. **Best feature:** Wonderful full-length view of Windermere seen from a vantage point north-west of the Ordnance Survey column.

Beacon Fell: One-page bicycle wheel. **Summary:** Nice array of Lakeland fells north-east, plus closer-up views of the Coniston fells, plus a full-length view of Coniston Water. **Best feature:** The view south to Morecambe Bay, where the Crake and Duddon estuaries make great indentations into the coastline.

Blawith Knott: Two-page bicycle wheel, plus outline of the Coniston fells. **Summary:** As much of interest away from Lakeland as the fells in the northern arc, including the Howgills and

the Yorkshire Dales peaks of Great Coum (actually in Cumbria but part of the Dales), Whernside and Ingleborough. **Best features:** The lower valley of the Crake and, especially, the Duddon Estuary.

Caw: Two-page bicycle wheel, plus outlines of the Coniston fells and the Scafell range. **Summary:** An abrupt summit gives Caw views of great depth as well as distance. **Best features:** The full-length prospect of Upper Duddon, and looking past Hard Knott and Harter Fell to the head of Eskdale and the majestic peaks of Scafell Pike and Scafell.

Black Combe: Two-page bicycle wheel, plus outlines from north through to east-north-east (Haycock to Grey Crag). **Summary:** One of the finest views in the country – the mix of Lakeland fells, lovely foothills, sandy estuaries and seascapes is intoxicating. **Best feature:** The Morecambe Bay shoreline, all 30 miles of it.

CAW VALUES: Esk Pike, Bowfell, Crinkle Crags and (far right) Grey Friar, seen from Caw, looking up the Duddon Valley past Seathwaite. The Walna Scar road snakes down from the right. 8/7/09

WALES on the HORIZON

On a clear day from many of Lakeland's summits the hills of **Scotland, Snae Fell** on the Isle of Man and Yorkshire Dales favourites such as **Ingleborough** and **Whernside** look close enough to touch. The mountains of **Northern Ireland** – over 100 miles away – can sometimes be seen from the summit of **Scafell Pike**. This amazing view is from **Coniston Old Man**, showing the Welsh mountain **Carnedd Llewelyn** (3491ft, 91 miles away) with, just behind it to the right, the top of 3560ft **Snowdon** (98 miles).

20/1/11

CLOUGH HEAD VIA FISHER'S WIFE'S RAKE: The steep route cuts diagonally across the fell's western flank. The picture shows the line of the rake from midway in the walk. 7/9/09

RAKE'S PROGRESS

Relationships can be so tiring

One of the most interesting ascents in BOOK ONE is the first (alphabetically) to feel the dry humour of AW's pen. In the introduction to the **Clough Head** chapter, referring to the adventurous ascent via Wanthwaite by way of Fisher's Wife's Rake and Jim's Fold, he writes:

> ... the merely curious traveller may content himself by puzzling out why and for what purposes Fisher's wife trod so persistently that remarkable path to Jim's fold.

Well, we've got an answer to that. Just take a look at the picture below and the scene along the far horizon: she obviously loved the view!

GOING UP: (Left) the rising rake. 7/9/09

COMING DOWN: The remains of Jim's Fold. 17/8/11

THE THIRD PORTRAIT (The fourth portrait is on page 152)

WATCH YOUR STEP...

By the time BOOK THREE rolled around, AW was starting to develop a rather self-deprecating sense of humour.

He justifies the inclusion of a self-portrait in the Raven Crag chapter on the grounds that a corner needed filling up on 'THE VIEW' page because conifers were obscuring a segment of the panorama. He writes: *The space thus saved by the lop-sided diagram is devoted, as a special treat to readers, to a picture of the author apparently contemplating the view (but more likely wondering if it's time to be eating his sandwiches) from a precarious stance on the edge of Raven Crag.*

NOTE: The same socks, the same knapsack – but no pipe this time.

A FELL WITH A VIEW: The same excellent viewpoint over Thirlmere appears to have fewer trees than when AW drew his self-portrait. 13/5/09

ROCK and WATER...

The combination that gives Dale Head a BOOK SIX edge

AN OASIS: Dale Head Tarn from the slopes of High Spy.   14/1/09

There are a number of factors that contrive to make Dale Head one of the most significant mountains in the north-western fells (a little like **Red Screes** over in the eastern fells, in fact): It sits perfectly at the head of one of the prettiest valleys in Lakeland and is the cornerstone fell of one

The direct climb from Dalehead Tarn is rough and steep and tiring. Much easier is the long loop left to join the path coming up from Honister. Both routes are well cairned.

ALL TOGETHER NOW: In this extract from Dale Head 8, you can see Dalehead Tarn, Launchy Tarn and three unnamed tarns (Three Tarns Mark II perhaps?) clustered together at High Scawdel.

of the best ridgewalks – one that made AW's 'favourite' list in his *personal notes* to BOOK SEVEN; its best rockface, Gable Crag, is one of the finest faces of 'clean' rock in the north-western area; it has one of the finest summit cairns (both its position and its structure); and it has one of the simplest and easiest routes of ascent for a fell of its height (2473ft), from Honister Pass.

And it has the only proper tarns in the north-western Fells – five of them, including two with names (**Dalehead Tarn** and **Launchy Tarn**). This is because, as AW explains, Dale Head is exactly at the position where the softer Skiddaw slate that characterises nearly all of the rest of the fells in the group (except perhaps neighbouring High Spy) ends and the volcanic rock of central Lakeland begins. Volcanic rock = tarns, which explains why Rigg Head and High Scawdel host five sheets of water between them.

131

THE RIDGE WAY

At the end of BOOK SEVEN, in his *personal notes in conclusion*, AW named what he considers to be the best ridge walks in Lakeland. There were 11 of them. The other three categories in his final comments to the PICTORIAL GUIDES – best fells, best summits, most exciting places – all featured six picks, which is a fair indication of how much he loved getting up on to the ridges of Lakeland.

Here are his favourites:

THE FAIRFIELD HORSESHOE (Ambleside)
THE HIGH STREET RANGE (Garburn Moor Divock)
THE MOSEDALE HORSESHOE (Wasdale Head)
CAUSEY PIKE–WHITELESS PIKE
GRISEDALE PIKE–WHITESIDE
ESK HAUSE–WRYNOSE PASS via Bowfell
THE ESKDALE HORSESHOE (Slight Side–Bowfell)
THE HELVELLYN RANGE (Grisedale Pass–Threlkeld
THE HIGH STILE RANGE with Haystacks
CATBELLS–DALE HEAD–HINDSCARTH SCOPE END
THE CONISTON ROUND (Old Man – Wetherlam)

And then he added something that, for the love of me, I cannot fathom. It was: (*not in order of merit*). It was puzzling, first, because in the three other lists he didn't add such a rider. Only in his 'best fells' is there an

AW picked 11 favourite walks
– but he appreciated many more
... the secret is to get on the ridges

acknowledgement that there really was a 'best' – of Scafell Pike he wrote: *Contrary to general opinion (which would favour Great Gable), the grandest of the lot is Scafell Pike.* Second, by suggesting that the order in which he presented the ridge walks was NOT in order of merit, he was implying that he did have in his mind a clear order.

And what was that? My money is on number six (Esk Hause-Wrynose Pass), not because that is my favourite (I prefer Wall End-Pike o'Blisco-Crinkle Crags-Bowfell-Great Slab-Climbers Traverse-The Band-Stool End), but because of a short line in the Crinkle Crags chapter (page 13) when describing the Bowfell-Crinkle Crags ridge walk: *Introducing Lakeland's best ridge-mile!*

The more you think about AW's list of top ridges, the stranger it is. Some ridges start from ground level, so to speak: Ambleside, Threlkeld, Wrynose Pass; some start from 'halfway up': Garburn, Moor Divock, Grisedale Pass; the others start and finish with fells. There is a lack of consistency here: the Helvellyn Range should start at Dollywaggon Pike and end at Clough Head, or Causey Pike-Whiteless Pike should mention the low-level start and finishing points (Stair and Buttermere respectively).

SIDEWAYS: Froswick, Ill Bell and Yoke, the first three fells on the Kentmere Horseshoe (done clockwise), as seen from Harter Fell, further along the walk. Kentmere Reservoir is the water in the mid-distance. Way in the background (right) are the Coniston fells.
12/11/08

133

But enough of the nit-picking. Now on to some of the fine ridge walks that did not make the final pages of BOOK SEVEN.

The obvious one to start with is **The Kentmere Horseshoe**, generally accepted as one of the finest of the stride-out-all-day type of ridge walk. Not only that, it also has some highlights along the way, particularly the hump-backed stretch from Yoke, over Ill Bell and Froswick and on to Thornthwaite Crag. There are splendid views of upper Kentmere along the way and a crossing of the pass that AW considers Lakeland's finest – Nan Bield Pass. Enough, surely, for it to make the ridge-list round dozen? Apparently not.

In the same category, a couple of other ridge walks way out west should appeal to the stronger walker. The first links the fells on the north side of Ennerdale, starting with Great Borne and continuing over Starling Dodd, Red Pike, High Stile and High Crag. The second is along Ennerdale's southern fringe, from Crag Fell to Caw Fell, then on to Haycock, Scoat Fell and Pillar. Supermen could link the two, throwing in Haystacks for good measure, to complete The Ennerdale Horseshoe.

Still out west, another 'horseshoe' that links good ridge walks in grand scenery would certainly have impressed AW, in my opinion. This is: Yewbarrow-Red Pike-Scoat Fell-Haycock-Seatallan, starting from and finishing in Wasdale.

A closer look at the list of best ridge walks reveals three each from The Southern Fells and The North Western Fells, two each from **The Eastern**

WORTH WATCHING: And worth climbing! From the rocks known as Watches, The Edge leads to Ullock Pike, Long Side, then to Skiddaw (in clouds). 15/3/07

Fells and The Western Fells, and one from The Far Eastern Fells. There is nothing from the north and central parts of Lakeland, and it's the absence of any from the former that is probably the most surprising, because there really is a fine ridge north of Keswick which AW eulogises in The Northern Fells; this is the Ullock Pike - Long Side - Skiddaw ridge, incorporating the very attractive edge known as The Edge (no resemblance to any Irish rock guitarist is intended).

The area described in The Central Fells isn't terribly well stocked with exciting ridges. It has, of course, around its edges some of the most attractive of the low- and mid-level fells in Lakeland, but there are few significant ridges. Except, perhaps, that linking Helm Crag-Gibson Knott-Calf Crag, which, if combined with Tarn Crag, could probably best be described as The Easedale Horseshoe. And the other 'horseshoe' that springs to mind (involving two fells

UPS AND DOWNS: 'The Little Dale Horseshoe' would see the ascent of Robinson (seen above from Blea Crags and below, right), crossing Littledale Edge, then descending Hindscarth (below left), finally down the ridge to Scope End (below, foreground). 27/9/06 (above), 5/11/07 (below)

with long north-eastern ridges) features those two lovely twins in The North Western Fells either side of the deep valley between them known as Little Dale. Robinson-Hindscarth (in that order) is an excellent ridge walk (both routes are among AW's favourite ascents). And at least it is a true ridge walk. Nearby Catbells-Hindscarth cannot not truly be described as such; the High Spy to Dale Head section involves such a descent to Dalehead Tarn that it is, more properly, jumping from one ridge to another.

There are some great ridges in the PICTORIAL GUIDES that probably were not considered for the ridge list because of their short length. Near the top of the tree is the great walk between Allen Crags and Glaramara, which, if it continued to Rosthwaite Fell with a well-defined path and down to Borrowdale, would surely be one of the finest ridge walks in Lakeland, being in such a splendid situation. As it is, AW was enthusiastic about this walk when it came into being: A delightful walk along a fascinating new

BREAKING: *Looking to Illgill Head from the Whin Rigg ridge. The gullies of the Screes clearly eat into the fell. In the background: Yewbarrow, Kirk Fell and, partially in cloud, Great Gable at the head of Wasdale.* 2/2/07

See 'More exciting places' 153-158

ON THE EDGE: *Whin Rigg from the path to Illgill Head.* 2/2/07

path. Of course, the path isn't so new these days!

Another top-drawer ridge walk, from the same guidebook, is that between Illgill Head and Whin Rigg (the two fells that occupy the length of the Screes alongside Wast Water). *A magnificent walk*, says AW, with three places where the path skirts big gullies down which are spectacular views. Two viewpoints which are illustrated on Whin Rigg 8 – one can clearly be seen above – show what a place this is. See Super views starting on page 114 and More exciting places starting on page 153.

Last, but by no means least, another short walk up in the north-west deserves to be mentioned: in both the Ard Crags and Knott Rigg chapters AW was quite downbeat about the one-mile ridge walk between them; but in the ascents of the fells he was much more positive. In fact, the full traverse from Rigg Beck to Newlands Hause is an absolute delight on a lovely summer's day and fellwalkers unfamiliar with it are definitely missing out – but that's only one man's humble opinion (mine).

HOW WELL DO YOU KNOW YOUR FELLS?

Quiz time: test your knowledge of the guidebooks

C1: NAME THIS FELL: AW describes it simply as: *The odd man out.*

C2: NAME THIS FELL: It has three main ridges, a subsidiary summit, a major crag and an occasionally used alternative name, and it is the only English home of an alpine flower.

C3: NAME THIS TARN: It is the source of the River Derwent.

C4: NAME THIS FELL: It has ridge routes to Arthur's Pike and Loadpot Hill.

C5: PICTURE QUESTION (right): Name this peak, for which AW coined a catchy nickname.

C6: NAME THIS FELL (where the blanks are): *The slender soaring lines of .... and its aloof height and steepness endow this fine mountain with special distinction. It stands on a triangular base and its sides rise with such*

30/11/10

regularity that all its contours assume the same shape, as does the final summit-plateau.

C7: NAME THIS ROCK FEATURE: *No ropes, pitons, etriers and other gadgets are needed to scale this fine rock monolith. (It is only four feet high).*

C8: NAME THIS OUTLYING FELL: A fell rated highly by AW . . . *amongst the most delectable of the lesser heights of Lakeland;* part of the Blawith Fells, it has a tarn named after it.

C9: NAME THIS FELL: Where you will find The Oracle. Clue: not Matrix Crags!

C10: NAME THESE FELLS: Both feature ascents beside a series of watercourses known as Tongues Gills (both plural).

THE ANSWERS are on page 344, but before you go there, there are OTHER QUIZZES: on pages 86, 108, 159, 205, 216, 239 and 259.

OH, DREARY ME...

Twenty fells that left AW distinctly underwhelmed

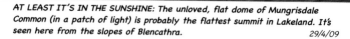

AT LEAST IT'S IN THE SUNSHINE: The unloved, flat dome of Mungrisdale Common (in a patch of light) is probably the flattest summit in Lakeland. It's seen here from the slopes of Blencathra.
29/4/09

In the introduction to BOOK ONE, AW writes: *Surely there is no other place in this whole wonderful world quite like Lakeland . . . no other so exquisitely lovely, no other so charming, no other that calls so insistently across a gulf of distance.*

Well, perhaps not quite. From the descriptions of the fells in this chapter – which has a self-explanatory title – one might be tempted to think that AW was engaging in a little 1950s example of a 21st-century art . . . spinning. Or, more likely, just writing it as he saw it – that all fells are wonderful but some are far, far, far more wonderful than others.

Even the subjects of this chapter might well be beauty spots if they were elsewhere in England (no suggested locations will be forthcoming from me . . . well, not in writing, anyway. Though I have some in mind!). Anyway, here they are – 20 of the 330 fells that didn't particularly impress AW. There is at least one from each book (which is a little hard on Brim Fell, but we'll get to that later). They are in chronological order.

Great Rigg: *No topographical surprises or secrets,* says AW, adding: *It is a plain, straightforward and uninteresting fell.* For a 'dull' fell, however, it is remarkably well-climbed, but only because it is part of the Fairfield Horseshoe.

Little Mell Fell: *. . . barely merits* inclusion in this book. *It is a fell – its name says so – but it is not the stuff of which the true fells are made.* Isolated on the edge of Lakeland, with 'alien' characteristics to Lakeland, why did AW include this in BOOK ONE? Best guess: because of its proximity to the much better (hence its prefix) . . .

Great Mell Fell. AW, despite his gruff reputation, can still be something of a softy, even if this is a backhanded compliment: *There is good in all, however, and its heathery top is a fine place for viewing the (greater) merits of other fells.*

Wether Hill: *The top . . . is quite without interest.* But fells are not just the top, and the steeper western side of the fell gets an honorary mention, as do the valleys surrounding it (Fusedale, Martindale, Cawdale Beck and Measand Beck).

Armboth Fell: *It can be said of very few fells that they are not really worth climbing; Armboth Fell is one of the few.* This, of course, was written around 16 years before THE OUTLYING FELLS and AW's remark

about Ponsonby Fell (overleaf), so perhaps he truly did mellow with age! Whether he did or not, he still didn't like Armboth Fell much, highlighting a number of drawbacks: . . . *walkers may justifiably consider its ascent is a waste of precious time and energy . . . a flat desolate top . . . little better than quagmire . . . a tangle of swamp and heather and mosses.*

High Seat: AW admits it has a fine situation and good approaches, but is less than enamoured of its upper plateau (*extreme dreariness . . . universal swampiness*). Of its approaches, the waterfalls in Ashness Gill get high marks, as does Shoulthwaite Gill . . . [it] *should find a place in every walker's itinerary.*

High Tove: *It is hard to imagine that anybody feels any affection at all for High Tove, apart perhaps from the sheep whose natural heaf it is.* Wet, wet wet is the problem here, but the fell does have on unique aspect – the summit path that links Watendlath with Thirlmere, which prompts the question: *Where else is a summit used as a pass?*

Thunacar Knott: It's a good job AW was a whizz with pen and ink, because he manages to draw a picture of Thunacar Knott (completely unphotogenic), a fell he further describes as being *quite deficient in interest.*

Ullscarf: Another fell whose upper slopes disappoint: *quite featureless and inexpressibly dreary.*

Brim Fell: It seems rather mean to pick out Brim Fell as the only 'dull' fell in BOOK FOUR – but that is probably more of a

CAIRN AT THE TOP: The summit of Wether Hill. 25/5/11

TWO FOR THE PRICE OF ONE: High Tove from Armboth Fell summit.   13/5/09

BRIM FULL OF PROMISE: The summit of the not-as-bad-as-all-that Brim Fell, looking towards Swirl How (centre) and Great Carrs (left).   24/11/10

tribute to the interest of the fells in the southern part of Lakeland rather than a reflection of its own shortcomings. A lot of the fell (particularly its rough eastern aspect and the tarns of Levers Water and Low Water) is of considerable interest. But its top is described as *featureless* and *without interest,* and thus becomes the token southerner in this list.

Brae Fell: Bare and grassy, Brae Fell is a good viewpoint, AW admits, but with little else of interest. This is how he puts it . . . *if all hills were like Brae Fell there would be far fewer fellwalkers.* Of the ascent from Green Head, he writes: *One wearies of the search for anything interesting during this overlong and featureless grassy trudge.*

Great Cockup: *First impressions are confirmed by a tour of exploration, the fell underfoot proving no more attractive than the fell at a distance.*

Mungrisdale Common: *[Its] natural attractions are of a type that appeals only to sheep: it is more an upland prairie than a hill.* This appears to be a trifle harsh on 'The Common', as it is known locally, which features a fine waterfall in Simon Gill and a rock outcrop called the Cloven Stone. Not enough for AW, however, who justifies the lack of any diagrams of ascent with: *There is little point in providing diagrams of ascent that will never be used.*

Broom Fell: Once again, the valleys take the honours (Wythop and Aiken Beck), with the upper reaches getting far lower marks: *There is little of interest on this rounded grassy hill, and nothing to justify a special visit to the summit.*

Sail: In the very first sentence of the chapter, AW spells it out: *Sail is the least obtrusive of the 2500-footers, being completely dominated by its vaster and more rugged neighbour, Eel Crag, and an absence of attractive or interesting features adds to its inferiority complex.* He describes its

140

position on the fabulous Causey Pike-Whiteless Pike ridge as *an unavoidable obstacle*. I wonder what his description would have been of the rebuilt path from Sail Pass to the summit which was, back when he wrote the chapter, *a very clear path being eroded into a trench*. Now it is the zig-zaggiest path in Lakeland, visible from miles away, and, when underfoot, seems more suited to a promenade in Blackpool than a fell in Lakeland.

Personal view:

It really is something of an abomination.

Burnbank Fell: *This is a dull hill, with little to suggest the grandeur of the mountain masses piled inland from it and nothing to divert the attention of a passing traveller. Next!*

Hen Comb: Another of the Loweswater fells, this also fails to stir the pulses: *It is the sort of fell sometimes climbed, but rarely twice. It is unfortunate in having Mellbreak as a neighbour.*

SCARRED FOREVER: The rebuilt zig-zag path from Sail, looking towards Scar Crags (also with three zigs and three zags) and in the distance Causey Pike.   2/6/11

Green Quarter Fell: A featureless, grassy height . . . but has *a perfectly-balanced and lovely view of upper Kentmere . . . that cries aloud for a camera. This apart, the long easy climb is without excitement and its accomplishment is gratifying only as evidence that there is life in the old dog yet.*

Hesk Fell: *Its appearance promises nothing at all of interest and the trudge to its featureless summit confirms first impressions.* AW says its one merit is honesty . . . What you see is what you get!

Ponsonby Fell: *There are no fells not worth climbing, but Ponsonby Fell is very nearly in this category.* No beating about the bush there, then! Although there is the splendid approach through Blengdale Forest that compensates for the climb. *Blengdale makes the climb worth while. But only just.*

Cold Fell: *Unremarkable . . .* but the fell is sufficiently close to the lovely Matty Benn's Bridge (*the most charming of Lakeland's packhorse bridges*) to elevate its status. There's more about this particular bridge on page 285.

JUST HOW STEEP IS IT?

It's the walk AW did on all fours. But is it really as tough as he described?

KIRK FELL FROM WASDALE HEAD: The walk AW described on Kirk Fell 4 *goes straight up the ridge on the left with only three places to stand upright: just above the small crag (black splodge); at Highnose Head (light patch of grass); and, finally, a grass ridge at the top of the scree (angled from low right to higher left, not far from the horizon).*   19/3/08

142

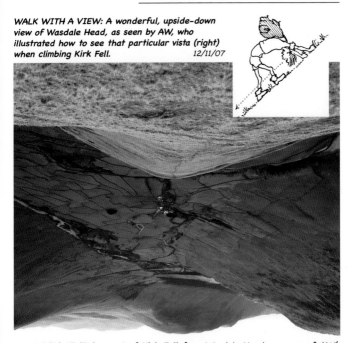

WALK WITH A VIEW: A wonderful, upside-down view of Wasdale Head, as seen by AW, who illustrated how to see that particular vista (right) when climbing Kirk Fell.
12/11/07

The BOOK SEVEN ascent of Kirk Fell from Wasdale Head was one of AW's classic pages – because he didn't just tell readers how steep was the ridge straight up the mountain . . . he **showed** them. And he used one of his most effective ways of doing so: with an amusing drawing! He did the same thing to get across how tough it was to finish his *personal notes* to BOOK FOUR with the famous sketch of a puppy nipping at his ankles as he was trying to write. Here's how he summarised the ascent of Kirk Fell, direct from Wasdale Head:

> *A straight line is the shortest distance between two points. This route is the straightest and therefore the most direct ascent in Lakeland. It is also the steepest – a relentless and unremitting treadmill, a turf-clutching crawl, not a walk. There are only three opportunities of standing upright, three heaven-sent bits of horizontal, before the slope eases into the summit plateau.*

Then came the drawing (shown at the top of this page), and the words:

> *Looking backwards (between one's legs) there is a superb upside-down view of Wasdale Head.*

So how steep is this climb? Well, overleaf you'll find a picture that shows very definitely that this, indeed, is an ascent that is not to be trifled with.

HERE'S EXACTLY HOW STEEP IT IS: From Yewbarrow, the sunlit ridge to Kirk Fell is seen in its full glory (if that is the word), from bottom right to upper, centre left. The small crag is visible early in the climb.   19/3/08

The picture is taken from way across Mosedale, and clearly shows the unremitting steepness of the climb. Fans of The Western Fells might point to Great Gable in the background, with the ascent via the grass ridge of Gavel Neese looking even steeper. It's not. Neither as steep nor as long, as the description on Great Gable 20 shows. Finally, it's worth noting how much AW's intrepid climber (the man on the previous page and right) aged between 1966 and 1974 (the period between BOOK SEVEN and THE OUTLYING FELLS). Here (left) is how he looked eight years later (on the back page of AW's last Lakeland guidebook).

ASCENT FROM WASDALE HEAD
2330 feet of ascent : 1¼ miles

KIRK FELL

A straight line is the shortest distance between two points. This route is the straightest and therefore the most direct ascent in Lakeland. It is also the steepest — a relentless and unremitting treadmill, a turf-clutching crawl, not a walk. There are only three opportunities of standing upright, three heaven-sent bits of horizontal, before the slope eases into the summit plateau. Apart from steepness, there are no difficulties or hazards of any sort.

natural dyke

third halting place (small delectable grass ridge as the top of the scree)

second halting place (crest of steep grass slope)

Back buttons cannot stand the strain, and wearers of braces are well advised to profit from a sad experience of the author on this climb and take a belt as reserve support.

first halting place (top of small crag)

Looking backwards (between two points) there is a superb upside-down view of Wasdale Head

Two alternative routes are available and more generally used. Either (a) proceed to the top of Black Sail Pass, thence climbing the north ridge, or (b) go up to Beck Head and ascend Rib End. In both cases the top of the fell is reached after an interesting scramble on a stony track alongside the watershed fence.

looking north

bracken

Wasdale Head

Row Head

Leave Wasdale Head by the Black Sail path, starting through the yard of Row Head, up the lane from the hotel.

THE PAGE: From the Kirk Fell chapter.

TONGUE TWISTER

What is unique about this modest little Troutbeck fell?

NICE VIEW: Troutbeck Valley and Windermere from Troutbeck Tongue.   31/7/09

What do the following 25 fells have in common? **Arnison Crag | Glenridding Dodd | Gowbarrow Fell | Great Mell Fell | Heron Pike | High Hartsop Dodd | Little Mell Fell | Low Pike | Nab Scar | Stone Arthur | Arthur's Pike | Froswick | Hallin Fell | Hartsop Dodd | The Nab | Sallows | Shipman Knotts | Sour Howes | Steel Knotts | Troutbeck Tongue | Thunacar Knott | Black Fell | Hard Knott | Holme Fell |** and **Mungrisdale Common.**

Sharp cookies among you will probably reel off the answer straight away. They are the fells in the first seven Lakeland guidebooks that do NOT feature ascent diagrams. Notice how many are from the first two books (ten each), before AW decided enough of that (almost!). After BOOK TWO, only two of his least-favourite fells (aesthetically) got such treatment (**Mungrisdale Common** and Thunacar Knott), plus three in the jam-packed BOOK FOUR (**Black Fell** and **Holme Fell**, both of low height with simple ascents, and **Hard Knott**, where an ascent diagram was sacrificed to make way for that of a Roman fort – a kind of reverse Monty Python moment – what has AW ever done for the Romans!)

Even sharper cookies might ask: What about THE OUTLYING FELLS? Well, this is where everything is turned on its head; only one fell DOES have an ascent diagram. That fell is Caw, and even then it warrants barely half a page.

Now on to the question that might blunt even the sharpest cookie in the biscuit barrel: of the fells listed above, what makes the ascent of **Troutbeck Tongue** unique? Clue: it's not that Sean McMahon's dog Casper completed his 214th 'Wainwright' on this summit! Here is the answer: it's the only fell for which AW's description of its ascent starts from the summit. Here's how it begins: *A prominent rock rib descends southwards from the summit and indicates the quickest and pleasantest route to the top.*

So, modest little Troutbeck Tongue, as well as being a lovely little hill with great views of nearby mountains, the Troutbeck Valley and Windermere, also has a claim to fame within the famous series of Lakeland guidebooks written by

AWainwright

A HALF-DOZEN IS

So here is a
TOP TWENTY
list of 'best
fells' that AW
might have
chosen (he
had already
named eleven
of his absolute
favourites)

*AS GRAND AS IT GETS: High
Stile, overlooking Bleaberry
Comb and Tarn, is the
centrepiece of one of the finest
'walls of fells' in Lakeland.
On the facing page, TOP:
Overlooking Burtness Comb and
Buttermere; MIDDLE: Chapel
Crags and Bleaberry Tarn;
BOTTOM: High Stile and Red
Pike above the lake.*

*28/6/11 (main picture),
31/3/08, 4/10/10 and 30/7/11*

Six years before BOOK SEVEN – the
final PICTORIAL GUIDE – was published
in 1966, AW revealed that he had a 'best
half-dozen' in mind. On the 'natural
features' page of the Bowfell chapter,
after lauding this magnificent mountain
at the head of Great Langdale, he dropped
in this line: *Rank Bowfell among the best
half-dozen.* Right below this, he added:

*The author is not prepared to say, at this
stage, which he considers to be the other
five. This opinion will be given in the last
pages of Book Seven.* But he couldn't wait

JUST NOT ENOUGH

that long. Two years after letting slip one of his best six, he revealed another in BOOK FIVE: **Blencathra**.

Four years later, in the final pages of BOOK SEVEN, he kept his fans guessing for one more page, with this (now famous) teaser: *I now give,*

after much biting of finger-nails, what I consider to be the finest half-dozen:

Be quick, turn over

And when you do, the best half-dozen awaiting are in this order: Scafell Pike, Bowfell, Pillar, Great Gable, **Blencathra** and Crinkle Crags. Then came some more surprises: in his opinion Great Gable wasn't the grandest of the lot; Scafell Pike was. Which suggests the best-six list WAS actually in order (with

Bowfell second, followed by the two western giants, Blencathra then Crinkle Crags). And then came some other revelations: Scafell would have been number seven if there had been seven in the list, and it grieved AW to leave out Haystacks (most of all), Langdale Pikes, Place Fell, Carrock Fell and *some others* . . . Those last two words might make you think (it certainly did me), what others?

Well, we've got his best six, his number seven and four others, which, if you count the Langdales as one fell, equals a nice round figure of eleven (!) So let's see if we can find nine more fells that AW would have included in his top 20. Without even having to think too hard, one of the nine is pretty obvious: High Street. AW really had a soft spot for this fell. He loved it being the clear overlord of its group of fells; he loved its history (a Roman road on the summit, which was also a former racecourse); he loved the extensive views from its summit which, because of its easterly position, includes an unparalleled vista of the Pennines; and he loved the ascent from Mardale direct via Rough Crag and Long Stile, a way up the fell that is generally known as The Connoisseur's Route (with initial caps).

HIGH-LEVEL: The wonderful ridge from Hopegill Head to Whiteside.   1/5/07

Next, on to a BOOK SIX fell that, you can tell from the 'natural features' page, AW really rated. The high mountain range of Hopegill Head *leaps like a rainbow from the woods and fields of Brackenthwaite and arcs through the sky for five miles to the east, where the descending curve comes down to the village of Braithwaite. This ridge has three main summits, of which the central one (and the finest, but not the highest) is known locally as Hobcarton Pike and to mapmakers as Hopegill Head. This ridge is, of course, the* Whiteside-Hopegill Head-Grisedale

EASTERN DELIGHT: The best flank of High Street, and Blea Water.   12/11/08

Pike traverse, which is one of AW's favourites. Hopegill Head has another great ridge, that from the subsidiary summit of Ladyside Pike; not far from the parent fell's top this ridge passes by The Notch – an exciting feature that is looked at in some detail on page 155. And then there is the huge Hobcarton Crag (see page 247), a wonderful sight in summer or winter and home to a rare alpine flower. This is, indeed, the grandest of the fells in the north-west.

Grandeur is the central theme of another splendid mountain that, I'm sure, most people would plump for when choosing their AW top 20. In that respect, High Stile has a lot in common with Blencathra. In fact, when you think about it, the Red Pike-High Stile-High Crag range's alpine-like wall overlooking the Buttermere valley is much like Blencathra's dominance over Threlkeld. And, like Blencathra too, the range has *perfect architecture* – in that High Stile is the centre (and highest) of the three fells, overlooking the central (and best) of the three great combs (Ling Comb, Bleaberry Comb and Burtness Comb), with a tarn – Bleaberry Tarn – *in the central recess like a jewel.*

Now to pleasures of a different

Grange Fell 1363'

King's How, from Shepherds Crag

PRETTY: Page one drawing.

nature, and a fell – Grange Fell – that not only features one of the prettiest page one drawings, but also one of the grandest introductions: *Grange Fell is nothing on the map, everything when beneath one's feet.* It really casts a spell over AW (it's on the edge of his famous Castle Crag 'thick black line', remember), and it features two interesting summits in King's How and Brund Fell, plus a jumble of other rocky tors and crags across a half-mile summit plateau that is flecked with heather (he loved his heather!). At 1363ft it's one of the lower fells – but not as low as Loughrigg Fell (a mere 1101ft) but which has to be included in this fantasy list for reasons that have been given elsewhere in this book (see

FULL OF INTEREST: Carrock Fell features various stony antiquities. 25/2/11

149

pages 63 to 67 and page 78).

That leaves four more. Now it's starting to get a little more difficult. Ah, but there's an obvious candidate, I hear you say! I agree. For all the indignities man has heaped upon Coniston Old Man it is still a grand old fell, and throughout its chapter there is an unmistakable air of affection about AW's writing. I'm 99.9 per cent sure he would have included it in his top 20.

I'm not quite so sure about Esk Pike because it really is one of those underrated fells, but think about it: it is lofty (2903ft); it is in a grand location (rubbing shoulders with Great End and Bowfell, a stone's throw from the Scafells); it has the famous Esk

Hause pass close by (and the infamous 'false' Esk Hause); it has a lovely view of Derwent Water (unlike Bowfell, which is lauded as one of Lakeland's finest vistas); it has a long and interesting south ridge that perfectly splits one of Lakeland's most beautiful valleys (Eskdale) . . . It has a whole lot going for it, including this ringing endorsement: *Did it but stand alone, away from such enticing neighbours, Esk Pike would rank highly among the really worth while mountain climbs.*

That leaves just two more. I've made the decision (tough one, this) that AW would have preferred St Sunday Crag over its near-neighbour Fairfield. In the Fairfield chapter he acknowledges its height, its

HUGELY UNDERRATED: At 2903ft Esk Pike is lofty and set in the middle of a fantastic array of mountains. Its south ridge (left) is well seen from Bowfell. 26/7/11

FAMOUS FEATURE: An interesting view of Helvellyn's Striding Edge ridge, taken from the ridge leading from the summit to Nethermost Pike. 12/10/10

A PICTORIAL GUIDE
TO THE
LAKELAND FELLS
being somewhere between inspired guesswork and unavoidable subjectivity, an attempt to work out what

awainwright

would have considered to be the twenty finest fells in Lakeland

Here they are, in order of merit (up to number seven only). After that, they're alphabetical.

SCAFELL PIKE
BOWFELL
PILLAR
GREAT GABLE
BLENCATHRA
CRINKLE CRAGS
SCAFELL
CARROCK FELL
CONISTON OLD MAN
ESK PIKE
GRANGE FELL
HAYSTACKS
HELVELLYN
HIGH STILE
HIGH STREET
HOPEGILL HEAD
LANGDALE PIKES
LOUGHRIGG FELL
PLACE FELL
ST SUNDAY CRAG

Any disagreements about this list should (ideally) be sorted out in the pub over a pint or two of the landlord's finest.

position at the head of one of the most popular of Lakeland's ridge walks, the grandeur of its northern crags – but I didn't detect any particular note of enthusiasm in all this praise. In contrast, St Sunday Crag is lauded for its *slender, soaring lines*, its fine ridges, and its soaring height above Deepdale. This is the sort of enthusiasm that you will never quite see in the Fairfield chapter: *Altogether this is a noble fell. Saint Sunday must surely look down on his memorial with profound gratification.*

That leaves just one mountain, and this decision is the hardest of the lot. Nah, just kidding! It's a shoo in. Helvellyn, of course, is one of the finest mountains in Lakeland (despite its dull western slopes). It has one of the most extensive views; it has probably the most exciting ascent (Striding Edge); it has a spectacular eastern flank overlooking a wonderfully evocative tarn (Red Tarn); it has another superb ridge (Swirral Edge) linking it to the fine peak of Catstycam; it has memorials (three of them), a shelter and a well near the summit; it has legend and poetry (there we go again!). My guess is it would have been number eight on AW's 'best six' list.

NOTE: AW chose his list of best fells eight years before he wrote THE OUTLYING FELLS. I would be surprised if any of the fells contained in that book would have made it into a top 20 list, but perhaps Whitbarrow, Beacon Fell and Scout Scar might have been given honorary mentions.

A GILL WITH A VIEW: Great Gable and (way in the distance) Skiddaw, as seen from this spectacular location on Scafell.
25/6/09

WISE MAN SAY...

BOOK FOUR's self-portrait was in one of the most exciting locations in Lakeland . . . right at the top of Deep Gill on Scafell, where the West Wall Traverse emerges from its exciting route up the face of Scafell Crag from Lord's Rake. The pillar of leaning rock AW is admiring is known as the Pinnacle. He describes the scene thus: *The Pinnacle (left centre) and the Oracle (bottom right).* As in most of the portraits of himself, AW is wearing those socks (hope they got washed now and then) and is in that typical bent-leg pose. No knapsack this time, though.

Great Slab
and Climbers
Traverse –
plus five
more 'best
places' for a
fellwalker

REST of the BEST

A DARKER SHADE OF PALE: Covered in snow and hidden from the sun,
Bowfell's Great Slab still contrives to skip the light fandango.   11/2/10

At the back end of BOOK SEVEN AW reveals his 'six best places for a
fellwalker' (no, not the bar at the Dungeon Ghyll Hotel!). By 'best' he meant
because of their exciting situations, and he chose:

STRIDING EDGE, **Helvellyn**

First col, LORD'S RAKE, Scafell

MICKLEDORE, Scafell

SHARP EDGE, **Blencathra**

SOUTH TRAVERSE, Great Gable

SHAMROCK TRAVERSE, Pillar

BOOK ONE:
Striding
Edge.

He tells readers: *Off course I haven't forgotten Jack's Rake on Pavey*
Ark. I never could. But this is a place only for men with hair on their
chests. I am sorry to omit Great Slab and Climbers Traverse on Bowfell.
Well, we don't have to – and we won't: this chapter features **Great Slab**
and Climbers Traverse, plus five more exciting places that impress AW.

Turn the page for more about this great place, and the other five

CLIMBERS TRAVERSE and GREAT SLAB, Bowfell

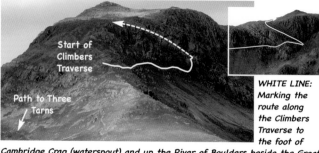

Start of Climbers Traverse

Path to Three Tarns

WHITE LINE: Marking the route along the Climbers Traverse to the foot of Cambridge Crag (waterspout) and up the River of Boulders beside the Great Slab of Flat Crags. *25/5/07 (main picture) and 18/10/07 (inset)*

The Climbers Traverse and Great Slab on **Bowfell** is the most exhilarating way up one of the best mountains in Lakeland, leading to one of the best summits in Lakeland, one that enjoys one of the best views in Lakeland. An enthusiastic AW describes it *as a very enjoyable high-level route leading to excellent rock-scenery*, and draws this detailed diagram of the latter stages of the ascent:

BB : Bowfell Buttress
CC : Cambridge Crag
FC : Flat Crag

REFRESHING: The Cambridge Crag waterspout. *15/10/08*

He adds that *the path is quite distinct and perfectly easy, with a little very mild scrambling, hardly worth mentioning*. It includes a visit to the most refreshing rockface in Lakeland: at the base of Cambridge Crag is a waterspout – nothing better ever came out of a barrel or a bottle. From there, turn left up the River of Boulders (an apt name indeed) which ascends to the right of the Great Slab. At the top, the summit is a short walk.

Personal view

I think AW missed a trick here. Sure, the Climbers Traverse and Great Slab isn't as spectacular as, say, Mickledore – but it's far more interesting and enjoyable.

THE TRAVERSE: Looking to Bowfell Buttress. *29/8/07*

WHIN RIGG and the VIEW OF WASTWATER SCREES

RED MARKS THE SPOT: The best two places to look down the Screes and on Wast Water. 26/2/07

TAKE YOUR PICK: The promontory or the arête behind it.   *11/1/06*

The views from **Whin Rigg** down onto Wastwater Screes and Wast Water made AW positively drool. He writes: *This is dramatic scenery, quite unique, and with an abiding impression of grandeur that makes the ascent of Whin Rigg a walk to be remembered and thought about often.* All you have to do is venture out onto the promontory in the picture left, or the arête behind it. Watch where you put your feet.

THE NOTCH, Hopegill Head

The Notch is an interesting and unexpected feature not far from the summit of Hopegill Head on the ascent via Ladyside Pike, a square cleft in the vertical rock wall of Hobcarton Crag that bites into the final arête leading to the summit. AW liked this so much he drew a picture (right) that made the front cover of BOOK SIX. And he adds: *Note The Notch. The finish above this point is excellent: the sort of place where one turns back to do it again out of sheer delight. You know!*

THE RIDGE: The final arête leading to the summit. The location of The Notch is indicated by the arrow (right).

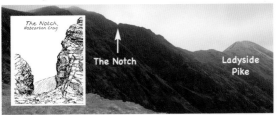

The Notch — Ladyside Pike

THE RIDGE: From Ladyside Pike to Hopegill Head. 2/6/11

DRAMATIC VIEW: *The huge cleft in the side of Yewbarrow, aptly named Great Door, offers sensational views of Wasdale, Wast Water and, in the background, Scafell.*   19/3/08

BELOW: *How Great Door fits into the Wasdale landscape in a view that features another 'door' (of a different spelling) way in the background.*   26/5/10

SCAFELL PIKE

SCAFELL

Mickledore

YEWBARROW

Great Door

GREAT DOOR, Yewbarrow

If The Notch (previous page) can be described as unexpected, **Great Door** on Yewbarrow is positively jaw-dropping.

It certainly qualifies as the most dramatic cleft in Lakeland that is anywhere near a path, and AW takes full account of this on Yewbarrow 5 in his description of the ascent of the fell from Overbeck Bridge.

His 'overview' reads: *Here illustrated is the best route to the top of Yewbarrow, a beautiful and interesting climb highlighted by the moment of arrival at the huge cleft of Great Door.* And earlier, he writes: *At the top of the gully* [to the right of Dropping Crag]*, on an open slope, climb half-right to reach the ridge exactly, suddenly and dramatically at Great Door: a thrilling moment.*

The huge cleft is perfectly safe to view from the path.

SWIRRAL EDGE, Helvellyn

GOOD ALTERNATIVE: Swirral Edge, climbing to Helvellyn. 1/6/09

A steep rock stairway . . . a fine rock ridge . . . AW is surprisingly generous (by BOOK ONE standards) with his praise for the ridge leading from the depression between **Catstycam** and **Helvellyn**. Let's be clear about this, **Swirral Edge** is not as long, as sharp, as photogenic or as exciting as Striding Edge – the other side of the deep hollow containing Red Tarn. But it is a fine ridge, nevertheless, and has to be treated with as much respect. And as an alternative way of ascending Helvellyn (if you're sick of queuing up to get down The Chimney on Striding Edge – sounds like a Christmas Eve climb!) it has a lot to recommend it.

WESTMORLAND CAIRN, Great Gable

The name of this magnificent viewpoint does not come from the former county. Great Gable used to be in Cumberland anyway! **Westmorland Cairn** gets its name because it was built in 1876 by a pair of Lakeland brothers of that name. They constructed the cairn to mark what they considered to be the best view in Lakeland – and as AW writes on Great Gable 4: *The aerial aspect of Wasdale is often described as the finest view in the district, a claim that more witnesses will accept than will dispute.*

TWO VIEWS: Left, to Wasdale Head and Wast Water; right, to Red Pike, Scoat Fell, Steeple and Pillar, beyond Kirk Fell. *both 12/11/07*

HOW WELL DO YOU KNOW YOUR FELLS?

Quiz time: test your knowledge of the guidebooks

D1: NAME THIS FELL: AW describes it simply as the *fell with the prosaic name.*

D2: NAME THESE FELLS: Name the peaks that make up the Langdale Pikes, in height order (highest to lowest).

D3: NAME THIS TARN: It has a number of stone shelters beside it.

D4: NAME THIS FELL: It has ridge routes to Red Pike and Great Borne.

D5: PICTURE QUESTION (right): These well-built twin cairns (the second is further down the slope behind the small cairn right) can be found on what fell?

25/5/11

D6: NAME THIS FELL (where the blank is): *A mountain has added merit if its highest point can be seen from the valley below, instead of being hidden behind receding upper slopes as is often the case, for then the objective is clear to the climber, there is no deception about the height or steepness, and the full stature from base to summit can readily be comprehended. Such a mountain is ....*

D7: NAME THIS ROCK FORMATION (AND FELL): Named after a 19th-century British politician who liked walking.

D8: NAME THIS OUTLYING FELL: On its summit is a prominent permanent structure known as The Hospice.

D9: NAME THIS FELL: Where you will find a rock-step right beside a wall?

D10: NAME THIS FELL: It features a prominent broken rockface called Dead Crags, and is also home to an impressive waterfall.

THE ANSWERS are on page 344, but before you go there, there are OTHER QUIZZES: on pages 86, 108, 137, 205, 216, 239 and 259.

BARF TIME

Big clean-up for The Bishop and his sidekick reveals the power of AW's pen

TOUGH GOING: Main picture – the steep slope up to The Bishop on the direct, full-frontal ascent of Barf. AW describes it as a very stiff scramble. 24/2/12
INSET: Way above the Bishop is the distinctive shape of Slape Crag, a barrier on the direct route that is bypassed by a rock traverse. 24/2/12

One of the best of AW's small drawings can be found in the chapter on the rugged Barf, the 1536ft of hill that overlooks Bassenthwaite Lake and the main Keswick-Cockermouth road as if a sentinel. It's from a little way up the fearsome eastern flank of the fell, looking down on the hamlet of Beckstones from a position directly behind **The Bishop of Barf**.

This is a proud 8ft monolith that is regularly given a lick of white paint which, because of its position against a backdrop of Skiddaw slate screes, makes it stand out for miles around.

AW told his BOOK SIX readers that the rear of **The Bishop** also had a paint job – but the drawing to the right (the one mentioned above) seems to suggest that the 'other side' wasn't quite given the diligent treatment its full-frontal valley view received.

A sidekick of the cleric – a curving pillar of rock called **The Clerk** – also looked in need of a paint-job (see below). And compared to his esteemed colleague he didn't get such a glowing write-up: *In comparison with the commanding figure of the Bishop, the Clerk is a poor drooping individual who attracts little attention to himself.* Not any more! These days, as the picture (left) shows, even **The Clerk** is a white-on guy.

It just goes to show the power of the AW pen in getting things done – or should that be the brush-stroke!

THE NAKED TRUTH: How the rear of The Bishop used to look when the paint wore off.

SHABBY: The Clerk, then.

BRIGHT: The Clerk, now.

ALL WHITE NOW: Baby it's a lick of paint for the rear quarters of The Bishop. 24/2/12

ALL THE FULL-PAGE DRAWINGS

The 76 that comprise AW's finest sketches of the Lakeland landscape

There are hundreds of pen-and-ink drawings in AW's eight Lakeland guidebooks, ranging from tiny sketches up to double-page spreads.

All 214 chapters in the PICTORIAL GUIDES had an introductory drawing, as did each of the 56 chapters in THE OUTLYING FELLS – but only the highest and mightiest fells (with the exception of rugged little Barf) were given an uncluttered full-page drawing to kick off the chapter. All of those are featured in this section; counting Barf, there are 16 of them – the others are **Helvellyn**, **High Street**, **High Raise**, **Bowfell**, **Coniston Old Man**, **Scafell Pike**, **Skiddaw**, Grasmoor, Grisedale Pike, Hopegill Head, Great Gable, Haycock, High Stile, Kirk Fell and Pillar.

In addition, AW uses seven full-page drawings as the frontispiece pages to the PICTORIAL GUIDES, all of which are included here. That leaves the three double-page spreads (Great Slab on Bowfell, Wastwater Screes in the Whin Rigg chapter, and the view towards the Scafells from Grasmoor). The rest were scattered throughout his books, featuring crags, waterfalls, valleys . . . everything beautiful.

NOTE: AW's two full-page self-portrait drawings (Harter Fell 10 and Yewbarrow 9) are not included in this chapter.

Frontispiece

Catstycam 6

Dove Crag 10

<u>Hart Crag 10</u>

from the east ridge, St Sunday Crag

Hart Crag 10

Helvellyn   3118'

from the south-west ridge of St Sunday Crag

Helvellyn 1

High Hartsop Dodd 3

Dove Crag and Hogget Gill, from High Hartsop Dodd

High Hartsop Dodd 3

Fairfield 14

The north face of Fairfield

Fairfield 14

Glenridding Dodd 4

Ullswater and Birk Fell

Glenridding Dodd 4

St Sunday Crag 8

Ullswater

St Sunday Crag 8

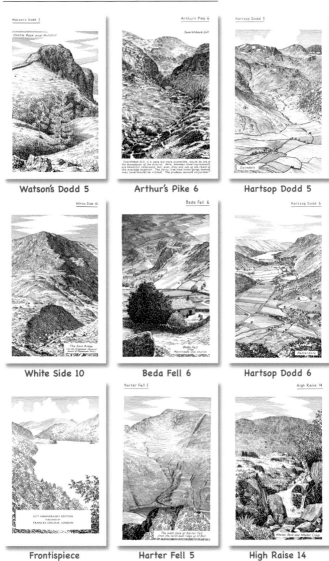

Watson's Dodd 5

Arthur's Pike 6

Hartsop Dodd 5

White Side 10

Beda Fell 6

Hartsop Dodd 6

Frontispiece

Harter Fell 5

High Raise 14

High Street 1

Wansfell 10

Frontispiece

Kentmere Pike 10

Wether Hill 12

High Raise 1

Tarn Crag 8

Yoke 10

Loft Crag 2

Pavey Ark 10

Tarn Crag 10

Bowfell 1

Sergeant Man 12

Frontispiece

Bowfell 10

Tarn Crag 3

Bowfell 13 and 14

Coniston Old Man 1

Winn Rigg 9 and 10

Dow Crag 12

Lingmell 11

Scafell Pike 1

Great End 3

Rossett Pike 5

Frontispiece

Bakestall 7

Blencathra 19

Skiddaw 1

Blencathra 11

Blencathra 23

Ullock Pike 9

Blencathra 15

Knott 8

Frontispiece

Barf 1

Causey Pike 9

Grisedale Pike 1

Grasmoor 9 and 10

High Spy 12

Catbells 10

Grasmoor 1

Hopegill Head 1

Sale Fell 6

Base Brown 3

Haycock 1

Whinlatter 3

Great Gable 1

High Stile 1

Frontispiece

Great Gable 28

Kirk Fell 1

Pillar 1

Latterbarrow (page 87)

Howes (page 232)

Pillar 4

Steeple 8

Howes (page 233)

WHERE DID ALL

There were 95 of them in **BOOKS ONE** and **TWO**

THE HIMALAYAS? No, the wall of rock wreathed in cloud in the far distance is

Whatever happened to all those blue skies? It's a common refrain as one gets older and looks back with, well, perhaps not rose-tinted spectacles – maybe sun-tinted shades . . .

The PICTORIAL GUIDES were originally, of course, a totally black-and-white venture (apart from a couple of coloured bands on the dust jackets, the colours of which were chosen by the printers and not by the author) and AW generally drew blue skies as white. But looking at his earlier books, you would be forgiven for thinking he only ever walked under a canopy of grey or, at best, big bunches of fluffy white clouds. In BOOK ONE alone **44** of his drawings featured a drawn sky, usually involving cloud of one form or another. In BOOK TWO he went even sky crazier, with an astonishing **51** drawings featuring some form of cloud detail. Then, like a sudden stock exchange collapse, the clouds simply disappeared (I'm not sure that's the correct analogy!).

Here's how the blue skies came back as the guidebooks rolled inexorably forward (remember, a blank sky equals a blue sky – or at least that's how I'd like to think of it): BOOK THREE: **35** drawings with sky detail; BOOK FOUR: **16** drawings; BOOK FIVE: **8** drawings; BOOK SIX: **13** drawings (a little increase there, but the trend is still downwards); BOOK SEVEN: **3** drawings; THE OUTLYING FELLS: **1** drawing.

Here are the chapters where you will find them:

BOOK ONE: Frontispiece, **Arnison Crag**, **Birkhouse Moor** (x2), **Birks** (x2), **Catstycam** (x2), **Clough Head** (x2) including a self-portrait of AW

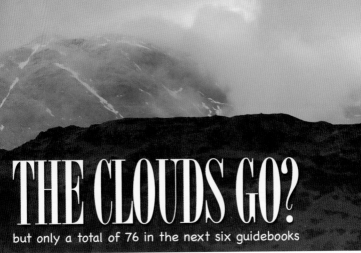

THE CLOUDS GO?

but only a total of 76 in the next six guidebooks

not Nanga Parbat or Kangchenjunga – it's Crinkle Crags.   28/1/11

looking towards **Blencathra**, Dollywaggon Pike, Glenridding Dodd, Great Dodd (x2), **Great Mell Fell**, Hart Crag (x3), Hart Side (x2), Helvellyn (x3), **High Hartsop Dodd** (x2), **High Pike**, Little Hart Crag, Middle Dodd, Nethermost Pike, Raise (x2), Red Screes (x4), St Sunday Crag, Seat Sandal, Sheffield Pike, Stone Arthur, Stybarrow Dodd (x2), Watson's Dodd (x2), **White Side**. Red Screes (with 4) manages to get another claim to fame (see Red Screes 11 for its others). 26 of the book's 35 fells have at least one image with a drawn sky.

BOOK TWO: Frontispiece, **Angletarn Pikes** (x3), **Beda Fell**, Branstree, Brook Crags, Caudale Moor (x4), Gray Crag, Grey Crag, Harter Fell (x2) including a self-portrait of AW looking towards Haweswater, Hartsop Dodd (x2), **High Raise** (x3), **High Street** (x3), Ill Bell, Kentmere Pike (x3), Kidsty Pike, Loadpot Hill (x4), Mardale Ill Bell (x2), Place Fell, Rampsgill Head, Rest Dodd, Sour Howes, Tarn Crag, Thornthwaite Crag (x2), Troutbeck Tongue (x2), Wansfell (x3), Wether Hill (x3), Yoke (x2). Again, 26 of the book's 36 fells have at least one image with a drawn sky.

BOOK THREE: Frontispiece, Armboth Fell, Bleaberry Fell (x3), Blea Rigg, Calf Crag, Eagle Crag, Grange Fell (x3), Harrison Stickle (x3), Helm Crag (x2), High Raise, High Rigg (x2), High Seat, Loft Crag, Pavey Ark (x2), Pike o'Stickle, Raven Crag, Sergeant Man (x2), Sergeant's Crag, Silver How, Steel Fell (x2), Tarn Crag, Thunacar Knott, Ullscarf, Walla Crag. 23 out of 27 fells have at least one drawn sky.

BOOK FOUR: Bowfell (x3), Brim Fell (x2), Coniston Old Men, Dow

Crag, Great End, Grey Friar, Illgill Head, Lingmell, Lingmoor Fell, Pike o'Blisco (x2), Scafell, Slight Side. 12 out of 30 fells have at least one drawn sky.

BOOK FIVE: **Bakestall, Bannerdale Crags, Blencathra** (x2), **Knott, Latrigg** (x2), **Ullock Pike.** 6 out of 24 fells.

BOOK SIX: Barf, Castle Crag, Catbells (x2), Causey Pike (x3), High Spy, Hindscarth, Ling Fell, Outerside, Sale Fell, Whinlatter. 10 out of 29 fells.

BOOK SEVEN: Fellbarrow, Grike, Pillar. 3 of 33 fells.

And finally, THE OUTLYING FELLS: Latterbarrow. Just 1 of 116 tops; 1 of 56 chapters.

Those are the facts. Now for the 64,000-dollar question: why did the clouds disappear?

Here is a theory. The really significant drop occurred between BOOKS THREE and FOUR – from 35 down to 16. BOOK FOUR was a monster of a book – the biggest, the most detailed (see page 42 for a discussion about this point), and, presumably, entailed the most work. Perhaps AW could no longer spare the time to continue drawing cumulus clouds and shading in deep 'blue' skies.

And then, when he sat back and flicked through THE SOUTHERN FELLS (and many would say it is the finest of the PICTORIAL GUIDES), perhaps he realised he didn't have to spend so much time and effort trying to achieve realism in his drawings.

Or perhaps around the period of the late 1950s and early 1960s there was some localised global warming we never knew about which resulted in a glut of cloudless skies.

Stybarrow Dodd 2770' approx.

from Brown Crag

Fellbarrow 1363'

from the slopes of Burnbank Fell above Waterend

Waterend, a scattered hamlet, is really mis-named. Here is Loweswater, true, but this is the head (the beginning) of the lake, not the foot, which is properly the end, the exit, the place of outflow.

SKIES: From BOOKS ONE and SEVEN.

174

PULL UP AN EASEL

A place beloved of artists and, naturally, of guidebook writers

Birkhouse Moor is best known as the fell you walk past (and through a hole in one of its walls) on the way to Striding Edge and **Helvellyn**.

But away from the crowds heading west across its flank, its far eastern extremity is a rugged little enclave overlooking Ullswater with a little top known as Keldas, of which AW says: *Artists and photographers will vote Keldas the loveliest and most delightful place amongst the eastern fells.* Nearby is Lanty's Tarn (named after Lancelot Dobson, a member of a local landowning family). But the cairn that was once on the summit of Keldas (as seen on Birkhouse Moor 7) is no longer there. No matter; Keldas is still delightful.

Ullswater from Keldas

PINING FOR ULLSWATER: The view from Keldas, **DRAWING: From** Birkhouse Moor 4.

13/2/12

As a solitary fellwalker, AW much preferred to avoid the crowds, and he rarely ever engaged in the habit of

PEOPLE WATCHING

Here are all the guidebook drawings of people (other than himself):

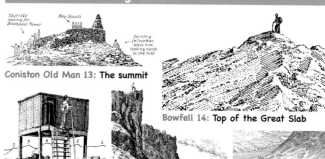

Coniston Old Man 13: **The summit**

Bowfell 14: **Top of the Great Slab**

Whin Rigg 8: **Two places to view Wast Water**

Bigland Barrow (page 72): **The viewing structure on the top of the 630ft fell: the view looking to the Coniston Fells**

Caermote Hill (page 208): **Looking to Binsey**

St Sunday Crag 8: **View of Ullswater**

Irton Pike (page 183): **The man in the uniform looks a little like Postman Pat . . . He's working for the Ravenglass and Eskdale Railway at Ireton Road Station, helping lots of passengers.**

Exciting places

Helvellyn 14: Looking to the summit from the ridge of Striding Edge

Dow Crag 12: Heading past a frozen and snow-covered Goat's Water

Helm Crag: The top of the rocks known as The Howitzer is the true summit of the fell. It was a summit that AW never visited, as he admitted on page 8 of the chapter

Great Gable 12: Left, Napes Needle, one of the most famous rocks in Lakeland. Next to the figure, AW drew an arrow from the words: *definitely not the author!*

Great Gable 12: Below, a tiny figure on the top of High Kern Knotts

Pillar 5: Left, three adults on Pisgah survey the top of Pillar Rock

Pillar 6: Right, the same three adults on the west face of the massive rock

You have to be bold to get to the top

Blea Rigg 3:
**The Split
Boulder**

Coniston Old Man 10:
**The Pudding
Stone.** AW: *The
figure up
aloft is not
the author*

**The Wet
Sleddale
Horseshoe
(page 244):
Gray
Bull**

Yoke 9:
**Badger
Rock**

West face   *East face*

Here's where all the book fivers ended up

Skiddaw 16: Right, on the western slopes of
this northern giant three people pose for
two drawings. No wonder there were no
other people illustrated in BOOK FIVE –
they were all up above Randel Crag!

*Concave and
convex slopes*

Concave slopes are
honest; convex
slopes are
deceitful.

concave

When ascending a concave
slope the summit can be seen at
all stages; on a convex slope it
seems to be visible but what the
climber sees is a skyline
that recedes as
he gains height.

convex

The final
slope of Skiddaw
above RandelCrag
is an exasperating
example of convexity

A whole town can fit in this cave

Loughrigg Fell 7: Left, one man
surveys the gloomy entrance to
Rydal Cave, which, it is said, could
shelter the population of Ambleside

But not many could fit in this shelter

Walna Scar (page 118): Right, a woman
checks out the entrance to a
stone shelter on the Walna Scar road.
A very similar shelter, perhaps the
same one, is illustrated on Dow Crag 4,
with the caption . . . *just big enough
for one person or a honeymoon couple*

178

VIEW FROM THE OUTSIDE: There is nothing between Binsey and the Solway Firth, but to the south Skiddaw and Bassenthwaite Lake are both prominent. 2/7/10

A BRIT OF HUMOUR

NICE DAY IN THE NORTH: It must have been for AW to be wearing rolled-up sleeves on the most northerly of the 214 fells.

On the summit of **Binsey** – the fell right on the very edge of Lakeland – is a pile of stones believed to be a prehistoric tumulus . . . which gave AW the chance for another slice of deprecating humour in his BOOK FIVE self-portrait. The caption to his drawing reads: *Prehistoric Tumulus and Ancient Briton.* That left-leg extension is now back. The big question is: will we ever see the knapsack again?

PANORAMA: The summit of Beacon Fell looking towards Dow Crag, Coniston Old

THE FELL THAT RINGS A BELL

It's lower than Castle Crag, it's off the beaten track, but, as a place for a family day out, it punches way above its weight

Beacon Fell is one of those Lakeland mountains that, family-wise, punches so much above its weight it's a veritable pocket heavyweight.

It's THE OUTLYING FELLS' Hallin Fell or Loughrigg Fell; it's the deep south's version of the northern gem Latrigg; it's the nearest thing in AW's eighth guidebook to Catbells, the ultimate family fell. In fact, its similarities to Catbells are rather uncanny. Both offer a round-trip walk of about three miles; both feature a little bit of mountaineering near their summits; both offer splendid views of lakes – Coniston Water and Derwent Water – but Beacon Fell has one attraction that Catbells cannot match – a tarn! And not just any tarn, either. **Beacon Tarn** is

A LITTLE BIT OF MOUNTAINEERING: The ascent of Beacon Fell includes a rocky gully close to the summit, which matches the excitement of the final rock stairways on the climb to Catbells from Hawse End. 16/3/06

Man, Wetherlam and the full length of Coniston Water.   25/8/11

ENTICING WATER: Beacon Tarn and a view
of Dow Crag and Coniston Old Man.   11/10/11

LANCASHIRE NAMESAKE

Another **Beacon Fell** in the north-west of England is possibly better known than the Lakeland version. Beacon Fell, on the edge of the **Forest of Bowland**, is also a popular family destination and, at 873ft to the Outlier's 836ft, is similar in altitude as well. **Beacon Fell Country Park** comprises 271 acres of woodland, moorland and parkland and was established in 1970. It even includes its own stretch of water, named **Beacon Fell Tarn**.

one of those stretches that water that just begs to be swum in at the back-end of a hot summer's day on the fells. AW, of course, never had much call for that sort of thing, dismissing the tarn in 12 words: *There is a tarn, too, hidden in a fold of the hills.* It's the fell he focuses on . . . *Beacon Fell ranks amongst the most delectable of the lesser heights of Lakeland. It is an epitome of all that appeals to fellwalkers . . .*

It also has a summit secret that can capture the imagination of youngsters whose parents may, just may, have used it to persuade their offspring that a half-day walk was better than a stint on a PlayStation. It's a little metal box hidden somewhere in the cairn (it's usually there, so I'm reliably informed) containing a visitors' book. You can read some of the remarks online at **www.beaconfellblogspot.co.uk**

181

COLOUR COLOUR EVERYWHERE: Watendlath Tarn and farm, an oasis of blue in the fells above Borrowdale, looking towards Great Gable (left, distance) beyond Base Brown. 3/5/07

WATER, WATER, EVERYWHERE

Lakes and tarns that gladden AW's heart

The Lakeland guidebooks were all about the fells – the summits, the ascents, the crags and the hidden upland places . . . right? Not quite. AW's eight guidebooks feature 330 fells (214 + 116) and an astonishing 180 pen-and-ink drawings of lakes and tarns (cue Michael Caine and his trademark phrase!).

Waterfalls and cascades attract his attention, too, earning 89 drawings in the eight guidebooks (see chapter beginning on page 286). He often explained the necessity of walking alone so as to be able to make a detour to take a photograph of a cascade that, back at home, he would fashion into a drawing.

Head and shoulders above all the water featured in the guidebooks is one place that was particularly close to his heart. Two of its waterside paths get high marks in his books (see page 224), and he drew it 37 times. The only other stretch of water that came remotely close didn't even come close at all, with a paltry (in comparison) 13 drawings.

Which lake is AW's favourite? Turn the page to find out

A BEAUTY: Ullswater, the lake AW drew 37 times, seen from Birkhouse Moor, with Glenridding in the foreground. 19/9/07

AW's favourite lake (or at least the one he liked to draw more than any other) was **Ullswater**. In BOOK ONE he sketched it 22 times, including three full-page drawings: from **Glenridding Dodd** (one of the classic viewpoints); from **St Sunday Crag** (a famous sketch with a young woman looking towards the lake); and for the **frontispiece** (the page opposite the details of the publisher). In BOOK TWO he sketched it 13 times, two of which were full-page drawings: again, for the frontispiece; and in a view of Patterdale from **Hartsop Dodd**. And in THE OUTLYING FELLS he drew the lake twice. Limping in in second place was **Haweswater**, with 12 of its 13 sketches in BOOK TWO (the lake is slap bang in the middle of this book's geographical area) and with one in THE OUTLYING FELLS. Another of AW's most recognisable full-page drawings features himself looking out over the lake in the **Harter Fell** chapter.

GET THE CAMERAS OUT AT SWINESIDE KNOTT

In both the **Hart Side** and **Stybarrow Dodd** chapters, AW points out that Swineside Knott is the best viewpoint for Ullswater. On Stybarrow Dodd 6 two arrows point to a location: *Here the keen camera enthusiast will suffer a paroxysm of enthusiasm.*

Here is a breakdown of the numbers of sketches of the lakes (and the books in which they appear): **37**: Ullswater (22 13 2); **13**: Haweswater (12 1); **8**: Brothers Water (4 4); **7**: Wast Water (4 3), Crummock Water (6 1); **5**: Grasmere (3 2), Thirlmere (1 4), Hayeswater (5), Windermere (3 2); **4**: Bassenthwaite Lake (1 2 1), Buttermere (1 3), Derwent Water (3 1); **2**: Ennerdale Water (2); **1**: Elter Water (1), Esthwaite Water (1), Loweswater (1), Over Water (1), Rydal Water (1); **0**: Coniston Water ('view' drawings don't count), and Devoke Water (the drawing in the Circuit of Devoke Water chapter is really of the boathouse, not the lake).

PRIDE OF KESWICK: Derwent Water from the slopes of Maiden Moor. 1/11/10

BOOK BY BOOK: HOW THE WATER BEGAN TO DRY UP

The north-western areas of Lakeland are the driest (in terms of tarns), and it is not surprising that BOOKS FOUR and FIVE have the fewest sketches of standing water among the eight guidebooks. BOOK FIVE features just six drawings: two each of **Bassenthwaite Lake** and Bowscale Tarn, one of **Scales Tarn** and one of **Over Water**. BOOK SIX also features six drawings of water: two of **Dale Head Tarn** and one each of **Buttermere, Crummock Water, Derwent Water** and **Launchy Tarn**. Book by book, the trend is shrinkage!

The Eastern Fells
39 drawings:
31 of lakes;
8 of tarns.
The Far Eastern Fells
44 drawings:
35 of lakes;
9 of tarns;
The Central Fells
21 drawings:
10 of lakes;
11 of tarns.
The Southern Fells
20 drawings:
5 of lakes;
15 of tarns.
The Northern Fells
6 drawings:
2 of lakes;
4 of tarns.
The North Western Fells
6 drawings:
4 of lakes;
2 of tarns.
The Western Fells
24 drawings:
15 lakes;
9 tarns.
The Outlying Fells
20 drawings:
6 lakes;
14 tarns.

Most popular tarns (3 drawings each):
Blea Water | Sprinkling Tarn |
Stickle Tarn.

MORNING LIGHT: The sun shines on Harter Fell and High Street on the far side of Haweswater, but The Rigg (trees) is still largely in shade. 12/11/08

TRUE BLUE: Wast Water from the slopes of Yewbarrow. 23/6/09

HEAD OF THE LAKE: Pillar and Steeple beyond Ennerdale Water. 28/6/11

UNNAMED TARNS

There are hundreds of pools and tarns featured in the guidebooks that are not named. Some of them were great favourites of AW – he wrote about them, sketched them; a few of these tarns are featured in the section starting on page 194.

CAMERAS OUT: For picturesque (Langdale) Blea Tarn, one of the most photographed of Lakeland tarns. 2/4/09

JEWELS OF THE FELLS

The lakes – the meres and the waters and Bassenthwaite Lake – of the valleys may have given the Lake District its name, but it's the mountain tarns, formed by extreme glacial action, that give it an added aura of magic.

When the Victorians began their first tentative exploration of Lakeland it was initially to see the lakes; then the lower-level tarns, then further up the fells, before the mountains themselves became the object of attention. Tarns may not be so fashionable these days – certainly not the objective of a walk – but they light up walking routes like sunshine breaking through low-level cloud, and many of the finest mountain walks feature a visit to one or more tarns, many of them set in the most breathtaking and romantic surroundings.

This section is about the tarns of Lakeland. Without them, it would be North Wales or the Scottish Highlands. With them, as AW might say, they help create a little piece of heaven.

So, sit back and just imagine you're beside Dock Tarn. It's August, the heather is out, it's warm and sunny . . . it really *is* heaven.

TARNS WITH A NAME and the chapters in which they feature

Alcock Tarn: Heron Pike. Allan Tarn: Top o'Selside. **Angle Tarn: Angletarn Pikes** - one of AW's favourites. See following pages. **Angle Tarn: Bowfell | Esk Pike** - see following pages. **Arnsbarrow Tarn:** Top o'Selside. **Barfield Tarn:** Black Combe. **Barngates Tarn:** Black Fell - only named on map in second edition. **Beacon Tarn:** Beacon Fell. **Blackbeck Tarn: Haystacks** - an AW favourite. See following pages. **Bleaberry Tarn: High Stile | Red Pike** - a picture of this popular tarn can be seen on page 146. **Blea Tarn: Armboth Fell. Blea Tarn: Lingmoor Fell | Pike o'Blisco** - one of the most picturesque of all tarns. See facing page. **Blea Water: High Street | Mardale Ill Bell** - AW liked this one, and the nearby Small Water. See following pages. **Blind Tarn: Dow Crag | Walna Scar** - very interesting. See following pages. **Boo Tarn: Coniston Old Man** - *a small reedy pool.* **Bowscale Tarn: Bowscale Fell** - one of two northern gems. See following pages. **Broadcrag Tarn: Scafell Pike** - supposedly the highest tarn in Lakeland. See page 208. **Brownrigg Tarn:** Calf Crag. **Burney Tarn:** Burney. **Burnmoor Tarn: Illgill Head | Scafell | Boat How. Carlside Tarn:** Carl Side. **Codale Tarn: Sergeant Man | Tarn Crag** - *a wild and impressive location.* See following pages. **Cunswick Tarn:** Scout Scar. **Dalehead Tarn: Dale Head | High Spy** - see OFF-TRACK, page 131. **Dock Tarn: Great Crag** - another AW favourite. See following pages. **Easedale Tarn: Blea Rigg | Tarn Crag** - another charmer. See following pages. **Eel Tarn:** Scafell. **Floutern Tarn: Gavel Fell | Great Borne | Hen Comb. Foxes Tarn:** Scafell - higher than Broadcrag Tarn? See page 208. **Goat's Water: Coniston Old Man | Dow Crag** - one of the best. See following pages. **Greenburn Reservoir: Great Carrs | Swirl How. Greendale Tarn: Haycock | Middle Fell | Starling Dodd** - underrated. See following pages. **Greycrag Tarn:** Tarn Crag. *A marsh that masquerades as a tarn.* **Grisedale Tarn: Dollywaggon Pike | Fairfield | Helvellyn | St. Sunday Crag** - similar to Angle Tarn (Bowfell). See following pages. **Gurnal Dubs:** Potter Fell. **Hard Tarn: Nethermost Pike** - a surprise awaited AW on a visit to this tarn. See following pages. **Harrop Tarn: Armboth Fell | Ullscarf. Haskew Tarn:** Seat Robert. **High Dam:** Finsthwaite Heights. **High House Tarn: Allen Crags | Glaramara. Highnook Tarn: Blake Fell | Gavel Fell. Holehouse Tarn:** Stainton Pike. **Innominate Tarn: Haystacks** - a location of some considerable significance. See following pages. **Keppelcove Tarn: Catstycam | Helvellyn | White Side** - now dry. See OFF-TRACK, page 214. **Kemp Tarn:** Reston Scar. **Kirkfell Tarn:** Kirk Fell. **Lambfoot Dub: Great End** - scenic pool in a tremendous location. See following pages. **Lang Tarn:** Blawith Knott. **Lang How Tarns:** Silver How. **Lanty's Tarn: Birkhouse Moor. Lanty Tarn:** Steel Knotts. **Launchy Tarn:** Armboth Fell. **Levers Water: Brim Fell | Swirl How. Lily Tarn:** Loughrigg Fell. **(The) lily tarn:** Latterbarrow. **Lincomb Tarns: Allen Crags | Glaramara. Lingmoor Tarn: Lingmoor Fell. Little Langdale Tarn: Great Carrs | Lingmoor Fell | Wetherlam. Loughrigg Tarn: Loughrigg Fell** - see picture on page 66. **Low Birker Tarn: Green Crag. Low Dam:** Finsthwaite Heights. **Low Tarn: Red Pike (W)** - a western gem. See following pages. **Low Water: Coniston Old Man** - a hugely popular route passes this scenic tarn. **Moss Eccles Tarn:** Claife Heights. **Potter Tarn:** Potter Fell. **Redcrag Tarn:** High Raise. **Red Tarn: Catstycam | Helvellyn** - five-star location. See following pages. **Red Tarn: Cold Pike | Crinkle Crags | Pike o'Blisco. Rough Hill Tarn:** Loadpot Hill. **Scale Tarn:** Claife Heights. **Scales Tarn: Blencathra** - anothern gem of the north. See following pages. **Schoolknott Tarn:** School Knott. **Seathwaite Tarn: Dow Crag | Grey Friar. Skeggles Water:** Green Quarter Fell. **Small Water: Harter Fell | Mardale Ill Bell** - a very fine tarn indeed. See following pages. **Snipeshow Tarn:**

Bleaberry Fell. **Sprinkling Tarn:** Allen Crags | Great End | Seathwaite Fell – one of the best. See following pages. **Stickle Tarn:** Blea Rigg | Harrison Stickle | Pavey Ark | Sergeant Man | High Raise – and another of Lakeland's finest. See following pages. **Stickle Tarn:** Stickle Pike. **Stony Tarn:** Scafell. **Styhead Tarn:** Great End | Great Gable | Green Gable | Scafell Pike | Seathwaite Fell – huge for foot traffic. See following pages. **Tarn at Leaves:** Rosthwaite Fell. **Tarn Hows:** Black Fell. **Tewit Tarn:** Scoat Fell. **Three Dubs Tarn:** Claife Heights. **Three Tarns:** Bowfell | Crinkle Crags – frequently visited; photogenic. See following pages. **Tom Tarn:** Newton Fell South. **Tosh Tarn:** Buckbarrow – 'look over the wall to see it'. **Watendlath Tarn:** Armboth Fell | Grange Fell | Great Crag | High Seat | High Tove – pictured on pages 182 and 183 at the start of this chapter. **Wise Een Tarn:** Claife Heights. **Wythburn Head Tarns:** Calf Crag | High Raise | Ullscarf – *an ambitious name for slight widenings of the beck into pools.* **Yew Tree Tarn:** Holme Fell.

TARNS WITH NO NAME which AW thought worthy of mention

ROCK AT THE TOP: The summit tarn of Haystacks with (right) its tiny rock island.   12/7/11

Summit tarns, ridge tarns, tarns in passes, rock pools ... AW had an eye for drama and beauty. Here are some of the tarns that caught his eye. First, the summit cairn of Haystacks, his favourite fell. It's one of four significant stretches of water on the summit plateau (one nameless, **Blackbeck Tarn** and, of course, **Innominate Tarn**), and it's the one with the tiny rock island. Another summit with a tarn right at the summit is Wetherlam. And Red Screes and Blea Rigg have a close proximity to water, too. No other Lakeland summits have tarns so close to the very top. Most 'summit' tarns are more of a 'summit plateau' tarn or a 'close-to-the-summit' tarn – examples of these are:

ICED POOL: Left and below, the summit of Wetherlam.   9/11/10

MORE ICE: The top of Red Screes.   10/12/08

NEAR WATER: The summit of Blea Rigg, a fell which also hosts a great rock pool (see page 190).   9/1/07

PLATEAU TARN: On Seathwaite Fell, looking to Great Gable. 26/6/07

DEPRESSION TARN: At Dore Head, Yewbarrow. View of Pillar. 2/3/10

Seathwaite Fell (a tarn little over 100 yards from the top); Grey Knotts (four small sheets of water); Kirk Fell (**Kirkfell Tarn** – yes, it's named – slap bang between the main top and the north top), **Blencathra** (a shallow tarn in the saddle between Hall's Fell Top and Atkinson Pike, the top of Foule Crag); Tarn Crag; Thunacar Knott; Place Fell; and Sheffield Pike.

Other tarns that have achieved some prominence in the guidebooks might have done so because of geographical positioning, such as being in a pass or a depression between two fells. The classic such tarns are, of course, **Three Tarns** between Bowfell and Crinkle Crags (see page 87); others of this type can be found at **Gillercomb Head** between Brandreth and Green Gable, and the prominent tarn at **Dore Head** between Yewbarrow and Red Pike.

The tarn that SHOULD have a name – Gem Tarn, perhaps

Then there are the tarns that just happen to be there, including one of AW's absolute favourites, an unnamed tarn in the depression on the splendid ridge walk between Allen Crags and Glaramara (see

THE TARN WITH NO NAME: Among a clutch of tarns with names halfway along the ridge between Allen Crags and Glaramara. In the Glaramara chapter AW called it 'a gem of a tarn'. 26/6/07

or even...Wainwright Tarn

picture above right). He really loved this one. *A perfect mountain tarn . . . a splendid subject for an artist's canvas. Only the very brave will attempt the full circuit of this tarn at the waterline.* Doesn't it seem such a shame that this tarn has no name? How about **Perfect Tarn**, or **Gem Tarn** (the Glaramara chapter described it as *a gem of a tarn*). Or perhaps even **Wainwright Tarn**. Now wouldn't that be a good way to christen this lovely stretch of water?

Which leads very nicely to another water feature, this one again being on Blea Rigg (which is a fell packed with interest – see page 228).

It cannot be described as a tarn – in fact, AW called it what it was, a rock pool. It's on the pleasant ridge walk between Blea Rigg and Sergeant Man, a little less than a mile west-north-west of Blea Rigg and about 200 yards short of a crossroads of paths, just to the right of the main path. AW's comments (right) are self-explanatory. The question is really: what made him deviate from the path to find this pool?

SERGEANT MAN

A few yards to the right of the ridge path, about a furlong short of the 'crossroads', is a miniature pool entirely enclosed in an outcrop of handsome rock. This is a delightful natural feature (a great favourite of the author) and all gardener-walkers who see it must covet it for their backyards at home

STICKLE TARN

COLOURED PATH

EASEDALE TARN

The 'crossroads'

BLEA RIGG

TARNS WITH A NAME which AW thought of some interest

Three Tarns is one of the most evocative names in Lakeland. It's the location of . . . three tarns; it's the midway point between two of AW's favourite mountains (Bowfell and Crinkle Crags); it's a fantastic viewpoint for the Scafell range (helped by the foreground); and it's part of the wonderful Bowfell-Crinkle Crags ridge walk.

ONE OF A TRIO: The view to Scafell and Scafell Pike from one of the (frozen) Three Tarns. 10/2/06

One of the very best lines from BOOK FOUR

Is it 'Crinkle Crags IS . . .' or 'Crinkle Crags ARE . . .'?
Is it 'Three Tarns IS . . .' or 'Three Tarns ARE . . .'?

IS sounds right but looks wrong!

There is something very unusual about Three Tarns, which is featured in an OFF-TRACK chapter – see page 87.

Unusual is also the right word to describe **Blind Tarn**, which sits in a comb below Buck Pike, two-thirds of a mile south of Dow Crag. It is called Blind Tarn because (unless there has been a recent

NO WAY OUT: Blind Tarn, below Brown Pike. 20/7/10

DREAMS ARE MADE OF THIS: Heathery slopes surround Dock Tarn   7/3/07

deluge) it has no outlet beck, an oddity that AW notes on Dow Crag 4: *Blind Tarn is one of the few tarns without an outlet – hence its name.*

Let's not forget, of course, that the Lakeland guidebooks were about the fells, and AW was pithy with his comments on the tarns, even the ones he so clearly loved. Here's what he said about **Dock Tarn** in the Great Crag chapter (beside a small drawing, above): . . . [when] *the upper slopes are ablaze with heather, Dock Tarn is a place to lie dreaming, and life seems a sweet sweet thing.* He didn't like the name, though.

A tarn that didn't quite get such a good write-up from AW falls into this category. In the Seatallan chapter **Greendale Tarn** is described as *unattractive,* yet in the ascent of Haycock from Greendale AW says the first stage of the walk (up to and just beyond Greendale Tarn) *is pleasant and interesting.* This discrepancy might be something to do with whether the sun was out or not! It certainly looks a delightful place, judging by the pictures below.

COLOURFUL: Greendale Tarn; and (left) the tarn below Middle Fell.   15/9/09 (above) and 26/2/07 (left)

Two stunning tarns in spectacular locations – turn the page

LOCATION, LOCATION, LOCATION plus some local scenery!

JUST OFF THE BEATEN TRACK: The wonderful location of Lambfoot Dub, on a shelf above the Corridor Route and below Great End and Broad Crag. Picture taken from Great Gable's south traverse.   *28/2/11*

Lambfoot Dub is perched on a shelf just a five-minute detour away from one of the most popular paths up Scafell Pike, but probably not one person in a thousand would turn off the Corridor Route to seek out its charms. And charms it has in spades, being surrounded by terrific mountains including – across the great gulf occupied by Lingmell Beck – Great Gable.

It is from Great Gable that the picture above was taken. The tarn isn't big enough to even make an appearance – as the two pictures below show.

But what a location . . . although its merits don't even get a mention in BOOK FOUR! AW visited it; in the Great End chapter he drew a small sketch of Long Pike *from near Lambfoot Dub.* But I guess with so much good stuff to cram into the biggest guidebook in the series, little Lambfoot Dub bit the dust. Well, here we're righting a wrong – let's hear it for the tarn with the cool name!

BELOW: Striking scenery. *24/9/10*

LEFT: Looking across to Great Gable and Green Gable. *24/9/10*

IT'S BEHIND YOU: Hard Tarn is situated the other side of Nethermost Pike's east ridge (diagonal, left to right).   15/9/11

TINY TARN: View from the east ridge looking down on Hard Tarn. Dollywaggon Pike is in the background.   15/9/11

Hard Tarn has more claim to fame than just being one of the shyest tarns in Lakeland. The pool of water that hides in a comb (Ruthwaite Cove) just south-east of the summit of Nethermost Pike also happens to be the subject of one of the few drawings in the guidebooks that is oval-shaped. Here it is:

DELECTABLE: AW's verdict on Hard Tarn, here basking in the sunshine.   15/9/11

AW didn't think much of this tarn at first sight, but that was clearly from a distance. This is what he writes on Nethermost Pike 6: *From the heights above, Hard Tarn appears to be a dreary, unattractive sheet of water. On closer acquaintance it will be found to be a delectable place.* As these pictures prove.

OVER THE LIP: The outlet of Hard Tarn is interesting; it flows over the edge of a rock lip.   15/9/11

Grandest Lakeland tarns (according to AW) — turn the page

THE TWIN TARNS

It's not just Scales Tarn and Red Tarn that have amazing similarities – check out all these AW favourites with a lot in common

SPOT THE DIFFERENCE: Scales Tarn (top), looking to Sharp Edge, and (above) Red Tarn, looking to Striding Edge. 17/5/10 and 1/6/09

MIRROR IMAGES: Scales Tarn (main picture) from Blencathra with Sharp Edge to the left; (above) Red Tarn from Helvellyn, with Striding Edge, right.   17/5/10 and 15/9/11

He drew them, he wrote about them, they featured in many of his ascent diagrams – the tarns in this section are those AW liked the best; they are the tarns that most discerning fellwalkers would say were the best.

And we're starting with two of the very best; two tarns that bear a remarkable similarity to each other. First, **Scales Tarn**, which nestles in a comb on the eastern side of **Blencathra** and is enclosed by the eastern flank of the mountain and the spectacular Sharp Edge to the north of the tarn. This is a tarn which AW calls *one of the most characteristic mountain tarns in the district.* Of course, he wrote that in BOOK FIVE and by that time he was somewhat more fulsome with his comments than in BOOK ONE, when he was positively frugal. How else could you explain no such assessment of **Red Tarn** (Helvellyn), which has everything that Scales Tarn has to offer –

and more. It has, of course, a dramatic situation, but with two spectacular ridges flanking it – Striding Edge, and Swirral Edge leading to **Catstycam**. And the rugged, rocky backdrop of Helvellyn's eastern face is even more impressive than the corresponding corrie headwall behind Scales Tarn.

Everyone knows that **Innominate Tarn** on Haystacks is one of AW's favourite Lakeland spots. Yet, in the chapter on his favourite fell, he doesn't single out Innominate Tarn for any more or less praise than its near-neighbour on the summit plateau, **Blackbeck Tarn**. Or even the nameless tarn between Innominate Tarn and the summit. Instead, he waxes lyrical about the heavenly nature of the summit area (see Super summits, page 99).

DOUBLE DELIGHT: Innominate Tarn, looking to Pillar (left) and Blackbeck Tarn, looking to Great Gable and Green Gable.   both 12/7/11

Another great double act features **Scoat Tarn** and **Low Tarn**, on the southern flanks of Scoat Fell and Red Pike respectively, separated only by the broad south-western ridge of Red Pike. AW describes this place as *an extensive area jewelled by Scoat Tarn and Low Tarn*. These are no equal partners, however. **Low Tarn** is in a quiet and infrequented grassy basin and the suggestion here is that it is a very pleasant place to be on a sunny day. About **Scoat Tarn** there is no ambiguity. On Scoat Fell 5, the introduction to the ascent from Netherbeck Bridge states: *The biggest attraction en route is Scoat Tarn, the grandest of the western tarns, and itself sufficient to justify the walk.*

A GRAND PLACE TO BE: An AW favourite, Scoat Tarn.   15/9/09

WESTERN GEMS: Scoat Tarn and Seatallan (left), with AW's split boulder prominent in the view; RIGHT: A frozen Low Tarn looking to Middle Fell.　　　15/9/09 and 2/3/10

Way across the other side of Lakeland are a couple of doppelgangers! They are both splendid mountain tarns; they are both separated by a ridge of one fell – in this case **Mardale Ill Bell**; and they are both splendid places to visit. They are, of course, **Blea Water** (the deepest tarn in Lakeland – only Wast Water and Windermere are deeper, in fact) and **Small Water**, the tarn with the stone shelters. In the introduction to the ascent from Mardale on Mardale Ill Bell 5, AW writes: *Of the many excellent climbs available from Mardale*

EASTERN DELIGHT: Blea Water, shaped like a teardrop, seen from the High Street range. The ridge from Mardale Ill Bell comes down from the right of the picture.　　　12/11/08

Head the direct ascent of Mardale Ill Bell ranks high, the walk being favoured by striking views of two of the finest tarns in Lakeland, each set amongst crags in wild and romantic surroundings.

COSY: Small Water nestles to the east of the High Street range. Whether AW's shelters (left) are cosy or not is another question.

Now on to a trio of tarns that, although given no particular praise by AW (though there is absolutely nothing wrong with any of them scenically or location-wise), appear in many ascent diagrams – simply because they are crossed by some of the busiest paths in Lakeland. In that respect, **Styhead Tarn** is the leader, with the popular paths from Wasdale, Borrowdale and Great Langdale/Eskdale all meeting at nearby Sty Head Pass, and plenty of grand fells (Great Gable and Great End among them) in close proximity.

SUPER HIGHWAY: Styhead Tarn is among Lakeland's busiest. 4/11/08

It's the same story over in **The Eastern Fells**. **Grisedale Tarn** is right beside Grisedale Hause and a number of important walkers' highways, and with high fells such as Fairfield, St Sunday Crag and Dollywaggon Pike breathing down its neck. The tarn has some ancient and more recent history. Legend has it that beneath its waters lies the crown of the kingdom of Cumbria, taken there in 945 by soldiers of the last king, Dunmail, after he was killed in battle.

JUNCTION: Important paths cross near Grisedale Tarn. 9/12/08

Nearby is the **Brothers Parting Stone**, marking the place where William Wordsworth last saw his brother John (see Monuments & memorials, starting on page 262).

The third tarn in this category, **Angle Tarn**, below Bowfell's northern summit Hanging Knotts and Esk Pike, is a stone's throw from Rossett Pass, another important pedestrian route. A path from Stake Pass meets the route at the tarn.

BUSY PLACE: Angle Tarn, below Hanging Knotts on Bowfell. The important Rossett Pass-Esk Hause path passes by (right to left), joined by a path from Stake Pass (centre left) the other side of Rossett Pike. 26/7/11

SHAPELY: The other very lovely Angle Tarn. 5/5/11

There is, of course, another **Angle Tarn**. One which, says AW, *in scenic values . . . ranks alongside the best of Lakeland tarns*. It is so good a fell was named after it – **Angletarn Pikes**. The beauty of this tarn is its beauty, and it's rather unusual for a Lakeland tarn in having islands and bays – more like a mini lake, in fact. It's situated on a delightful plateau midway between Angletarn Pikes and Brock Crags.

Across the district is a magical tarn that has all the atmosphere, shape and interest of Angle Tarn, plus a sensational location. **Sprinkling Tarn** – formerly

Sparkling Tarn – is one of the best-known, best-loved and best tarns in the Lakes, and gets added kudos for its position in the thick of things (Great Gable, Esk Pike and, of course, the dark northern cliffs of Great End). The tarn is the source of the River Derwent and is the highlight of a visit to its parent fell – Seathwaite Fell; AW writes: *Sprinkling Tarn, which, with lesser sheets of water, provides the interest of a wide, undulating plateau.*

HIGHLIGHT: Sprinkling Tarn seen from the slopes of Great End. 1/4/09

Here is the introduction to the Tarn Crag chapter in BOOK THREE: *Ever since it first became fashionable to behold the scenic wonders of the English Lake District* **Easedale Tarn** *has been a popular venue for visitors: a romantic setting, inurned in bracken-clad moraines with a background of craggy fells, and easy accessibility from Grasmere, have combined to make this a favourite place of resort.* You'd never think this was a chapter about a mountain! And poor Tarn Crag (quite a fine fell, actually) even has to put up with another sheet of water stealing its thunder: *Easedale Tarn is not the only jewel in Tarn Crag's lap. A smaller sheet of water,* **Codale Tarn**, *occupies a hollow on a higher shelf.*

TWO TARNS: Codale Tarn (left) and Easedale Tarn, split by the rocky peak of Belles Knott which, from this angle, appears just to be an outcrop. Fairfield and the Helvellyn range occupy the background. 18/10/07

Easedale Tarn was a great favourite of the Victorians, as was the northern gem **Bowscale Tarn**, in a hollow of crags north-east of **Bowscale Fell**, which is said to have two immortal fish swimming in its cool waters! That wasn't why 19th-century tourists visited it, however. It was because . . . *the setting is wild and romantic and very impressive; and Bowscale Tarn remains one of the best scenes of its kind in the district.*

ROMANTIC: The impressive Bowscale Tarn was an 1800s favourite. 13/7/05

The two tarns in Lakeland's finest settings – turn the page

PERFECT COMBINATION: The majestic cliffs of Dow Crag deserve nothing more than the splendid foreground offered by Goat's Water. 17/12/07

SPECTACULAR: (Right) One of the things that makes Stickle Tarn such an impressive sight is the sudden view of Pavey Ark as the top of its outlet beck, Stickle Ghyll, is reached. 13/8/07

MARVEL: (Below) It's not just the view of Pavey Ark that is a marvel – from various places around the tarn there are great views of Harrison Stickle and (bottom) towards Sergeant Man. both 8/9/08

Goat's Water barely gets a mention in the chapter on Dow Crag – yet it shimmers in front of one of the grandest crags in lakeland, Dow Crag, like a jewel in a crown. The crag is lauded left, right and centre . . . but how less impressive a place it would be without the evocative stretch of water in front of it. The full-page drawing (right) sums up this close

Dow Crag from Goat's Water

link between rock and water (even though, in the drawing, the tarn is frozen. It's still water!).

THE OLD ONE-TWO

There was no need for **Goat's Water** to be lauded in BOOK FOUR – it got plenty of praise in BOOK THREE in the chapter on **Pavey Ark**. The praise was, however, of the backhanded variety, because AW placed the Dow Crag-**Goat's Water** combination in second position in the rock-and-water category.

This is what AW says in the Pavey Ark introduction: *In an area where crags and precipices abound, here is the giant of them all, and, scenically, it is the best. The view of the Ark across the waters of **Stickle Tarn**, at its foot, is superior to all others of this type in Lakeland, having an advantage over the principal rival team of Dow Crag-Goat's Water in that the scene, being invariably reached by the steep climb from Dungeon Ghyll, bursts upon the eye with dramatic effect.*

NOTE: The huge cliff of Pavey Ark (seen above behind a shivering Stickle Tarn) features in the LANDSCAPES: Big Crags chapter, which begins on page 242 (just another 41 pages, so there's not long to wait!).

LITTLE DOUBT ABOUT IT

There is a drawing in the Scafell Pike chapter that I had never quite believed was accurate.

It shows the hanging valley of Little Narrowcove on the eastern flank of England's highest mountain, with the following caption: *Not many readers, not even those who are frequent visitors to Scafell Pike, could give a caption to this picture. It is, in fact, a scene in the unfrequented hollow of Little Narrowcove, looking up towards the summit of the Pike (the top cairn is out of sight). The crags, unexpected on the usual routes, are a great surprise.*

I have not climbed Scafell Pike from Eskdale (Borrowdale x2, Wasdale and Great Langdale have been my starting points), so could never vouch for the drawing – but somehow it just seemed not quite right . . . Surely that big pointed cliff (let's christen it **Narrowcove Pike**) couldn't be *that* pointed; and the shading (all that cross-hatching) looked a bit odd as well.

How wrong I was, as Sean McMahon's picture above proves. Sean, of course, has climbed Scafell Pike from Eskdale a number of times, including via Little Narrowcove (straight from the River Esk) and via the subsidiary peak of Pen.

In his notes about the ascent of the Pike from Eskdale, AW comments: *It seems remarkable that England's highest mountain has no direct path to its*

YES, IT DOES LOOK LIKE THE DRAWING! This view of Little Narrowcove looking towards the summit of Scafell Pike (out of sight from here) shows just how accurate AW's drawing (facing page) was. The cluster of boulders in the foreground of the drawing is also in the picture, bottom left.
25/6/09

summit on this, its finest side. It is not merely steepness that has kept walkers away from it, but rather the unavoidable, inescapable shawl of boulders covering the final 500 feet, where progress is not only painfully slow but carries a risk of displacing stones that have never before been trodden on and may be balanced precariously and easily disturbed. There is no fun in pioneering routes over such rough terrain, which is safest left in virgin state.

His comments about the 'shawl of boulders' could, of course, easily apply to the tourist path over Broad Crag col, or the grind up from Lingmell col, or the torturous climb from Mickledore to the summit. And, of course, they were made back when AW was compiling BOOK FOUR (from the end of 1957 to the end of 1959) when he probably didn't carry on to the fells a camera equipped with a high-powered zoom. But Sean does, and overleaf you will see four of his photographs that reveal the possible way of a new route up Scafell Pike's grandest flank – albeit steep, most certainly challenging and adventurous, but perhaps not with quite as much ascent through a field of boulders as AW envisaged when he wrote those words at the foot of Scafell Pike 22.

A new way up Scafell Pike! Turn the page for details

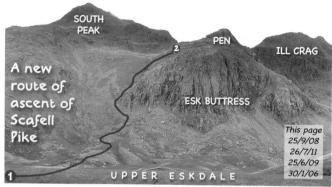

SOUTH PEAK

PEN

ILL CRAG

A new route of ascent of Scafell Pike

ESK BUTTRESS

UPPER ESKDALE

1

2

This page
25/9/08
26/7/11
25/6/09
30/1/06

Here it is! And the inspiration comes from AW himself (Scafell Pike 22): *Note the dotted line on the diagram . . . a shorter way that skirts the left edge of Dow Crag [Eskdale Buttress], crosses a col near the rocky peak of Pen and enters Little Narrowcove at mid-height.* He went on to suggest climbing up the cove to Broad Crag col before joining the path from Esk Hause. But here is another way: **TOP PICTURE:** From the River Esk ❶ follow AW's very steep route up to ❷, a grassy col beside Pen. Then, instead of dropping down into Little Narrowcove . . .

PICTURE RIGHT: Pick your way across a broken band of crags ahead, and follow the rough slope alongside the edge of the crags looking over Little Narrowcove, to ❸. This is the gully immediately the far side of Narrowcove Pike (see ❸ **PICTURE NEAR RIGHT**), at a point looking down a scree gully (**PICTURE FAR RIGHT**) towards the hollow of Little Narrowcove and Ill Crag. Continue past the South Peak of Scafell Pike and across the field of boulders on the summit to the cairn on the highest point ❹. All this, of course, is **just a suggestion . . .**

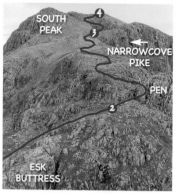

SOUTH PEAK

4
3

NARROWCOVE PIKE

PEN

2

ESK BUTTRESS

3

NARROWCOVE PIKE

LITTLE NARROWCOVE

ILL CRAG

NARROWCOVE PIKE

3

HOW WELL DO YOU KNOW YOUR FELLS?

Quiz time: test your knowledge of the guidebooks

E1: NAME THIS FELL: AW describes it as being *Curved like a scythe.*

E2: NAME THESE FELLS: Skiddaw's eight satellites, all of which are '214' fells (not in height order! It's a tough enough question anyway).

E3: NAME THIS TARN: The 'other' named tarn on AW's favourite fell.

E4: NAME THIS FELL: It has ridge routes to Graystones and Lord's Seat.

E5: PICTURE QUESTION (right): Name the community in the sunshine, and its valley.

4/10/11

E6: NAME THIS FELL (where the blank is): .... *has received scant mention in Lakeland literature, and admittedly is mainly of nondescript appearance, yet one aspect of the fell is particularly good and appeals on sight to all who aspire to a little mild mountaineering. This is to the north-east, where a boulder-strewn shoulder leaves the summit and soon divides into two craggy ridges enclosing a rocky corrie . . .*

E7: NAME THIS ROCK FORMATION: It's in Great Langdale . . . and it's singular (but only just).

E8: NAME THIS OUTLYING FELL: *Couches of lovely heather make this tiny top a near-perfect solace for reminiscences of past happy days on the higher fells.*

E9: NAME THIS FELL: On its northern face is a gully named after a man who fell to his death there.

E10: NAME THIS FELL: On its flank is a prominent rock outcrop named Calfhow Pike.

THE ANSWERS are on page 344, but before you go there, there are OTHER QUIZZES: on pages 86, 108, 137, 159, 216, 239 and 259.

Treasure map

1200
1300
1700.
▲ LANK RIGG
1775'
△ ⊗ tarn
× tumulus
×fold
1500
1600
1400
Ho[

Buried Treasure on Lank Rigg
    The only exciting experience in the lonely life of the Ordnance column occurred on a gloriously sunny day in April 1965, when it was a mute and astonished witness to an unparalleled act of generosity. In an uncharacteristic mood of magnanimity which he has since regretted, the author decided on this summit to share his hard won royalties with one of his faithful readers, and placed a two-shilling piece under a flat stone: it awaits the first person to read this note and act upon it. There is no cause to turn the whole top over as though pigs have been at it — the stone is four feet from the column. If the treasure cannot be found at this distance it can be assumed that a fortunate pilgrim has already passed this way rejoicing. The finder may be sufficiently pleased to write in to the publishers and confirm his claim by stating the year of the coin's issue. If nobody does so before the end of 1966 the author will go back and retrieve it for the purchase of fish and chips. It was a reckless thing to do, anyway.

GOLD IN THEM THAR HILLS

Hidden doubloon makes this fell very valuable

It may not look it, but little Lank Rigg (above), measuring up at just 1775ft, 24th highest out of 33 in BOOK SEVEN, 153rd out of the 214 fells in the PICTORIAL GUIDES, is **the most valuable fell** in Lakeland.

Not by much, it has to be admitted; not always, either, according to reports from very reliable sources. It all started in 1965 when AW – either because of an innate sense of generosity, or perhaps because a space needed filling on Lank Rigg 7 – decided to deposit a **two-shilling piece** (a.k.a. **two-bob bit** or a **florin**) under a stone 4ft away from the summit Ordnance Survey column (as the 'recently unearthed' map, left, explains in full). Since then it has become a tradition to leave a coin during a visit. Sometimes this doesn't quite work out, as Sean McMahon explains at the start of his section on Lank Rigg on www.stridingedge.net.

He writes: 'There was some money under a stone near the summit when I was there in 2003. It was gone by 2004 but back in 2009!'

FLORIN: Actual size of the defunct coin, which was worth two shillings in pre-decimalisation money (ten pence now).

A HIGH WATER MARK...

Highest-tarn statistic that AW appears to have got wrong

The sheet of water known as **Broadcrag Tarn** doesn't get much of a mention in the chapter on Scafell Pike. And why should it? The chapter is about the highest mountain in England, the roughest, toughest and grandest of Lakeland's fells. Broadcrag Tarn is *small and unattractive*, says AW, *but, at 2725 feet, can at least boast the highest standing water in Lakeland.*

For as long as I can remember, that was the accepted wisdom. But perhaps not. It seems that Broadcrag Tarn is NOT the highest tarn in Lakeland. According to Sean McMahon, that honour belongs to the tarn on the top of the Crinkle Crags which, although strictly nameless (it was when AW was wrote his guidebooks), is now generally known as **Crinkle Crags Tarn**.

Sean bases this on some technology he carries around with him that AW never had access to: a GPS (global positioning system), a space-based satellite navigation system maintained by the United States government that provides location (including height above

208

FAR LEFT: Crinkle Crags Tarn, just a short walk west of the summit of Crinkle Crags, looking towards Scafell and Scafell Pike (summit in cloud). 26/7/11

LEFT (ABOVE): Broadcrag Tarn, showing it is clearly lower than both the grassy shelf and Mickledore. 25/9/08

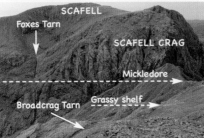

LEFT: The grassy shelf is visible below and left of Mickledore, which is some way lower than the location of Foxes Tarn. 25/9/08

sea level) and time information where there is an unobstructed line-of-sight view to four or more GPS satellites. That's why, in his 26 July 2011 walk, underneath the picture of Crinkle Crags Tarn (main picture) he was able to state: 'Crinkle Crags Tarn, at 854m it is the highest tarn in the Lake District and in England.'

If we go back three years, to Sean's walk of 25 September 2008, there are two photos that confirm Broadcrag Tarn isn't even the second-highest tarn in Lakeland – or the highest named tarn – but is a mere third in the height list (behind another named tarn in second place).

Underneath a photo of Broadcrag Tarn (above, top), his caption is: 'Broad Stand from Broadcrag Tarn - the highest tarn in the Lake District at 827m according to Birkett . . . but my mapping software shows Foxes Tarn at 837m and Long Top Tarn (Crinkle Crags - the tarn is unnamed on the OS map) at 854m.'

Look at the grassy shelf between the tarn and the ridge of Mickledore (top picture). It's higher than the tarn and lower than Mickledore. Clearly, Broadcrag Tarn is possibly 10 or 20 feet lower than Mickledore. Now look at the picture of Scafell Crag and Mickledore (immediately above), which shows the aforementioned grassy platform. Now look at the location of **Foxes Tarn**: it's some way higher than Mickledore, some way higher than Broadcrag Tarn.

I hope that's sorted things out! This, therefore, is the (unofficial) one-two-three of the highest tarns in Lakeland, based on the figures quoted above:

1.	CRINKLE CRAGS TARN	2801ft (854m)
2.	FOXES TARN	2746ft (837m)
3.	BROADCRAG TARN	2725ft (830m)

RETURN OF THE PIPE

GREEN GABLE
GREAT GABLE
RANNERDALE KNOTTS
HIGH CRAG
HIGH STILE
RED PIKE
Hause Point
Crummock Water
Lanthwaite Wood
Lanthwaite Hill
Harris tweed
looking south-south-east from Lanthwaite Hill

For the first time since BOOK TWO, AW's pipe was back for his self-portrait in the Grasmoor chapter in BOOK SIX. Sales must have been going well, too, because by now he was wearing a Harris Tweed jacket!

Lanthwaite Wood

Lanthwaite Hill

Natural fur

LITTLE BIG FELL: Rannerdale Knotts from Lanthwaite Hill, with the larger Buttermere fells and the distant Gables in cloud beyond Crummock Water.   24/2/12

LAKE, VILLAGE & FELL: Coniston Water, Coniston and its Old Man.   5/3/12

LOVE & MARRIAGE

go together like the Old Man and Coniston; Mellbreak and Crummock Water, Helm Crag and Grasmere . . . and many more, according to AW

The fictional children in Arthur Ransome's 1931 novel *Swallowdale* called it Kangchenjunga. AW likens it to the Matterhorn (sort of!). And while it's more than 25,000ft lower than the world's third-highest mountain, and nowhere near as shapely as the Alpine giant, Coniston Old Man holds a special place in the hearts of Coniston folk, and everyone across the south

Lakeland area that it dominates. AW loves the mountain, and here's what he writes about it in BOOK FOUR:

The highest (by a few feet) and the best-known of the Coniston fells is the Old Man, a benevolent giant revered by generations of walkers and of particular esteem in the eyes of the inhabitants of the village he shelters, for he has contributed much to their

211

prosperity. The Old Man is no Matterhorn, nor is Coniston a Zermatt, but an affinity is there in the same close links between mountain and village, and the history of the one is the history of the other. Coniston without its Old Man is unthinkable.

Flicking through the PICTORIAL GUIDES and THE OUTLYING FELLS, you will find many more Old Men and many more Conistons – valleys and communities which have an almost spiritual relationship with the fell just up the road/lane/track. Here are a few of them, the first with another Alpine analogy.

Whiteless Pike is no great shakes when it comes to height (2165ft and 106th in the list of 214 fells), and is overtopped by nearby Wandope, yet is sufficiently shapely for AW to dub it *the Weisshorn of Buttermere*. Strictly speaking, that should be 'the Weisshorn of Rannerdale' because it is from the road near **Rannerdale Farm** that it exhibits its pyramid-like outline – above Rannerdale and its famous bluebells fields it really does have Alpine qualities. **Buttermere** village, of course, really has a close affinity with a number of fells: Fleetwith Pike, despite its position at the other end of the lake, or more likely because of its position, giving the village a classic outlook; and High Stile and Red Pike because of the wonderful rugged wall they present to the valley, the lake and the village.

One of the closest links is that between the village of **Grasmere** and Helm Crag, which AW acknowledges in BOOK THREE. On the description of the classic little climb from the village, he writes . . . *if it has a fault it is that it is too short. But for the evening of the day of arrival in Grasmere on a walking holiday it is just the thing: an epitome of Lakeland concentrated in the space of two hours – and an excellent foretaste of happy days to come.*

And another of AW's favourite fells also has pride of place in more than just his heart: namely, **Patterdale**. Of **Place Fell**, he writes: *Few fells are so well favoured as Place Fell for appraising neighbouring heights. It occupies an exceptionally good position in the curve of Ullswater in the centre of a great bowl of fells; its summit commands a very beautiful and impressive panorama. On a first visit to Patterdale, Place Fell should be an early objective, for no other viewpoint gives such an appreciation of the design of this lovely corner of Lakeland.*

Other well-known and well-loved companions identified by AW are:

Loughrigg Fell and **Ambleside**: The walk past the church and across the park is a delightful start to a wonderful walk to one of the finest small fells.

Latrigg and **Keswick**: The easy climb of this much-loved fell is more than rewarded with a very famous view over the Vale of Keswick.

Mellbreak and **Crummock Water**: AW described this combination as

P-PARTNERS: Patterdale and Place Fell (seen from Arnison Crag).   13/9/11

ALPINE: Whiteless Pike above Rannerdale bluebells.   1/5/07

BUTTERMERE FELL: Fleetwith Pike might lay claim to this title, thanks to this fantastic view of the lake, village and Crummock Water . . . 7/6/06

. . . and also its distinctive outline at the head of the valley, as seen from Mellbreak's south top. 25/02/08

essential partners in a successful scenery enterprise, depending on each other for effectiveness.

Low Fell and Loweswater: In a nice position overlooking the lake and the village of the same name (also known as Kirkstile), this is a lovely low fell (sorry about that!) that AW thought rather highly of, with two charming ascents and a view to die for.

Wastwater Screes (Illgill Head and Whin Rigg) and Wast Water: The classic backdrop to the grandest of the dales occupied by a lake.

And these: Yoke and Kentmere; Barrow and Braithwaite; Ullock Pike and Bassenthwaite Village; Hallin Fell and Ullswater; Wetherlam and Little Langdale; Catbells and/or Walla Crag and Derwent Water; Caw and Seathwaite; Scout Scar and Kendal; School Knott and Windermere.

FELL AND VALE: Helm Crag and Grasmere. 9/7/08

TWIN PEAKS: Mellbreak, with south and north tops, and Crummock Water. 1/5/07

SHATTERED: The remains of
the Keppelcove Tarn dam.
The burst banks of the
original moraine can be seen
just behind the dam. 22/3/11

WHERE LIGHTNING DID STRIKE TWICE

The story behind a double disaster at Keppel Cove

Three of the chapters in BOOK ONE – **Catstycam**, **Helvellyn** and **White Side** – feature ascents past the burst dam of Keppelcove Tarn, a location AW describes as *where man tried to tame nature*. The dam is still there, still with a gaping hole where, in 1931, its waters cascaded down the valley of Glenridding Beck in a repeat of what had happened four years earlier. All that's left of the tarn these days is a boggy green marsh.

In 1927 the natural tarn, whose waters were held in place by a typical terminal moraine, was part of a burgeoning mining operation going on two miles downstream. Lead was first discovered at Greendale in the mid 17th century but it was not until 1825 that mining became a serious local industry, following the formation of the Greenside Mining Company. At the time, the reserves of lead at Greenside were thought to be the world's second largest.

Before the end of the century engineers at the mine identified the waters of Keppelcove Tarn as a rich resource further up the valley, and a hydro-electric scheme to power electric winding gear at the mine was commissioned in 1891, the first such scheme in the country.

The early part of the 20th century saw peak production at the mine, which

THE HAND OF MAN section starts on page 262

214

THE BREACHED DAM: Between Catstycam (left) and Raise (right), with White Side behind. Twice in four years a huge flood swept down this valley to Glenridding.
22/3/11

KEPPELCOVE TARN
AND ITS ENVIRONS
— a study in devastation

The burst banks

The breached dam

Keppelcove Tarn is now a marsh. Formerly it served as a reservoir for the Glenridding lead mine. In October 1927, following a cloudburst, flooded waters burst the banks of the tarn, carved out a new ravine, and caused great damage. The dam was breached later, in 1931, and has never been repaired.

BOOK ONE REPORT: In the Catstycam chapter, how AW described what happened at Keppel Cove.

is thought to have produced 350,000 tons of lead in its lifetime. But disaster was to strike on Saturday, 29 October 1927. A sustained period of heavy rain caused a massive breach in the moraine where it had been weakened by the extraction pipe. A wall of water flooded down the valley, swamping homes and businesses in the village of Glenridding and sweeping animals into Ullswater. Miraculously, no one died.

Within two years a concrete dam was built a few yards downstream from the original breach (still there, too); but poor construction or design (or both) and more heavy rain caused the breach in the wall of the dam that remains today. It's a sad sight.

MINING CATASTROPHES

Sat., 29 Oct. 1927: Keppelcove Tarn moraine fails. In Glenridding houses and bridges are damaged by the flood. Animals swept into Ullswater.

Wed., 21 Nov. 1928: Whitehaven man James Story is killed when a tractor hauling cement for the reconstruction of the dam overturns.

1929: Concrete dam completed.

1931: More torrential rain causes a breach in the concrete dam. It is never repaired.

Mon., 7 July 1952: Four miners die after a fire in the north shaft.

1960: Two men die after being overcome by gas.

Jan. 1962: The mine closes.

HOW WELL DO YOU KNOW YOUR FELLS?

Quiz time: test your knowledge of the guidebooks

F1: NAME THIS FELL: . . . *like the legendary sea serpent, the top is quite unmistakable.*

F2: NAME THESE FELLS: The five Loweswater fells south of the lake of that name, which AW says *fan out like the fingers of a hand.*

F3: NAME THIS TARN: The deepest tarn in Lakeland (a fact not mentioned by AW, so this is some general knowledge).

F4: NAME THIS FELL: It has ridge routes to White Side and Stybarrow Dodd.

F5: PICTURE QUESTION (right): This distinctive gap in the mountains is known as what?

20/9/06

F6: NAME THIS FELL (where the blank is): *From north and south and east and west, ... is completely unphotogenic, and the best that any illustration can produce is a slight roughness of the slowly-swelling curve that forms its broad summit. This uninspiring characteristic extends to the whole fell, which is quite deficient in interest* . . .

F7: NAME THIS ROCK FORMATION: A rock pillar with two names, one of which incorporates the valley in which it is situated; the other has the definite article.

F8: NAME THIS OUTLYING FELL: Its summit features a well-built circular cairn which incorporates a tablet with an inscription.

F9: NAME THIS FELL: It features a 'hinterland' in which are situated Joe Banks's Fold, an amphitheatre, two rakes and a rocky outcrop called Minum Crag. Oh, and the fell also has three other names.

F10: NAME THIS FELL: Another fell with an a.k.a., plus a separate name for its summit, and SIX ridges.

THE ANSWERS are on page 344, but before you go there, there are OTHER QUIZZES: on pages 86, 108, 137, 159, 205, 239 and 259.

THE PICTORIAL FINALE

The last self-portrait to appear in the PICTORIAL GUIDES was, rather appropriately, the final page of BOOK SEVEN (right ahead of the *personal notes in conclusion*).

It features AW on one the most important routes in the whole of The Western Fells – the path from Wasdale Head, through Mosedale and up the rising slopes towards Black Sail Pass alongside Gatherstone Beck.

The knapsack is back as AW sits on a rock and surveys the dramatic shape of Yewbarrow on the other side of the valley. Meanwhile, two sheep look back in his direction. The first says: *First time we've seen him with a cap on.* The second replies: *He must be going bald or something.*

AW, of course, did one other drawing of himself in the PICTORIAL GUIDES (in the final notes to BOOK FOUR), but there might have been others – see page 250.

FINAL IMAGE: The last drawing in the Pictorial Guides was based on this view of Yewbarrow and Dore Head from Gatherstone Beck.   17/9/08

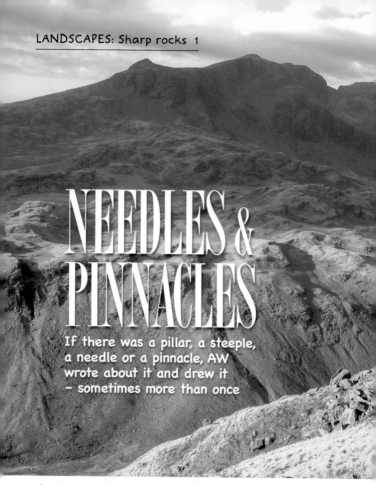

NEEDLES & PINNACLES

If there was a pillar, a steeple, a needle or a pinnacle, AW wrote about it and drew it – sometimes more than once

If AW was to do it all over again, I'm pretty sure he would add another 50 pages to each of his guidebooks; not to put in extra ascents or panoramic views from every summit or wax lyrical about this or that, but to add more of the background detail that he loved so much but which, for whatever reason, never saw the light of day.

A few great places in Lakeland were, in my opinion, underplayed by AW. Striding Edge springs to mind; and Gable Crag, which never got the Scafell Crag/Dow Crag/Pavey Ark 'rockface' teatment – all of his rock detail in the Great Gable chapter was concentrated on the other side of the mountain, and even when he went into some detail, as in the Great Napes section, he missed out one famous landmark in particular. I still find it

SUPREME LOCATION: Eskdale Needle, also known as The Steeple, may be part of Hard Knott, but it's towards Upper Eskdale and the Scafells that it looks. AW told BOOK FOUR readers that it was 50ft high on its longest side (facing the valley). 16/11/11

hard to believe he wrote more about a small needle of rock on the south flank of Pike o'Blisco (we'll come to that later) than on the most iconic rock pinnacle in the country – the ascent of which was the catalyst for the start of modern rock climbing.

I'm referring to **Napes Needle** of course, about which he wrote . . . well actually, not that much. He described where to view it (from a nearby ledge

known as the Dress Circle), and he drew a picture of it with a climber nearing the top block (an arrow next to the figure came from a caption: *definitely not the author!*). And that is about it.

Napes Needle is, of course, no ordinary pillar of rock. It's THE rock feature that captured the imagination of young men (and women) from all over the country after its first ascent in July 1886 by Walter Parry Haskett Smith, followed by subsequent pictures of the needle by the Keswick-based Abrahams brothers. The solo climb by Haskett Smith – without ropes, pitons, carabiners or any other such modern climbing gadgets – was an astonishing feat of bravery and skill that kick-started rock climbing in the Lakes. In the graveyard of St Olaf's Church at Wasdale Head are the graves of many of the early rock pioneers – and it's all a little strange that AW never really went into this in any depth – at least with one of his trademark 'special pages'. I can only assume pressure of deadlines or space, or both, may have played a part in it all. And I'm not

Napes Needle

Sphinx Rock

Cat Rock

complaining. BOOK SEVEN is a wonderful jam-packed book, full of fantastic routes on wonderful mountains – with tales of buried treasure, of smugglers and secret tracks and favourite fells, of terrific drawings and much more.

This chapter is about the rock features that excite the imagination and heat up the blood, and, for a change, we're starting from BOOK SEVEN and then dotting around at random. Where else to start than on the Great Napes and with **Napes Needle** and the other great feature on the south-western face of Great Gable – the **Sphinx Rock**, also known as the **Cat Rock**. This, as everyone knows, is because of the two widely differing views of the rock – as AW illustrated on Great Gable 12; his illustrations are matched with the pictures on the facing page, which are:

Napes Needle: 28/2/11   *Sphinx Rock: 12/11/07*   *Cat Rock: 12/11/07*

Elsewhere in The Western Fells, the **Pinnacles** on Crag Fell get two close-up drawings in its chapter. They are sufficiently dramatic to be seen from way across Ennerdale Water – see red circle, below.

PINNACLES:
On Crag Fell.
22/8/07

(I haven't forgotten **Pillar Rock** on Pillar; however, this is such a big rock that it is featured in the Big Crags chapter which starts on page 242).

On a par (kind of) with the Crag Fell Pinnacles is **Oak Howe Needle** (left) on Lingmoor Fell. Like the pinnacles, it's on the north face of a mid-height fell; like the pinnacles it's halfway up a fellside; and like the pinnacles it is a splintered structure rather than a really solid piece of rock: *a strange survivor of the erosion that has tumbled much of the crag into a vast fan of scree and boulders*, writes AW. It certainly didn't much impress him, however. He adds: *As a spectacle it is scarcely worth the effort entailed by getting to it*. Which he did to make the sketch.

SPLINTERY:
Oak
Howe
Needle.

SHAPELY:
Gladstone's
Finger.

Further up Great Langdale, high above the Oxendale fork of the valley head, is the shyest pinnacle of them all – because apart from appearing as the frontispiece illustration in BOOK FOUR, **Gladstone's Finger** doesn't even get a mention in the Crinkle Crags chapter, where the crag of which it is a part – Gladstone Knott – only merits two words on a map. I was surprised AW didn't elaborate on this shapely looking pinnacle; it is only 300 yards off the well-blazed path from Red Tarn to the Crinkles and he could easily have moved the paragraph about 'cutting the corner' on

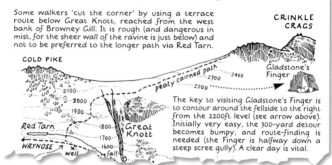

ASCENT FROM DUNGEON GHYLL (via RED TARN)
2600 feet of ascent : 4 miles

Some walkers 'cut the corner' by using a terrace route below Great Knott, reached from the west bank of Browney Gill. It is rough (and dangerous in mist, for the sheer wall of the ravine is just below) and not to be preferred to the longer path via Red Tarn.

CRINKLE CRAGS

COLD PIKE

Gladstone's Finger

peaty cairned path 2300 2400
2200
2100
2000
1900
Red Tarn 1800
1700
Great Knott
1600
WRYNOSE well fall

The key to visiting Gladstone's Finger is to contour around the fellside to the right from the 2200ft level (see arrow above). Initially very easy, the 300-yard detour becomes bumpy, and route-finding is needed (the Finger is halfway down a steep scree gully). A clear day is vital.

THE MISSING DETOUR: How Crinkle Crags 5 **could look.**

Crinkle Crags 5 to produce a page layout similar to that above. But he didn't, so that's so.

Perhaps he was too excited by his discovery just a mile away – at **Black Crag** on the south side of Pike o'Blisco – of a shapely pinnacle of rock he named **The Needle**, and about which he penned the following: *This smooth and slender pinnacle, detached from the face of Black Crag, is precariously balanced on a massive plinth of rock, 12ft high, the total height to the tip being 35ft. Well off the beaten track (although only a long half-mile from Wrynose Pass) it may have escaped the notice of the cragsmen, there being no evidence of ascent on the pinnacle or in the rock-climbing literature at present available for the area. It seems (to a novice who hasn't tried) that the tip may be gained by 'bridging' the gap with the main crag. He will be a good man who can stand erect on the point of the needle. The author feels rather proud of this 'discovery' and hopes people will not write to*

THE NEEDLE, BLACK CRAG: How AW drew it; and the same view more recently. 11/1/05

claim (i) a knowledge of the pinnacle (since they were

children), (ii) that they have climbed it (blindfolded), and (iii) stood for hours on its point (on their heads).

Since AW wrote those words (in 1958 or 1959) the crag has been 'discovered' by rock climbers, as the picture (right) shows.

That's Crinkle Crags and Pike o'Blisco dealt with. Now all that remains of this triangle of fells is Cold Pike, and a *grotesque* fang of rock (12ft of it) AW dubbed as **Cold Pike Tooth**, at the foot of a crag less than 200 yards west-south-west of the summit. This is what it looked like over fifty years ago (below) ... I suspect that in fifty years time a cold snap in the meantime will see the tip of this fang having its own snap!

That's really it for the significant pillars/steeples/ needles/ pinnacles. The best of them are in the south-

BLACK CRAG: An area of rocks and boulders on Pike o'Blisco's southern flank.   *14/7/11*

west corner of Lakeland (where you will find the harder, Borrowdale volcanic rock). Here's a round-up of the rest (or at least those featured in THE PICTORIAL GUIDES, either in drawings, or words, or both):

The Bishop of Barf and **The Clerk**: On belligerent Barf (see page 160);

Catbells **Pinnacle**: Just below the summit on the east ... but don't hold your breath – it's only 4ft high;

Moses' Finger: Great Gable;

Pinnacle: Blencathra, near the top of the ridge, ascent via Hall's Fell;

Pinnacle: Grasmoor, on the direct ascent from Lanthwaite Green;

Pinnacle: Lonscale Fell, east ridge;

Pinnacle: Yewbarrow, beside ridge from Dore Head to Stirrup Crag;

Pinnacle: Wandope, south ridge;

Pinnacle: White Side, on Brown Crag;

Pinnacles and spires: Lingmell, Piers Gill;

Summit rocks: Helm Crag, The Howitzer (in effect, a tilted pillar);

Two pinnacles: Skiddaw Little Man, south-west arête.

Some of the best walks in Lakeland are strictly on the down-low, and although the PICTORIAL GUIDES were about higher places than lakesides, that didn't stop AW having a say about some of his favourite low-level excursions.

The walk that got his most extensive coverage – wordwise – is seen here (right) in all its glory (if that's the word). The problem he highlighted on the walk alongside Wast Water below Wastwater Screes (Whin Rigg and Illgill Head) can be seen in the quarter-mile section where the path crosses a tilted boulder field . . . *compared with which the top of Scafell Pike is like a bowling green – here the screes take the form of big awkward boulders, loosely piled at a steep angle and avoidable only by a swim in the lake; it has been impossible to tread out a path here despite a brave effort by somebody to cairn a route . . . many a gentle pedestrian must have suffered nightmares in this dreadful place and looked with hopelessness and envy at people along the smooth road on the opposite shore.* Yes, he loved it!

WALKING ON AN ANGLE: The lakeside path along the foot of Wast Water Screes is at a steep angle and crosses boulder fields..   7/11/11

LET'S GO DOWN TO

A PLACE OF BEAUTY: The final section of the path below Place Fell and beside Ullswater.
12/3/09

THE WATERLINE...

There was no beating about the bush; no equivocation; no room for doubt. On page 3 of the **Place Fell** chapter AW minced no words about what he considered to be the best lakeside walk in the district: *It is the author's opinion that the lakeside path from Scalehow Beck, near Sandwick, to Patterdale (in that direction) is the most beautiful and rewarding walk in Lakeland.* A quick glance at the two pages allocated for the map of Place Fell will alert Patterdale-based walkers to an obvious excursion (probably so obvious there was no need to spell it out): ascend Place Fell, descend via Low Moss and Sleet Fell to Sandwick, and return to base via the lakeside path. Job done!

OFF-TRACK: Lakeside paths 3

Lakeside walks are all fine and dandy if you're not looking for an energetic day on the fells. But if you are, a lakeside walk as part of an ascent is surely one big bonus. AW recognised this in the climb of Walla Crag from the Borrowdale Road, which he called a *beautiful short climb*. He suggested a preliminary path should be taken from Keswick (largely beside **Derwent Water**): *If the starting point on the road is reached via Friar's Crag and Calfclose Bay, and if the return is made via Rakefoot and Brockle Beck, this becomes the best walk easily attainable in a half-day from Keswick.* From the upper slopes of Walla Crag this route of ascent is displayed in all its beauty.

BUTTERMERE FROM HIGH CRAG: The section of the lakeside walk (left, in trees) that includes a tunnel. 28/6/11

A waterside walk of similar beauty provides a marvellous beginning for a number of walks from **Buttermere** – via the south-west side of the lake to Scarth Gap (High Crag, Haystacks), or via the north-east water's edge if heading for Gatesgarth (the starting point for

The lakeside path passes through a 30-yard tunnel cut out of the rock below Hassness. These grounds were formerly private.

LEFT: The tunnel illustrated in the Robinson chapter.

226

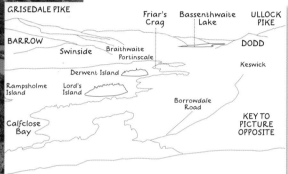

DERWENT WATER FROM WALLA CRAG: The walk suggested by AW leaves Keswick and follows the tourist path to the beauty point of Friar's Crag, then takes the Derwent Water lakeside path to Calfclose Bay before crossing the Borrowdale Road and beginning the climb proper.   28/6/10

GRISEDALE PIKE

Friar's Crag · Bassenthwaite Lake · ULLOCK PIKE

BARROW · Swinside · Braithwaite · Portinscale · DODD

Derwent Island · Keswick

Rampsholme Island · Lord's Island

Borrowdale Road

Calfclose Bay

KEY TO PICTURE OPPOSITE

climbs of Robinson, Fleetwith Pike and Haystacks). This latter route includes a 30-yard section through a tunnel that was illustrated in the chapter on Robinson. The two routes can be linked by the path across the flat meadows at the head of the lake to provide a memorable low-level walk. Further along the valley, a road occupies the eastern side of Crummock Water, but below Mellbreak is a striking lakeside walk on the western side that eventually links with the Buttermere lakeside path on that side of the valley.

A walk linking two lakes is also a feature of one of AW's favourite mountains, Loughrigg Fell. The popular Loughrigg Terrace path crosses the southern end of Grasmere (not exactly at the water's edge, it has to be admitted), then meanders its way 'around the corner' to Rydal Water on its way to Rydal and/or Ambleside. Follow this on Loughrigg Fell 7 and 8.

Finally, out on the eastern and western extremities are two contrasting lakeside walks. In the Hallin Fell chapter AW writes of another Ullswater path: *Incidentally (although this has nothing to do with fell-walking!) the lakeside path via Kailpot Crag is entirely delightful.* And on the south side of Ennerdale Water, in the Crag Fell chapter, he highlights the lakeside path below Anglers Crag. In the later A COAST TO COAST WALK (1973, second edition 2010) this route is given an enthusiastic recommendation.

The lakeside path below Anglers Crag was formerly regarded as dangerous, and walkers were recommended to take the longer route over the top. The passage of many boots, however, has smoothed out the difficulties, and today it is no more than a simple, rather rough, walk.

RIGHT: Anglers Crag on Crag Fell.

A TORRENT of BOULDERS

Anywhere AW saw a boulder he drew it, placed it on a map, or indicated it on an ascent diagram (or all three) – whether they were solid or split, perched or hanging, solitary or clusters... Check out a chapter overflowing with the hard stuff

RIVER OF BOULDERS: Yes, this IS the name for a rocky stream that 'flows' down the side of the Great Slab on Bowfell.   15/10/08

ROCK CENTRAL: BOOK THREE *is littered with boulders: Right, Blea Rock, The Split Boulder, Woodcock Stone and Great Crag's 'rock wall'.*

FIELD OF BOULDERS: In Dovedale, looking towards Dove Crag.   8/4/11

Fifty boulders hardly sounds like anything, does it? About three steps on the approach to the top of Scafell Pike; a couple of feet on the summit pyramid of Bowfell; a needle in a haystack in the recesses of Great Gable's Stone Cove.

But the boulders here are a cut above the thousands that litter the upper slopes of Lakeland giants; many of these 50 have names or occupy a place on a map or a point on an ascent diagram. These are the rocks and boulders that caught AW's eye and that he singled out from the many others that merited just squiggles on a diagram.

He took such great care in chronicling these mini-monoliths (some of them not so small) that it only seems right that every one of them should be listed in this chapter. They include

such famous names as the **Bowder Stone**, the **Pudding Stone** and **Badger Rock**; plus lesser-known boulders such as **Dumpy Stone** and **Binka Stone**.

They are listed on a book-by-book basis, and you probably won't have much difficulty in noticing the number of boulders that made appearances on the pages of BOOK THREE. The Central Fells are the lowest of the seven areas covered by the PICTORIAL GUIDES, but they make up for their lack of inches in many respects, not least with the number of rocks and boulders that stood out enough 'from the crowd' to make an impression on AW, four of which are featured right here on these two pages. Everyone who has ever read anything about AW will know that he loved his

Chapter on the Big Crags starts on page 242

maps. Indeed, he dedicated BOOK ONE to: *The men of the Ordnance Survey, whose maps have given me much pleasure both on the fells and by my fireside.* Night after night he poured over reissued Ordnance Survey 2.5-inch maps and old 6-inch maps, maps that were of sufficient detail to identify solitary boulders (and even a tree – see page 43), and it was perfectly natural that these boulders should make their way on to the maps and diagrams AW created in THE PICTORIAL GUIDES.

Boulders are, of course, relative. What would attract the attention on a grassy hill in the Caldbeck Fells wouldn't merit a second glance at Sty Head. And to be fair to AW, he made this point on a number of occasions. One such boulder was the wonderfully named **Great Stone of Blakeley**, which he drew in the Grike chapter, and about which he wrote: *The Great Stone of Blakeley, despite its grand title, is nothing more than an ordinary large boulder at the angle of the fence.* This theory of relativity is not confined to boulders; in the **Skiddaw** chapter, AW writes: *Gibraltar Crag and Randel Crag are merely steep loose roughnesses. Neither would earn the name of crag in the Scafell area.*

NOT SO . . .
Great Stone
of Blakeley.

ROCKS & BOULDERS: The list

BOOK ONE

The Kirk Stone: Illustration on Red Screes 4. *This fallen boulder stands about sixty yards to the left (west) of the road at the steep descent to the north* [of Kirkstone Pass]. *It is a prominent on the way up the pass from Brothers Water, having the appearance of a ridged church-tower.*

There are no other named or even unnamed boulders in this guidebook – quite a surprise considering the rough nature of much of the **Helvellyn** range's eastern flank, and the northern and eastern flanks of fells such as **Fairfield, Hart Crag, Dove Crag** and **Little Hart Crag.** It's perhaps not so much of a shock, however, if you remember that AW didn't start to draw scree and boulders in any great detail until BOOK TWO, further developing the style of later guidebooks in BOOK THREE. The main picture on page 229 shows that the field of boulders is right beside the path to Dove Crag AW described on Dove Crag 4, but the rocks get no mention in the first guidebook.

DISTINCTIVE OUTLINE: The Kirk Stone, looking to Brothers Water and Place Fell. 14/6/11

BOOK TWO

Badger Rock: also known as Brock Stone, a huge isolated rock just 50 yards from the Garburn Pass path just beyond the last buildings of Kentmere. The rock is illustrated on the opening page of the **Sallows** chapter, and is featured in more detail in the **Yoke** chapter: *A well-known local landmark, it has little fame outside the valley. Although the base of the rock is now silted up, there is little doubt that it is*

THE DRAWING: Badger Rock, on page one of the Sallows chapter.

THE PHOTO: Badger Rock with Sallows behind.   19/4/10

a boulder fallen from the fellside above, a theory supported by the cavities beneath (a refuge for foxes), and it may well be the biggest boulder in Lakeland. There are rock climbs on it of all degrees of difficulty.

Hollow Stone: An upright boulder (offering good shelter at its foot) at the bottom of the north ridge of **Branstree**, just west of Hopegill Beck near the Haweswater road.

Ull Stone (above): High on the south-western flank of

IN THE SHADOW: The Hollow Stone, left foreground, looking to Haweswater.   12/11/08

Harter Fell, this large rock juts into the valley of Kentmere below, about a quarter-of-a-mile above the excellent path from Kentmere to Nan Bield Pass.

BOOK THREE

Balanced boulder: A 12ft-high monolith alongside the Armboth-Watendlath footpath, featured on page 2 of the **Armboth Fell** chapter (illustrated below left).

Big boulders: Just off the Borrowdale Road and below Falcon Crag at the start of the ascent of **Bleaberry Fell** (page 4), including shelter.

The Split Boulder: In a field below Scout Crag on **Blea Rigg** (see the illustration on page 228), a well-known Great Langdale landmark.

A balanced boulder, 12 feet high, alongside the footpath from Armboth

Perched boulder: 300 yards east-south-east of the summit of **Blea Rigg** (plan of the summit, page 9).

The Shelter Stone: Another **Blea Rigg** boulder (right), this refuge from the elements is located at the base of a rocky tor 150 yards west of the summit, close to the path across the top. *The accommodation is*

THE SHELTER STONE: One of three boulders in the Blea Rigg chapter.

strictly limited.

Vegetation-crowned big boulder: Above Green Burn on Calf Crag 4 in the ascent from Grasmere. It is also featured on Gibson Knott 2.

A particularly big boulder: On the far (north) side of Wyth Burn shortly before Wythburn Head Tarns on the walk from Wythburn Church. It is featured on Calf Crag 5 and also on High Raise 6 where the adjectival intensifier (a bit of English grammar there!) 'particularly' is dropped.

Big boulders: On Eagle Crag 4 in the upper stages of the direct ascent from Stonethwaite (the close-up diagram).

The Bowder Stone: The most-famous of all Lakeland boulders is featured on maps on Grange Fell 2 and also in the 'thick-black-line' map that occupies Castle Crag 4.

Split boulders: On Grange Fell 5 above Watendlath in the ascent of Brund Fell (Grange Fell's highest point).

Boulder with wall: The wall illustrated on page 229 is no longer there. It was constructed above the boulder on the approach to Great Crag (page 3) to prevent sheep from falling into a pool at the foot of the boulder. That has become the fate of the wall!

BIG AS A HOUSE: The famous Bowder Stone in Borrowdale. 7/4/11

Woodcock Stone: Illustrated on page 229, this prominent rock is at the southern end of High Rigg (page 2) close to the A591 dual-carriageway.

Blea Rock: Illustrated on page 228. It is situated below Sergeant's Crag off the popular Langstrath path to Stake Pass, near Blackmoss Pot. It is named on the map (page 3) and ascent from Stonethwaite (page 3). It is also known as **Gash Rock**.

BOOK FOUR

Boulder Valley and **The Pudding Stone:** Boulder Valley is aptly named, consisting of dozens of huge boulders of all shapes and sizes littered across a shelf on the eastern slopes of Brim Fell just a short distance from the popular tourist pass to Coniston Old Man. A page (10) is devoted to this geographical phenomenon in the Old Man chapter, and it features a drawing of the very well-known Pudding Stone, the largest of the boulders. Boulders are not just confined to this location — there are a number of huge rocks in (literally) and around Levers Water.

Cairn on boulder: Shown in a diagram showing the geography of the Eastern

THE PUDDING STONE: AW's drawing, flanked by the largest boulder in a valley of them. 16/2/08

BOULDER VALLEY: The home of the Pudding Stone and many more.   16/2/08

Terrace, a diagonal rake across the flank of Crinkle Crags (page 17).

Cave in boulders: Near the top of the steep slope at the foot of the rockface of Dow Crag (page 3), not far from where the traverse to Goat's Hawse heads north and the path along the foot of the crag heads south towards South Rake. AW didn't apparently spot a similar feature some distance away – much closer to The Cove – where a similar grouping of boulders offers shelter when the weather is bad.

Sampson's Stones: If AW had had access to the internet when he was writing BOOK FOUR, he might have done some research on the cluster of big boulders on the floor of Eskdale immediately east of the steep flank of Scafell. He didn't – just mentioning them in passing (literally) on the way to the summits of Scafell and Scafell Pike – and thus missed what can only be described as an out-of-this-world experience. That's because the room-sized blocks of Borrowdale volcanic rock are a haven for rock-climbers and the routes are festooned with galactic names: The Asteroid, Stellar Dweller, Quasar, Quark Star, Crater Face, Light Speed, Event Horizon . . . Apparently, the location is seen among the rock-climbing fraternity as one of the best 'bouldering experiences' in the UK.

Cave in boulders DOW CRAG

GIMME SHELTER: The boulders below the main crag of Dow Crag (above), and a little way away, another cluster of boulders where it is possible to seek shelter.
both 20/7/10

Hollow Stones: The other side of Scafell from Sampson's Stones (and a bit higher up). Hollow Stones is a vast natural amphitheatre, and it is aptly named, being littered with boulders of all sizes and shapes, many of which must have fallen from the rockface of Scafell Crag. AW writes about this location on page 11 of the Scafell Pike chapter: *Hollow Stones is an excellent place for a bivouac, with a wide choice of overhanging boulders for shelter, many of which have been walled-up and made draught-proof by previous occupants.* He is obviously writing from experience, and he goes on: *Watch the rising sun flush Scafell Crag and turn a black silhouette into a* rosy-pink castle! (*This doesn't always happen. Sometimes it never stops raining*).

Boulder (shelter): Above the crag of Black Waugh on the ascent of Seathwaite Fell (page 3 in that chapter) from Seathwaite.

Perched boulder: In the hollow of Calf Cove, just south-east of the summit of Grey Friar (right), this feature was sufficiently interesting to warrant a drawing on Grey Friar 6 (though only a small drawing, so perhaps it's not so interesting – although in the caption to the sketch he added the word *big*). Elsewhere in the same chapter is the splendidly named . . .

Matterhorn Rock: This is another feature on Grey Friar which AW

HOLLOW STONES: AW's drawing from the Scafell Pike chapter, looking towards Pulpit Rock, Mickledore and Scafell Crag (right).

PERCHED: On Grey Friar.   14/9/10

named *pointed boulder* (on a summit map and a location drawing) in the first edition of BOOK FOUR. It's interesting that Chris Jesty revised both the map and the caption to the drawing to include the modern name for this pointed boulder in the second edition. My guess is that AW never viewed the rock from the same angle as Sean's picture (below); otherwise he surely would have at least mentioned the rock's uncanny similarity to the Alpine giant above Zermatt.

MATTERHORN ROCK: Looking towards Cold Pike and Pike o'Blisco, this boulder has an uncanny resemblance to the shape of the Alpine mountain.   14/9/10

GREAT CARRS   SWIRL HOW

from the pointed boulder

BOOK FIVE

White Stones: A strange outcrop of boulders; on page 1 of the **Carl Side** chapter. AW described them thus: *The south ridge, Carl Side proper, is unremarkable except for a distinctive rash of white stones at 1600' extending over several acres, unique in Lakeland and identifying the fell exactly in many distant views.*

WHITE STONES: Part of the unique feature on Carl Side. 26/8/10

GREAT NAME: Apronful of Stones. 25/2/11

LONE BOULDER: On the side of Great Cockup. 21/9/04

Apronful of Stones: A great name – but on the ground this is a bit of a disappointment if you're used to rocks and boulders in the southern and western areas of Lakeland. The feature is at the foot of the most popular ascent of **Carrock Fell**.

Boulder: Nameless, lonely (left, below); on the flank of **Great Cockup** (page 4) and also on the ascent of nearby **Great Calva** (page 5).

Dumpy Stone and **Howthwaite Stone:** Two boulders (right), both on the eastern flank of **High Pike**, both sufficiently standing out to be drawn on page 6 of the fell's chapter.

Cloven Stone: Just over half-a-mile west-south-west of the top of the unloved (by AW) **Mungrisdale Common**, this strange rock (below, right) is aptly named, and although not particularly large it stands out on a grassy slope.

Fox Bield: A cluster of boulders (below, right) high up on the southern frontage of **Skiddaw** (page 13), just above the 2500ft contour.

Boulders (a little Stonehenge): That's the grand description on page 15 of the **Skiddaw** chapter. I'm sure if it really was like Stonehenge, AW would have drawn it. He didn't. Some poetic license here, I suspect.

The two boulders: Underneath the drawing in the **Skiddaw Little Man** chapter (page 7) is the caption:

Two boulders

Dumpy Stone

Howthwaite Stone

Cloven Stone

Fox Bield

The two boulders – the only feature of note on the tedious climb from the weir (which emphasises the poverty of detail on this ascent). In the early stages they are conspicuous on the skyline, and the inexperienced walker who thereby assumes that they mark the top of the mountain will be disappointed in due course to find the slope going on and up behind them, endlessly. Not 'endlessly' of course, but for another 750ft until the strange cairn on Skiddaw Lesser Man is reached – we've all been on such slopes!

WATCHES: Looking up The Edge towards Ullock Pike and Long Side.   15/3/07

Watches: A grouping of boulders at the foot of The Edge (the ridge leading up to **Ullock Pike**). From page 2 of the chapter: *A strange and interesting congregation of upstanding rocks, huddled together as though assembled in conference, and suggesting, at first sight, a Druids' Circle. The formation is natural, however, but unusual and (being in the midst of grass) unexpected.*

Hanging Stone: Ordnance Survey large-scale maps give prominence to this feature, about 400 yards west of the summit of **Ullock Pike**, but AW wasn't so impressed, calling it *an unremarkable block anchored to the lip of a small crag.*

EDGY: Ullock Pike's Hanging Stone.

BOOK SIX

The Bowder Stone: Although mentioned in the Castle Crag chapter, this is strictly speaking (being on the eastern side of the River Derwent) a BOOK THREE boulder.

Father and mother of all boulders: A grandiose title for a pair of boulders close to the upper stretches of Newlands Beck on the ascent of Dale Head (page 6).

Speckled boulder: There are many of these in the valley of Rudd Beck (Ling Fell). There is an illustration of one of them (right) on page 1 of the fell's chapter.

SPECKLED: Boulder in Rudd Beck valley.

Two conspicuous white boulders: On open fellside above the Aiken Plantation in the ascent of Lord's Seat (page 8) from High Lorton.

NOTE: The **Bishop of Barf** and the **Clerk**, and **Catbells Pinnacle** are in the Needles & Pinnacles chapter of this section.

BOOK SEVEN

If there is, indeed, a 'father and mother of all boulders', then how else could one describe Base Brown's shattered remnants? The grandparents, perhaps? The north-east ridge of the fell, heading down towards Seathwaite, one of Lakeland's legendary

SLIPPERY SLOPE: Let's hope not! Base Brown's Fallen Stone clings on. 15/6/09

locations, is a shattered shoulder of rocks, with three boulders so significant that they each warrant a drawing in the opening chapter to BOOK SEVEN. Most prominent from the valley (it's in such a situation and it's so large that it can clearly be seen) is the **Fallen Stone**, a tremendous mass of rock that must at some time have fallen from it [the crag above], although silting now gives it the appearance of a natural outcrop. It has been badly fractured in the fall, and identifiable fragments from it can be found lower down the slope. The **Hanging Stone** is balanced on the crag above the Fallen Stone and, according to AW, is repeatedly featured conspicuously in successive editions of the Ordnance Survey maps, where its name is given as much prominence as that of the fell itself . . . The Stone occupies a startling position balanced on the rim of a crag, apparently half its bulk being unsupported and overhanging the void, but it is smaller than one is led to expect . . .

About sixty yards further up the ridge is the **Perched Boulder** (AW didn't name it, but such a moniker is entirely appropriate). This rounded rock is resting on a clutch of smaller stones.

Another BOOK SEVEN fell that

Near the top end of the rock several large boulders have tumbled together, forming caves and foxholes.

THE FALLEN STONE: AW's drawing of a rock that must have collapsed from a crag. 15/6/09

PERCHED BOULDER: Base Brown. 15/6/09

HANGING STONE: Also on Base Brown. Not a good place to stand below. 15/6/09

punches above its weight in the boulder department is Scoat Fell, with two prominent rocks (both split) on opposite flanks. On the approach via Mosedale and Blackem Head (Scoat Fell 6), the **Y Boulder** can hardly be missed (it's the best part of 10ft high). In the second edition, Chris Jesty included this titbit: *Y Boulder is named on O.S. maps. It is the shortest place name in the Lake District.* The other side of the fell close to Scoat Tarn is the well-named **Split Boulder**, one of the most distinctive of its kind in Lakeland, the victim of either frost or lightning (or perhaps both).

Y BOULDER: On the way to Scoat Fell. 10/11/10

Little Buckbarrow, close to 1400ft lower than Scoat Fell, has attempted its own brand of one-upmanship with a **perched and split boulder** (left), a combination which (naturally) caught AW's eye (and he produced a nice little drawing of it) and about which he writes: *obviously split after perching, probably by frost or lightning.* Perching seems to be the theme in BOOK SEVEN:

SPLIT: Close to Scoat Tarn. 2/3/10

Perched boulder: On the ascent of Fleetwith Pike (page 5) from Honister Pass, close to the Drum House.

Perched boulder: The famous one (a woman's face) featured on page 10 of the Haystacks chapter (left),

about which AW writes: *Note the profile in shadow. Some women have faces like that.*

Buck Stone: One mile south-west of the summit of Seatallan (page 3), close to Cat Bields.

Marble Stone: A big boulder on the ascent of High Crag (page 3) from Scarth Gap. It is named on the 2.5-inch Ordnance Survey map.

Whoap boulder: Marking the summit of this height one mile north-east of Lank Rigg (illustrated on Lank Rigg 3).

THE OUTLYING FELLS

Erratic boulder: On a limestone platform, featured in the chapter on Knipescar Common (illustrated on page 222 of THE OUTLYING FELLS).

Gray Bull: A 14ft-high monolith, featured in the chapter on The Wet Sleddale Horseshoe (illustrated on page 244).

Perched boulder: A boulder perched on a massive plinth of pink granite, with some confusion over its name. According to the Ordnance Survey it's **To Stone** or **To'other**, but it's possible it should be **One Stone on T'other** or **Top Stone on T'other**. It is featured in the chapter on The Wasdale Horseshoe (illustrated on page 251).

ERRATIC: And limestone.

GRAY BULL: 14ft high.

PERCHED BOULDER: That has one name or t'other.

HOW WELL DO YOU KNOW YOUR FELLS?

Quiz time: test your knowledge of the guidebooks

G1: NAME THIS FELL: . . . *the patron fell of its valley head, a distinction little recognised.*

G2: NAME THESE FELLS: The Fairfield Horseshoe, in clockwise order (starting from Rydal, finishing at Ambleside).

G3: NAME THESE TARNS: The only two (not man-made) with names in BOOK SIX.

G4: NAME THIS FELL: It has ridge routes to Armboth Fell and High Seat.

G5: PICTURE QUESTION (right): A well-known cairn. But on which sub-height, and which parent fell?

18/6/07

G6: NAME THIS FELL (where the blank is): .... *is nothing on the map, everything when beneath one's feet. In small compass, here is concentrated the beauty, romance, interest and excitement of the typical Lakeland scene. Here Nature has given of her very best and produced a loveliness that is exquisite . . .*

G7: NAME THIS ROCK FORMATION: Named after short-legged omnivores of the weasel family, this boulder has two names.

G8: NAME THIS OUTLYING FELL: The geographical feature known as Chapel Head Scar can be found on this fell.

G9: NAME THIS FELL: Which BOOK FIVE fell overlooks Skiddaw Forest yet still – by a geographical quirk – manages to have views of the low Windermere hills in the extreme south of Lakeland?

G10: NAME THIS FELL: 'Seldom Seen' is the name of what feature, and in what chapter?

THE ANSWERS are on page 344, but before you go there, there are OTHER QUIZZES: on pages 86, 108, 137, 159, 205, 216 and 259.

THE PAGE THAT MIGHT HAVE BEEN

Of all the drawings he could have chosen for the first page of the Blencathra chapter, why did AW pick this one?

HIGHLY VISUAL: The final part of the ridge to Hall's Fell top might have been a better visual subject for the Blencathra chapter start.

29/4/09

One of the most surprising pages out of the more than 2,000 in the guidebooks can be found in BOOK FIVE – the first page of the **Blencathra** chapter. It is surprising because of words that were written one book earlier; here's what AW wrote on page 2 of the Glaramara chapter in BOOK FOUR:

SIDEWAYS: The view of Blencathra from the summit of Souther Fell. From this angle you can see where its other name comes from.

11/9/07

The ancient and beautiful name really applies only to the grey turret of rock at the summit but happily has been commonly adopted for the fell as a whole, and it is pleasing to record that no attempt has been made to rob it of this heritage of the past, as in the case of Blencathra. Much of Lakeland's appeal derives from the vary lovely names of its mountains and valleys and lakes and rivers, which fit the scenery so well. Those names were given by the earliest settlers, rough men, invaders and robbers: they were there long before Wordsworth – but they, too, surely had poetry in their hearts?

AW didn't like the alternative name for **Blencathra** – Saddleback – and, to be fair to him, he makes that clear on the opening page, on which he writes: *better known, unfortunately, as Saddleback.* That's the first-edition comment; in Chris Jesty's second edition this has been revised to take account of the fact that Blencathra has finally won this long battle (helped in no small part by AW's views on the matter). Now, the comment reads: *better known, until recently, as Saddleback.* All of this leads nicely to what is truly surprising about Blencathra 1: and that's the drawing. Of all the views of Blencathra, and there are many: the view of its soaring ridges from Castlerigg Stone Circle; the

Blencathra   2847'

From Castlerigg Stone Circle

better known, unfortunately, as Saddleback.

THE PAGE THAT NEVER WAS: A possible opener for the Blencathra chapter.

towering Hall's Fell summit above Gate Gill or Doddick Gill; the massive south frontage as seen from St John's in The Vale – the view from the east (the view of the profile that gave it its so-unlovely former most-popular name) is the last view one would expect AW to draw on the opening page to a chapter about one of his favourite fells (*Blencathra joins Bowfell in the author's best half-dozen*).

So why did he draw it when he hated it so much? And what was it with the signpost? Answers on a postcard, please (or Facebook), because I have no idea.

NOTE: Elsewhere in the pages of BOOK FIVE you will find another Saddleback – an interesting geographical feature two-thirds of a mile north-west of **Brae Fell**. This Saddleback is probably a glacial moraine, but sufficiently distinctive (with a 'saddle'-type top) to have been so christened by local folk. AW writes, rather cuttingly: *In this case there can be no quarrel with the name.*

SNOW JOKE: Pavey Ark overlooking (a frozen) Stickle Tarn is one of the finest sights in Lakeland. The snow also highlights the route of the infamous Jack's Rake, diagonally across the rockface. Easy Gully is the gully to the right. 22/2/10

VERTICALLY CHALLENGED

AW loved the big crags and the steep gullies – but not climbing them (though that didn't stop him, occasionally)

242

When AW climbed – or more probably crawled and scrambled – his way up Jack's Rake on Pavey Ark he was a man fast approaching 50, and one who didn't much like that sort of thing. He much preferred to place his feet carefully than be forced to use elbows and knees in an ungainly and quite possibly painful fashion.

Take a look at the route up Pavey Ark on this page. It starts here and then snakes upward – steeply at first – in a groove and then, at various places, becomes much more exposed as it reaches the midpoint of the precipitous cliff. But it was classed as a 'walk' – albeit a scramble – so AW felt obliged to tackle it. It resulted in a memorable ascent diagram (Pavey Ark 6) and some marvellous writing. But then, most of what he wrote about the big crags of

LANDSCAPES: The big crags 3

Lakeland was memorable. They were places where he most likely felt in awe of the majesty of the exposed rock that formed the fells he loved. It didn't matter if the crags he described were scorned by rock-climbers; fractured Skiddaw slate was just as exciting for him as firm Borrowdale volcanic. Most people who walk the Lakeland fells – if their name's not Chris Bonington – would probably take that view.

Views are, of course, what most mere mortals get of the crags of Lakeland, and it is the number of places where it's possible to remain safe and secure on the horizontal while witnessing the vertical at close quarters that makes the district so delectable. Unlike on the Isle of Skye, there are no Inaccessible Pinnacles in Cumbria (there is one, actually, and we'll come on to that later). This chapter is packed with rock 'n' stroll, and to keep things clear and simple it's all done in chronological order (apart from Pavey Ark's massive cliff kicking off things on the previous page).

The first big rockface that caught AW's attention is in BOOK ONE, and it's the one that gives **Dove Crag** its name. The crag is about 300ft high at its highest point and is a popular venue for rock climbers and also for boulderers on some of the big blocks that have become detached from the main crag and lie at its foot. Hidden within the crags is a cave known as Priest's Hole, little over 15ft deep and given added protection for hardy souls planning an overnight camp by a low wall at the front. AW didn't mention the cave in the first edition, which suggests he didn't know about it, but in the second edition there is a paragraph that includes this information: *Inside there is a metal box containing a book in which visitors have written interesting messages.*

The Dove Crag chapter features a guide to the crag which, although not matching big crags in later books for depth of detail, does indicate the main features of the rockface. It's by far the biggest and most imposing crag to be found anywhere in BOOK ONE. There are

BEST IN THE EAST: Dove Crag probably offers the finest selection of rock climbs east of Dunmail Raise.   8/4/11

Dove Crag, from the south-east
1: Main face 2: South Gully 3: Easy Gully
4: Inaccessible Gully 5: Wing Ridge 6: Tree
*Easy Gully was so named by rock-climbers;
it is NOT a pedestrian route.*

a number of crags on the north face of **Fairfield** that feature good, clean rock, but perhaps the next best in the area of BOOK ONE is the extremely impressive **Castle Rock**, on the western flank of **Watson's Dodd** overlooking the Vale of St John, the top of which is accessible with care 'from the back'. AW calls it the fell's *especial pride and joy*, and from across the valley it looks like a kind of mini

AYERS AND GRACES: Castle Rock. 13/2/06

Ayers Rock (see picture, above right). Its profile is similarly striking, so much so that it clearly warranted a drawing – a full-page one, no less, in the Watson's Dodd chapter. This rock, with a car park just below, is one of the popular for rock-climbers in the Lakes; as usual, climbs have exotic and dangerous names, among them Rigor Mortis, Where Monkeys Dare, Wingnut and Romantically Challenged. No, I don't understand rock climbers either!

Further out east, the 'big daddy' of rockfaces in the Far East is the huge **Rainsborrow Crag** on the eastern flank of **Yoke**, a *formidable thousand-foot precipice . . . the safety of which is a subject of disagreement between rock-climbers and foxes.*

Away from **The Eastern Fells**, the other side of the great central trench of Lakeland beyond Thirlmere Dam, is the fell (and the rockface) of **Raven Crag**, one of a number of big crags that ring **The Central Fells** and the only one that gives its name to a mountain – one which hosted a self-portrait of AW no less (see page 130). Further south, but still on the edge of the area covered by BOOK THREE, is **Gimmer Crag**, on **Loft Crag** overlooking Great Langdale, which AW describes on the opening page of the chapter as: *Once the most popular of all climbing grounds.*

FELL & FACE: Raven Crag, above Thirlmere.   13/5/09

GIMMER CRAG: Below Loft Crag.   11/9/06

Of course, the grandest climbing in Lakeland can be found in the area covered by BOOK FOUR, with the biggest (and most well-known) crags both taking the name of the parent fell, or more like vice versa. **Dow Crag**, above Coniston, is one of those cliffs, with over 100 rock climbs, the longest of which is over 300ft. In the chapter on Dow Crag, AW does a detailed drawing of the cliff, much like that of Dove Crag three guidebooks earlier, but with more detail. He stresses that *The Crag is the preserve of rock-climbers, but walkers may visit the base of the cliff by taking the path from the outlet of Goat's Water.*

IMPRESSIVE ARCHITECTURE: The cliffs of Dow Crag from Coniston Old Man   11/9/06
RIGHT: The pattern of the gullies and buttresses.

Almost as impressive as Dow Crag is the northern front of Great End. The cliffs are nowhere near as steep (the average gradient is around 45 degrees), which means they are not of as much interest to rock-climbers, but winter ice-climbing in the gullies is very popular, so I'm told. I prefer my ice tinkling in a glass these days!

A rock-climbing feast is available on the 400ft **Esk Buttress** on Scafell Pike (also known, rather confusingly, as Dow Crag). This cliff is, as the crow flies, only one mile from the grandest rockface in Lakeland, **Scafell Crag** on Scafell, which AW described as a . . . *towering rampart of shadowed crags facing north and east below the summit, the greatest display of natural grandeur in the district, a spectacle of*

FEAST FOR CLIMBERS: Esk Buttress.   25/6/09

massive strength and savage wildness but without beauty, an awesome and a humbling scene. As usual, there is a splendid (and safe) place to take this all in: *A man may stand on the lofty ridge of Mickledore or in the green hollow beneath the precipice amongst the littered debris and boulders fallen from it, and witness the sublime architecture of buttresses and pinnacles soaring into the sky, silhouetted against racing clouds or, often, tormented by writhing mists, and, as in a great cathedral, lose all his conceit. It does a man good to realise his own insignificance in the great scheme of things, and that is his experience here. 'Here' in this case is close to the aforementioned ridge of Mickledore, seen to the left in this great picture (below) from Pulpit Rock.*

GRANDEST CRAG: Scafell Crag from Pulpit Rock. Broad Stand is far left; Lord's Rake is far right. Two climbers are circled in red, showing scale.   1/2/12
RIGHT: Key to the crag.

The maximum height of the crag is 600 feet
Scafell Crag, from Pikes Crag

Two more big crags are featured in BOOK FIVE: **Dead Crags** on **Bakestall** – a dark yet colourful rampart of buttresses and jutting aretes; and the rim of crags immediately below the summit of **Bannerdale Crags**. Both are substantial, both are shattered and splintered, offering little in the way of 'clean' rock. **Hobcarton Crag** on Hopegill Head falls into this category, but has even more botanic and geological interest – enough to warrant a whole page in BOOK SIX.

DEAD CRAGS: Just below Bakestall.   7/6/07

HOBCARTON CRAG: And Hopegill Head.   4/2/09

BANNERDALE CRAGS: One mile long.   8/2/11

Which leaves us with the two most striking crags in Lakeland – both in BOOK SEVEN - and they are striking because unlike most crags, which tend to merge in with the shape of the fell, these two stand out from steep slopes – literally.

The most impressive single cliff in Lakeland is, of course, **Pillar Rock** on the north face of Pillar, which caught the attention of William Wordsworth, no less, in his poem 'The Brothers':

You see yon precipice – it almost looks
Like some vast building made of many crags,
And in the midst is one particular rock
That rises like a column from the vale,
Whence by our Shepherds it is call'd, the Pillar.

From top to toe it's 600ft if it's an inch, and whether seen from side on (picture right) or head on (far right) it's an awesome sight.

Naturally, AW waxed lyrical about this astonishing physical feature, and he gave it 'the treatment', with three pages of drawings and diagrams.

Three miles away from Pillar, the astonishing array of crags on Great Gable also gets 'the treatment': a drawing of the very impressive **Gable Crag** (occupying the whole of the north face); a drawing of the beautifully clean slab of **Kern Knotts** on the south flank close to Sty Head Pass; and the best of the lot, the **Great Napes** high on the southern flank overlooking Wasdale. This unique feature includes the famous **Napes Needle** and **Sphinx (Cat) Rock** (see page 220), and was afforded four pages of space in the Great Gable chapter: *Unlike most crags, which buttress and merge into the general slope of a mountain, the Great Napes rises like a castle above its*

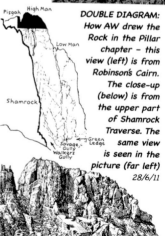

DOUBLE DIAGRAM: How AW drew the Rock in the Pillar chapter - this view (left) is from Robinson's Cairn. The close-up (below) is from the upper part of Shamrock Traverse. The same view is seen in the picture (far left) 28/6/11

HEAD-ON ROCK: As seen from High Crag, the other side of Ennerdale, not only is the rock itself an impressive sight, but the subsidiary buttress to the left – Shamrock – is also substantial.

28/6/11

FAR LEFT: The rock stands out in profile, looking west.

17/9/08

surroundings so that there is not only a front wall of rock but side walls and a back wall too.

The picture and diagram below show this quite clearly. The Great Napes do, indeed, rise like a castle high up the steep slope way above Wasdale, and they are accentuated by the flanking scree slopes of Great Hell Gate and Little Hell Gate (see diagram below, a part of a larger diagram on Great Gable 11).

CASTLE IN THE SKY: The distinctive outline of the Great Napes. 3/2/10

THIS WAS 8

(it was the fifth, really, but as it was a 'bonus' sketch we've added it on at the end!)

The very final page of the *personal notes* at the end of the mighty BOOK FOUR: The Southern Fells saw AW apologise to readers for the quality of his penmanship in those notes and blame a new puppy Cindy – recently introduced to the Wainwright household – for the problems. *It's Cindy's fault, not mine,* he laments. He illustrated the point with this drawing, which was also used on the back cover of the Hunter Davies-edited book (published in 2011) *The Wainwright Letters.*

AND 9

Surely that has to be AW making his way from BOOK ONE to BOOK TWO (final page of The Eastern Fells)!

Who is the lone man wearing glasses and smoking a pipe in the rear (open) carriage of a train ready to leave Irton Road Station on the Ravenglass and Eskdale Railway? Although the hair is a few shades darker than normal, it has to be AW occupying the left-hand edge of a drawing on the Irton Pike chapter (page 183). I've always wondered why there wasn't a self-portrait in THE OUTLYING FELLS – but perhaps there was after all. Perhaps he had taken to tinting his hair so he wasn't recognised on the fells (or the rails!).

WAS THIS NUMBER 10?

EIGHT PAGES of interesting stats & trivia start RIGHT HERE!

EVERYBODY NEEDS GOOD NEIGHBOURS

CLOSE: Stybarrow Dodd (left) and Watson's Dodd, in front of cloudy Helvellyn and the pointed Catstycam. 29/9/06

Apart from the same surname, what have **Stybarrow Dodd** and **Watson's Dodd** got in common? I stumbled across this while looking through the 'order of appearance' page in BOOK ONE. The answer: they are next to each other alphabetically and geographically:

| 13 | 9 | .. | STYBARROW DODD | .. | 2770 |
| 9 | 13 | .. | WATSONS DODD | .. | 2584 |

See what I mean? And that got me to wondering if there were any more instances of '214' fells being alphabetically and geographically adjacent. You're not going to believe how many – with an obvious pair of pairs to start things off: Great Gable/Green Gable and Skiddaw/Skiddaw Little Man. The others are: Crag Fell/Caw Fell, Grange Fell/Great Crag, Hard Knott/Harter Fell, High Crag/High Stile and High Seat/High Tove. And there are two more pairs that are alphabetically and geographically next to each other – as well as both being next to each other in one other category: height. Both Scafell Pike/Scafell and Grasmoor/Eel Crag are the highest and second-highest fells in their respective guidebooks – BOOK FOUR and BOOK SIX.

EVEN CLOSER: Scafell Pike (left) and Scafell, seen from Yewbarrow. 23/6/09

FIRST THINGS FIRST

We promised you stats – so stick on that anorak and get stuck in to some facts and figures! This chapter is mainly about where the ascents begin

POPULAR PLACES TO BEGIN: Wasdale Head, looking to Mosedale and Pillar (main picture); INSET: Patterdale.
Main picture: 3/2/10 Inset: 13/9/11

HAND OF MAN section starts page 262

FELL STATISTICS

Book by book: how many **ascents** (with significant **variations**); number of ascent **diagrams**; number of **starting points**; number of pages devoted to **chapters** about the fells.

	No. of ascents	No. of variations	No. of diagrams	No. of starting points	No. of chapter pages
ONE	95	50	47	20	276
TWO	93	36	51	21	274
THREE	70	19	61	23	236
FOUR	72	25	62	21	314
FIVE	69	26	67	28	273
SIX	74	18	74	29	274
SEVEN	87	28	75	30	301
OUTLYING	56	N/A	1	53	268

STARTING POINTS: THE TOP TEN

1	**Dungeon Ghyll**	(13, 12)	25
2	**Grasmere**	(8, 15)	23
3	**Patterdale**	(15, 6)	21
4=	**Seatoller**	(7, 2, 6)	15
	Wasdale Head	(9, 6)	15
6	**Buttermere**	(6, 8)	14
7=	**Boot**	(8, 1)	9
	Hartsop	(9)	9
	Stonethwaite	(6, 3)	9
10=	**Kentmere**	(8)	8
	Troutbeck	(8)	8

NOTES: Ascents from **Dungeon Ghyll** in BOOK THREE and BOOK FOUR incorporate the following starting points: **Dungeon Ghyll Hotel** (old hotel), **Dungeon Ghyll New Hotel, Stool End, Wall End** and **Mickleden** | In BOOK FOUR, seven of the eight ascents from **Seathwaite** originate at **Seatoller** | In BOOK FIVE, all eight **Threlkeld** ascents and four of the six ascents from **Scales** are of Blencathra | In BOOK SIX, most ascents are from the **Newlands Valley** (six locations: **Little Town, Newlands Church, Newlands Hause, Rigg Beck, Skelgill** and **Stair**); also, ascents from Coledale Hause are, in effect, from either **Braithwaite** or **Lanthwaite Green** | In BOOKS FOUR and SEVEN ascents from **Sty Head** could be classed as being from **Seathwaite** and **Wasdale Head** respectively | Only five starting points in THE OUTLYING FELLS have more than one ascent (two is the maximum). All ascents are walks except **Black Combe** with a choice of four ways up.

STARTING POINTS

TOP FIVE in each
PICTORIAL GUIDE

BOOK ONE

1	Patterdale	15
2	Grasmere	8
3	Glenridding	7
4	Ambleside	5
5=	Dockray	3
	Rydal	3
	Thirlspot	3

BOOK TWO

1	Hartsop	9
2=	Kentmere	8
	Troutbeck	8
4=	Mardale	7
	Martindale	7

BOOK THREE

1.	Grasmere	15
2	Dungeon Ghyll	13
3	Stonethwaite	6
4=	Watendlath	5
	Wythburn	5

BOOK FOUR

1.	Dungeon Ghyll	12
2	Wasdale Head	9
3=	Boot	8
	Seathwaite	8
5	Coniston	6

BOOK FIVE

1	Threlkeld	8
2	Scales	6
3=	Millbeck	5
	Mungrisdale	5
	Orthwaite	5

BOOK SIX

1	Buttermere	6
2=	Braithwaite	5
	Grange	5
	Stair	5
5=	Coledale Hause	4
	Little Town	4
	Rannerdale	4
	Thornthwaite	4
	Whinlatter Pass	4

BOOK SEVEN

1	Buttermere	8
2	Black Sail Y.H.	7
3=	Honister Pass	6
	Loweswater	6
	Wasdale Head	6

BEST NORTH WEST

The hills are easier to climb than their abrupt appearance suggest: the secret is to get on the ridges early, because it is the ridges, not the fellsides, that provide the best travelling underfoot, and give the area its special appeal. That's how AW summed up The North Western Fells in his closing comments to BOOK SIX, and, of course, it could apply to any area. But there IS something special about the north-west ridges: they seem sharper, and generally more defined than those in other areas. Look at the ridges in the picture below from Eel Crag (13/1/12), where there are two ways to reach Braithwaite: via Coledale Hause and Grisedale Pike, or Sail-Scar Crags-Outerside-Barrow.

RIDGE WALKS: MOST FEET OF ASCENT

BOOK ONE

1=	Hartsop above How-Hart Crag	1000ft
	Sheffield Pike-Stybarrow Dodd	1000ft
3	Seat Sandal-Fairfield	950ft
4	Little Hart Crag-Red Screes	900ft
5=	Birkhouse Moor-Helvellyn	850ft
	Birks-St Sunday Crag	850ft

BOOK TWO

1	Wansfell-Caudale Moor	1550ft
2	Steel Knotts-Wether Hill	1100ft
3=	Angletarn Pikes-Rest Dodd	700ft
	Branstree-Harter Fell	700ft
	Tarn Crag-Branstree	700ft

BOOK THREE

1	Great Crag-Ullscarf	1300ft
2=	Loughrigg Fell-Silver How	950ft
	Armboth Fell-Ullscarf	950ft
4	Walla Crag-Bleaberry Fell	900ft
5=	Sergeant's Crag-High Raise	850ft
	Silver How-Loughrigg Fell	850ft

BOOK FOUR

1	Rosthwaite Fell-Glaramara	1000ft
2=	Cold Pike-Crinkle Crags	850ft
	Crinkle Crags-Bowfell	850ft
	Lingmell-Scafell Pike	850ft
	Scafell Pike-Scafell	850ft

BOOK FIVE

1	Dodd-Carl Side	1075ft
2	Bakestall-Skiddaw	900ft
3	Bannerdale Crags-Blencathra	850ft
4	Carl Side-Skiddaw	780ft
5	Lonscale Fell-Skiddaw Little Man	675ft

BOOK SIX

1	High Spy-Dale Head	900ft
2	Barrow-Outerside	800ft
3	Catbells-Maiden Moor	720ft
4=	Dale Head-High Spy	550ft
	Robinson-Hindscarth	550ft

BOOK SEVEN

1	Yewbarrow-Red Pike	1350ft
2	Crag Fell-Caw Fell	1200ft
3	Kirk Fell-Pillar	1150ft
4	Haystacks-High Crag	1100ft
5	Seatallan-Haycock	1050ft

RIDGE WALKS: LEAST FEET OF ASCENT

ALL PICTORIAL GUIDES

1	Great Rigg-Stone Arthur	0ft
2	Stybarrow Dodd-Watson's Dodd	'Negligible'
3	Dove Crag-High Pike	'Few feet'
4	High Seat-High Tove	25ft
5	Heron Pike-Nab Scar	'downhill all the way' – est. 30ft
6	Rampsgill Head-Kidsty Pike	35ft
7	Skiddaw-Bakestall	40ft
8=	Brandreth-Grey Knotts	50ft
	Knott-Great Sca Fell	50ft
	Loadpot Hill-Arthur's Pike	50ft
	Loadpot Hill-Bonscale Pike	50ft
	Long Side-Ullock Pike	50ft
	St Sunday Crag-Birks	50ft
	Sergeant's Crag-Eagle Crag	50ft

> **DOUBLE TOP:** The summit of Wansfell, looking towards Caudale Moor. The ridge walk between them is the longest (4.5 miles) and has the biggest ascent (1550ft)
> 20/9/04

RIDGE WALKS: LONGEST

(miles)

1	Caudale Moor-Wansfell	4.5
2	Caw Fell-Crag Fell	3.5
3	Armboth Fell-Ullscarf	3
4	Great Crag-Ullscarf	2.75
5=	Blencathra-Souther Fell	2.5
	High Pike-Knott	2.5
	Kirk Fell-Pillar	2.5
8=	High Raise-Wether Hill	2.25
	Arthur's Pike-Loadpot Hill	2.25
10=	Too many to mention	2

RIDGE WALKS: SHORTEST

(miles)

1	Scoat Fell-Steeple	0.25
2=	Great Carrs-Swirl How	0.33
	Harrison Stickle-Loft Crag	0.33
	Kidsty Pike-Rampsgill Head	0.33
	The Knott-Rampsgill Head	0.33
	Loft Crag-Pike o'Stickle	0.33
	Long Side-Ullock Pike	0.33
8	Eel Crag-Sail	0.4
9=	Too many to mention	0.5

KEY TO PICTURE OPPOSITE

Binsey — Grisedale Pike — Skiddaw — Blencathra — Causey Pike — Helvellyn range — Barrow — Catbells — Coledale — Outerside — Scar Crags — Sail — Eel Crag

END OF THE LINE: Esk Pike is right at the head of Eskdale, flanked by Ill Crag (left) and Bowfell (right). As such, it's Lakeland's longest ascent. 26/7/11

You can tramp for hours on a single ascent, or be up and down in just an hour. Here is...

THE LONG and THE SHORT of it

Four of the five longest ascents in the PICTORIAL GUIDES can be found in BOOK FOUR – Esk Pike, Bowfell, Scafell Pike and Scafell – because the valley that AW thinks is the grandest in Lakeland – Eskdale – has no road going to its head (or even anywhere near it). At the head of the valley is Esk Pike, which is why it edges ahead of the other three southern fells listed above in the length of its longest ascent (see tables on facing page). Esk Pike is not the remotest of Lakeland fells. That 'honour' goes to Grey Crag, way out on the eastern fringe, with four ascents (7, 6, 5 and 5 miles) – see list, left. The shortest ascents in Lakeland are really short! The climb to High Rigg from St John's in the Vale, for instance, is just half-a-mile, a figure (this is an estimation) matched by Hallin Fell. There are very few climbs that

Grey Crag
Four ascents | Total **23 miles**
Average ascent **5.75 miles**
Esk Pike
Four ascents | Total **21.75 miles**
Average ascent **5.44 miles**
Caw Fell
Three ascents | Total **16.25 miles**
Average ascent **5.42 miles**
Scafell Pike
Six ascents | Total **31.75 miles**
Average ascent **5.29 miles**

LONGEST ASCENTS
BOOK BY BOOK (miles)

BOOK ONE
1	Helvellyn	7.25
2	Red Screes	6.5
3	Helvellyn	6.25
4=	Helvellyn	5.5
	Fairfield	5.5

BOOK TWO
1	Grey Crag	7
2	Loadpot Hill	6.5
3=	Caudale Moor	6
	Grey Crag	6
	High Street	6
	High Street	6
	Loadpot Hill	6

BOOK THREE
1	Sergeant Man	5.5
2=	High Raise	5
	Sergeant Man	5
4=	Calf Crag	4.5
	Calf Crag	4.5
	Gibson Knott	4.5
	Sergeant's Crag	4.5

BOOK FOUR
1	Esk Pike	8.5
2	Crinkle Crags	8
3=	Bowfell	7.5
	Scafell Pike	7.5
4=	Scafell	7.25

BOOK FIVE
1	Skiddaw	5.5
2=	Blencathra	5
	Skiddaw	5
4	Knott	4.5
5	Lonscale Fell	4.25

BOOK SIX
1	Causey Pike	4.5
2=	Broom Fell	4
	Dale Head	4
	Eel Crag	4
	High Spy	4
	Lord's Seat	4

BOOK SEVEN
1	Caw Fell	7.5
2	Pillar	6.25
3	Caw Fell	6
4	Pillar	5.25
5	Starling Dodd	4.5

LONGEST ASCENTS
TOP TEN and ties (miles)

1	Esk Pike	8.5
2	Crinkle Crags	8
3=	Bowfell	7.5
	Caw Fell	7.5
	Scafell Pike	7.5
6=	Helvellyn	7.25
	Scafell	7.25
8	Grey Crag	7
9=	Bowfell	6.5
	Loadpot Hill	6.5
	Red Screes	6.5

LOW AND BEHOLD: The ascent of High Rigg is a just a half-a-mile stroll – with a fantastic view of Blencathra at the end of it. both 20/11/10

match this brevity in THE OUTLYING FELLS OF LAKELAND, mainly because the last of AW's guidebooks tends to focus on walks involving more than one fell. There are, however, five outliers that have simple, 'straight-up-straight-down' or fairly short circular walks: they are Burney (1.5 miles, round walk), Cartmel Fell (1.75 miles, round walk), Cold Fell (1.25 miles there and back — so just a five-eighths of a mile ascent), Gummer's How (1 mile there, 1 mile back), and Hugill Fell (also 1 mile there, 1 mile back).

NOTE: The top 5 in each PICTORIAL GUIDE does not include ascents from 'passes' or other locations that have to be walked to first.

So, OUT are places such as: Sty Head Pass, Garburn Pass, Coledale Hause and Kentmere Reservoir. IN, because they are accessible by road, are locations such as: Honister Pass, Kirkstone Pass, Wrynose and Hard Knott passes, Newlands Hause, Watendlath etc.

In BOTH TABLES on this page, an asterisk (*) indicates no distance was given (note how frequent this was in the first two books). These distances have been estimated.

SHORTEST ASCENTS
TOP TEN and ties (miles)

1=	Hallin Fell	*0.5
	High Rigg	0.5
	Little Mell Fell	*0.5
4=	Arnison Crag	*0.67
	Bakestall	0.67
	Black Fell	*0.67
	Hartsop Dodd	*0.67
8=	High Hartsop Dodd	*0.75
	Stone Arthur	*0.75
10=	Barf	0.75
	Graystones	0.75
	Hard Knott	0.75
	Hartsop Dodd	*0.75
	Holme Fell	*0.75
	Steel Knotts	*0.75

SHORTEST ASCENTS
BOOK BY BOOK (miles)

BOOK ONE

1	Little Mell Fell	*0.5
2	Arnison Crag	*0.67
3=	High Hartsop Dodd	*0.75
	Stone Arthur	*0.75
4=	Glenridding Dodd	*1
	Great Mell Fell	*1
	Nab Scar	*1
	Stone Arthur	*1

BOOK TWO

1	Hallin Fell	*0.5
2	Hartsop Dodd	*0.67
3=	Hartsop Dodd	*0.75
	Steel Knotts	*0.75
5	Brock Crags	1

BOOK THREE

1	High Rigg	0.5
2=	Grange Fell	1
	High Tove	1
	Raven Crag	1
	Steel Fell	1
	Walla Crag	1

BOOK FOUR

1.	Black Fell	*0.67
2=	Hard Knott	0.75
	Holme Fell	*0.75
4=	Cold Pike	1.25
	Pike o'Blisco	1.25

BOOK FIVE

1	**Bakestall**	0.67
2	Binsey	1
3=	**Carrock Fell**	1.25
	Longlands Fell	1.25
	Souther Fell	1.25

BOOK SIX

1=	Barf	0.75
	Graystones	0.75
3	Barf	1
4	Dale Head	1.25
5=	Catbells	1.33
	Catbells	1.33

BOOK SEVEN

1	Grey Knotts	1
2	Fleetwith Pike	1.125
3=	Fellbarrow	1.25
	Loweswater	1.25
	Wasdale Head	1.25

HOW WELL DO YOU KNOW YOUR FELLS?

Quiz time: test your knowledge of the guidebooks

H1: NAME THIS FELL: *It is one of those fells that compels attention by reason of shapeliness and height.*

H2: NAME THESE FELLS: The seven Coniston fells, in height order (highest to lowest).

H3: NAME THIS TARN: *A place to lie dreaming, and life seems a sweet sweet thing.*

H4: NAME THIS FELL: It has ridge routes to Rampsgill Head and Wether Hill.

H5: PICTURE QUESTION (right): Name this tarn.

H6: NAME THIS FELL (where the blank is): .... *marks the end of roads and farmsteads, of woods and green pastures, as one proceeds into the upper recesses of* [valley name]. *It is the first of the rough and rugged heights extending to and around* [another valley name], *and introduces its*

18/7/10

hinterland excellently, being itself of striking appearance, gaunt, steep-sided, a pyramid of tumbled boulders and scree, a desert abandoned to nature.

H7: NAME THIS ROCK FORMATION: *A smooth and slender pinnacle 12ft high, balanced on a massive plinth of rock.*

H8: NAME THIS OUTLYING FELL: AW says this fell *was meant to be climbed.*

H9: NAME THIS FELL: It overlooks what AW describes as . . . *a perfect example of a hanging valley, quite the finest in Lakeland, and a remarkable example of natural sculpturing . . . The whole scene is a complete geography lesson without words.*

H10: NAME THIS FELL: In its chapter, AW has drawn a sign that reads: *Danger, WD Range. Keep Out.*

THE ANSWERS are on page 344. The OTHER SEVEN QUIZZES are on pages 86, 108, 137, 159, 205, 216 and 239.

THE GREAT ILLUSION

SECRET MOUNTAIN: Skiddaw looks like
a mountain at the head of the Wythop
Valley – but this is just an illusion – as
the diagram (below) reveals.

Of all the unusual
geographical features
that are highlighted in
the guidebooks, none
is as strange as the

shy **Wythop Valley**, which so intrigued AW that he devoted two pages to it in
the Sale Fell chapter in BOOK SIX. They say a picture is worth a thousand
words; a diagram can be even more valuable, especially when it so clearly
explains that the Wythop Valley, unlike typical Lakeland valleys, does not have
a head. This valley's head is a trench, in which sits Bassenthwaite Lake, and the
mountain at its head is, in fact, nowhere of the sort – **Skiddaw** is far away
the other side of the lake; the view from the valley towards this venerable
giant of the fells is so unusual, AW calls it *The Great Illusion*.

He rarely fails to spot strange little geographical quirks, the details of which
positively litter the pages of the PICTORIAL GUIDES. Such as the **valley of
Tarn Beck** (Grey Friar chapter), where he highlights the watercourse which
runs parallel to the River Duddon, separated from the river by a low ridge so
that, in effect, the Duddon Valley is split in two for some distance.

Oddly enough, this strange arrangement is mirrored across the district where
the low fell of **Troutbeck Tongue** splits the Troutbeck Valley in similar fashion.

See page 145 for another thing unique about Troutbeck Tongue

STRANGE BUT TRUE

The Big Hole (Banishead Quarry – Dow Crag and Walna Scar) is filled by a waterfall, but it has no outlet.

Tarn Crag on the flank of Dollywaggon Pike does not overlook the nearby Grisedale Tarn.

Aiken Beck (Broom Fell) is a valley enclosed on four sides.

The flanking becks of Knott Rigg (**Keskadale Beck** and **Sale Beck**) flow in opposite directions.

Sandbed Gill (Clough Head) has a stream in its rocky gorge but is empty at valley level.

The Great Central Fault, while no San Andreas, gives **Great Calva** extra significance.

Wythburn the hamlet and **Wythburn the village** are on opposite sides of Thirlmere (Steel Fell chapter).

The course of the **River Glenderamackin** is rather remarkable (Souther Fell chapter).

Raven Crag **deflects water** from Thirlmere (see page 2 of the chapter, which reveals a similar occurrence the other side of the valley).

Great Gable has roots only in Wasdale, and only then one mile from the head of the valley.

A tarn on the ascent of Silver How (page 5) issues at both ends after rain – something not supposed to happen.

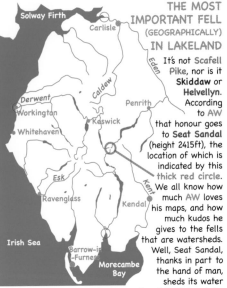

THE MOST IMPORTANT FELL (GEOGRAPHICALLY) IN LAKELAND

It's not Scafell Pike, nor is it Skiddaw or Helvellyn. According to AW that honour goes to **Seat Sandal** (height 2415ft), the location of which is indicated by this **thick red circle**. We all know how much AW loves his maps, and how much kudos he gives to the fells that are watersheds. Well, Seat Sandal, thanks in part to the hand of man, sheds its water at more divergent points than any other fell. AW explains this phenomenon on Seat Sandal 2: *This has been so since the diversion of Raise Beck to feed Thirlmere.* (Dollywaggon Pike shares this distinction only when Raise Beck is flowing south at Dunmail Raise.)

The map shows where the raindrops that fall on Seat Sandal end up (**thin red circles**): NORTH-EAST: **Grisedale Beck** leads to Ullswater, Penrith, the River Eden, Carlisle and finally to the **Solway Firth**; NORTH-WEST: **Raise Beck** leads to Thirlmere, the River Greta, the River Derwent and the **Irish Sea** at Workington; SOUTH: **Raise Beck** and **Tongue Gill** lead to Grasmere, Rydal Water, Windermere and, eventually, **Morecambe Bay**.

IT DOESN'T LOOK MUCH: But Seat Sandal, seen from the old gatepost on Dollywaggon Pike, is a highly significant fell in geographic terms. 12/10/10

PLACES TO REMEMBER

Beauty acts as an inspiration

It's not really surprising that every one of the eight guidebooks features details of at least one memorial or monument. The wish of **AW** himself was that his ashes were scattered at Innominate Tarn on his favourite fell, **Haystacks**; many other lives have been commemorated by friends and loved ones. Lakeland is a place where people yearn

to spend their lives, so why wouldn't they want to spend their afterlives high on the fells they loved; and why wouldn't the people they left behind want to remember them in such beautiful and wild settings?

Some of the stories that lay behind these fellside memorials are heartbreaking; some are uplifting; some have been lost in the mists of time.

BRAVE FLYERS: A simple memorial to the Canadian crew of a Halifax bomber who died on Great Carrs in 1944. For more details, see page 267.
15/11/07

BOOK BY BOOK:
All the monuments and memorials in the guides

Hart Side: Birkett Memorial.

Helvellyn: Dixon Memorial, Gough Memorial, Aircraft Memorial.

Seat Sandal: 'Coast To Coast' milestone house.

Caudale Moor: Mark Atkinson's Monument.

Bleaberry Fell, High Seat: Robert Graham (fellrunner) Memorial.

High Seat: Litt's Memorial.

Pavey Ark: Cairn with tablet.

Steel Fell: Manchester Corporation memorial stone.

Coniston Old Man: Charmer's Grave.

Great Carrs, Pike o'Blisco: Three Shire Stone.

Great Carrs: Canadian aircraft.

Rossett Pike: Packwoman's grave.

Scafell: Carved cross (in crag).

Blencathra: White cross.

Skiddaw: Hawell Monument.

Castle Crag: War memorial.

Sale Fell: White cross.

Fleetwith Pike: White cross.

Great Gable: War memorial.

Grey Knotts: John Bankes memorial.

Pillar: Robinson's Cairn.

Scout Scar: Darwin Leighton memorial tablet; King George V memorial shelter.

Orrest Head: View indicator.

Finsthwaite Heights: Royal Navy memorial tower.

Muncaster Fell: Henry VI monument.

Ponsonby Fell: Gosforth Cross.

Caermote Hill: Memorial boulder.

Fauld's Brow: John Peel's gravestone.

High Knott: Williamson's Monument.

Not in the guidebooks

Grisedale Tarn: Brothers Parting Stone. **Scafell:** White cross.

HONOURED ON HELVELLYN

As befits Lakeland's most-visited mountain, there are three monuments on **Helvellyn**, which AW outlined in the chapter on the fell thus:

Space was clearly at a premium in the 26-page chapter; otherwise surely he would have elaborated more on this unique feature of the fell. So let's do it for him and tell the story of **The Gough Memorial**, which is close by the path

The Gough Memorial

Erected 1890 on the edge of the summit above the path to Striding Edge.

This small stone tablet, 40 yards S of the shelter, commemorates the landing of an aeroplane in 1926. (Playful pedestrians may have hidden it with stones)

The Dixon Memorial 1858

Situated on a platform of rock on Striding Edge overlooking Nethermost Cove (often not noticed)

which comes up from Striding Edge, is well known, and inspired poems by Sir Walter Scott ('Helvellyn') and William Wordsworth ('Fidelity'). Charles Gough from Kendal fell to his death from Striding Edge while making his way from

THE DIXON MEMORIAL: *The memorial (2/6/08) is on a platform close to the top of High Spying How, below.* (9/12/08)

Patterdale to Wythburn on 18 April 1805. The skeletal remains of his body were not found until three months later – on 20 July – and were still being guarded by his emaciated dog, Foxie. The memorial was constructed in 1890.

Striding Edge also claimed the life of Roger Dixon. **The Dixon Memorial**, erected in 1858 on a platform on the south side of High Spying How (the edge's highest point), reads: *In memory of Robert Dixon of Rooking, Patterdale who was killed on this place on the 27th day of Nov 1856 following the Patterdale foxhounds.*

The third memorial is a tablet just south of the summit cross-shelter to celebrate the first **landing of an aircraft** on a mountain top in Britain by John Leeming and Bert Hinkler in 1926. An inscription reads: *The first aeroplane to land on a mountain in Great Britain did so on this spot. On December 22nd 1926 John Leeming and Bert Hinkler in an AVRO 585 Gosport landed here and after a*

HIGH SPYING HOW: At the far end of Striding Edge, its highest point. 9/12/08

THE GOUGH MEMORIAL: Above, looking towards the eastern flank of Helvellyn; below right, the view to Striding Edge (both 18/12/09); below left, the inscription reflects on the loyalty of Mr Gough's dog Foxie (the dog pictured is Sean McMahon's trusty sidekick Casper). 2/6/08

short stay flew back to Woodford. That's in south Manchester, some 90 miles away. But this doesn't tell the whole story. Apparently, Leeming nearly died of exposure on a reconnaissance visit to the summit; the recce was worth it, however, to rule out the summit itself and settle on an area south of the top. A few days later some friends of Leeming spent three days clearing boulders from the 'landing strip'. Three attempts were made (beaten

From 'Fidelity' by William Wordsworth

Yes, proof was plain that, since the day,
When this ill-fated Traveller died,
The Dog had watched about the spot,
Or by his master's side:
How nourished here through such long time,
He knows, who gave that love sublime,
And gave that strength of feeling, great
Above all human estimate!

From 'Helvellyn' by Sir Walter Scott

Nor yet quite deserted, though lonely extended,
For, faithful in death, his mute favourite attended,
The much-loved remains of her master defended,
And chased the hill-fox and raven away.

by bad weather and engine problems) before the plane landed and, luckily, there was a witness already on the summit sheltering by the cairn. Take-off was dicey, with the plane only just making it over Striding Edge.

THE PAIN OF PARTING

SITE OF SORROW:
The Brothers
Parting
Stone.
28/1/05

North-west of **Grisedale Tarn** is the **Brothers Parting Stone**, marking the place where poet William Wordsworth and his sister Dorothy last saw their brother John on 29 September 1800, Michaelmas Day. On 5 February 1805 John died aged 33 when the *Earl of Abergavenny* ship, of which he was captain, sank off Weymouth. Stricken by grief, Wordsworth carved some lines into the rockface. Some 80 years later a metal plaque was constructed above it. The words are now impossible to read, but this is what Wordsworth carved:

> *Here did we stop; and here looked round,*
> *While each into himself descends,*
> *For that last thought of parting Friends,*
> *That is not to be found.*
> *Brother and friend, if verse of mine,*
> *Have power to make thy virtues known,*
> *Here let a monumental Stone,*
> *Stand – sacred as a Shrine.*

AW didn't find space for this story in THE PICTORIAL GUIDES, but a description and a drawing appears in A COAST TO COAST WALK on page 35. Talking of which, in the **Seat Sandal** chapter (2nd edition) a house built in 1983 at Mill Bridge is identified, bearing the inscription: *St Bees Head 40, Robin Hood's Bay 150.*

4/3/09

29/9/06

Mark Atkinson's Monument is on the western edge of the summit plateau of **Caudale Moor** at the top of the ridge to Kirkstone. The landlord of the Kirkstone Pass Inn died in 1930 aged 60. It also honours his son Mark, who died in 1987 aged 83.

The Birkett Memorial has the name Birkett Fell inscribed on a stone close to the summit of **Hart Side**. The peer led a successful House of Lords revolt in 1962 to stop water being taken from Ullswater. He died two days after his famous speech.

SECRET GRAVES: The locations of two grave sites drawn by AW in BOOK FOUR were kept secret by the author. **Charmer's Grave** on Coniston Old Man, marked by a headstone, commemorates the death of a foxhound on Dow Crag in 1911. AW writes: *it is rather nice to know that the memory of a faithful dog was revered in this way. But some visitors have seen nothing sacred in the stone and it has been uprooted and cast aside on occasion. For this reason it has been thought best not to*

CHARMER'S GRAVE   12/12/11

reveal its exact location. The **Packwoman's Grave** (Rossett Pike chapter) is close to the path from Mickleden to Rossett Pass. It marks the final resting place of a woman who used to sell articles to Langdale farms – *it has suffered little disturbance down the years, but because so many folk nowadays seem unable to leave things alone the precise location is not divulged here.*

THE FATAL FLIGHT

THE MEMORIAL: *Incorporating part of the wreckage, looking towards the Scafell range.* 24/11/05

A moving memorial – rededicated in November 2005 – close to the summit of Great Carrs commemorates the eight crew members of a Halifax bomber who died when the plane crashed on the mountain on 22 October 1944. Halifax LL505, part of the No. 1659 Heavy Conversion Unit of the Royal Canadian Air Force 424 Transport and Rescue Squadron based at Topcliffe in North Yorkshire, came to grief on a night navigation exercise. The plane got lost in thick cloud and the pilot descended to try to get a visual fix. The aircraft crashed near the summit, killing all on board. It was too big to be removed, but so other aircraft would not report it, the remains of the plane were broken into pieces and pushed off the side of the mountain down Broad Slack, where much remains today, apart from two of the four Merlin engines, which are now in museums (Ruskin Museum in Coniston, and the RAF Museum in London) and bits which have been kept by fellwalkers as souvenirs. In the Great Carrs chapter AW speculates on what happened (though not quite accurately).

The dead were: pilot, FO John Johnston, aged 27; navigator, FO Francis Bell, 33; bomb aimer, PO Robert Whitley, 20; flight engineer, Sgt Harvey Pyche, 21; flight engineer, Sgt William Ferguson, 19; wireless operator/gunner, Sgt Calvin Whittingstall, 20; gunner, Sgt Donald Titt, 19; and gunner, Sgt George Riddoch, 20. All were Canadian except Sgt Ferguson, who was a Scot.

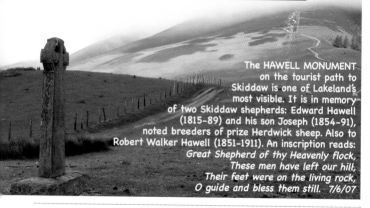

The HAWELL MONUMENT
on the tourist path to
Skiddaw is one of Lakeland's
most visible. It is in memory
of two Skiddaw shepherds: Edward Hawell
(1815–89) and his son Joseph (1854–91),
noted breeders of prize Herdwick sheep. Also to
Robert Walker Hawell (1851-1911). An inscription reads:
Great Shepherd of thy Heavenly flock,
These men have left our hill,
Their feet were on the living rock,
O guide and bless them still. 7/6/07

CROSSES MARK LOSSES

The story of the large white cross in the saddle at the summit of **Blencathra** is fully revealed in AW's chapter on the fell: *Formerly there was a very small cross of stones here (locally ascribed as a memorial to a walker who lost his life on a rough slope adjacent) and Mr*

THEN: How AW drew the white cross.

NOW: It's much bulkier. 17/5/10

[Harold] *Robinson, an enthusiastic lone hill-wanderer who has climbed his favourite Blencathra hundreds of times, collected more stones . . . and extended the cross to its present size of 16' by 10' during a succession of visits from 1945 onwards. The cross has grown (in bulk, if not in overall size) since* AW made his drawing, as the comparison (above) shows.

The Blencathra stone white cross is well known, but not as much as the prominent upright white cross just below Low Raven Crag on **Fleetwith Pike** in full view of traffic going up (or down) Honister Pass. An inscription reads: *Erected by friends of Fanny Mercer. Accidentally killed, 1887.* It is most likely she fell from a crag while descending.

Sixteen years later, the worst single mountain tragedy to hit Lakeland occurred on **Scafell**. On 21 September 1903 four rock climbers – Richard Broadrick from Windermere and three Yorkshiremen, Algernon Garrett, Henry Lupp and Stanley Ridsdale – died when they fell from Scafell Pinnacle. Broadrick is buried in his home town, the other three in the churchyard at St Olaf's, Wasdale Head. At the foot of the Pinnacle a stone cross is carved into the wall of the crag, along with the initials of the four men.

ROBINSON'S CAIRN: On the northern face of
Pillar, offering a sensational view of Pillar Rock.
On a nearby rock is a tablet bearing a
beautifully worded inscription. AW didn't quote it.
It reads:

> *For remembrance of John Wilson Robinson of*
> *Whinfell Hall in Lorton who died 1907 at*
> *Brigham. One hundred of his comrades and*
> *friends raised this. He knew and loved as none*
> *other these native crags and fells whence he*
> *drew simplicity, strength and charm.*
> *We climb the hills from end to end,*
> *Of all the landscape underneath,*
> *We find no place that does not breathe,*
> *Some gracious memory of our friend.* 17/9/08

BANKES TAKES A BASHING: When AW
worked on BOOK SEVEN, between 1963
and 1965, the John Bankes' memorial stone
on Grey Knotts (drawing, left) was in far
better condition than it is now (right).
Thanks to the wear and tear of age, part
of 'Bankes' is missing, as is the date. But at
least it's still there. By the way, efquier =
esquire. 15/6/09

Two more very important Lakeland memorials...

***At Orrest Head, the view indicator
reads:*** *'That day on Orrest Head
changed my life.' (A. Wainwright). Your
climb to this viewpoint at Orrest Head
follows in the footsteps of well-known
walker and author Alfred Wainwright.*
16/4/08

***At Buttermere Church, the plaque
reads:*** *Pause and remember Alfred
Wainwright. Fellwalker, guide book
author and illustrator who loved
this valley. Lift your eyes to Haystacks,
his favourite place. 1907-1991.*
4/10/10

THIS WAY UP

What drove AW to seek out the rough, remote and challenging lines of ascent . . . and then climb them?

LONG WAY DOWN: *Looking back on Loweswater, Crummock Water and Lanthwaite Hill from the fearsome Grasmoor direct route.*

13/1/12

270

One of the truly remarkable things about the first seven guidebooks is the number of 'off-piste' ascents AW made. He could quite easily have produced seven wonderful books based based on the way to the tops via the established paths and tracks and the old drove, mine and corpse roads, but he didn't; he could quite easily have taken the view that a man in his advancing years shouldn't be scrambling over rocks or up steep, slippery scree, but he didn't.

However, it's not surprising if you think about it. He was a 'map' man; he loved poring over the Ordnance Survey's finest. If there was a ridge or a hanging valley or a gill that looked as though it might lead to a summit it wouldn't have escaped AW's forensic eye. And he liked peace and solitude, which he was far more likely to find on a quiet side valley than on the Wasdale Head tourist path to Sty Head or the Grisedale Tarn route up Helvellyn from Grasmere.

As the PICTORIAL GUIDES were published one after another, I can imagine the excitement they generated, but it's doubtful that readers at the time really put them into context: here was a man well past the midpoint of his life climbing and clambering up Lakeland's steep and rugged places as if he was a 19-year-old; here was a man not only putting his 6ft, 14-stone frame through the special torture that is Jack's Rake (at 6ft 2ins and over 200lbs I can testify that the Spanish Inquisition would have loved this little baby in their armoury!) but also taking on some very challenging ascents without the

WHAT? NO JACK'S RAKE?

This is a chapter about 'off-piste' routes. The climb up Pavey Ark (clamber might be a better word) is a well-established path (if you can call it that!). More on Jack's Rake on pages 94-95.

The best of the wild ways

A mixture of steep ridges, rough scrambles and ingenious routes through rock scenery.

Dollywaggon Pike 7: Eastern flank, up narrowing ridge (The Tongue).
Fairfield 7: Link Cove and Greenhow End.
Hart Crag 6: Link Cove again – Hart Crag's *inner sanctuary.*
Nethermost Pike 6: Mirror image of Dollywaggon Pike ridge, but even better.
Ill Bell 5: Steep scramble up north-east ridge from Kentmere Reservoir.
Mardale Ill Bell 5: East and north ridges beside two of the best tarns in Lakeland (Small Water, Blea Water).
Eagle Crag 3-4: Direct ascent; very clever route finding.
Harrison Stickle 8: Scenic scramble up Dungeon Ghyll - see page 288.
Sergeant Man 6: Surprising shelf.
Dow Crag 3: Picking the brains of rock climbers - see page 273.
Great End 6: Branch Gully, scramble.
Bannerdale Crags 6: East ridge – scramble up narrowing arête.
Blencathra 12: Blease Gill. AW's famous wild-west 'gulch'.
Blencathra 20: Doddick Gill. *A route to recommend heartily to one's worst enemy.*
Lonscale Fell 5: North-east buttress. Steep final tower; surprisingly easy.
Skiddaw Little Man 8: South-west arête. Steep scramble; exhilarating.
Barf 6: Straight up rough frontage.
Dale Head 6: Clever route past old mines.
Eel Crag 7-8: Choice of ascents: Tower Ridge and Shelf Route.
Grasmoor 6: Direct route (picture on facing page) - see next page.
High Crag 6: Steep route from Burtness Comb via Sheepbone Rake.
High Stile 8: Also from Burtness Comb, via rocky north-east ridge.

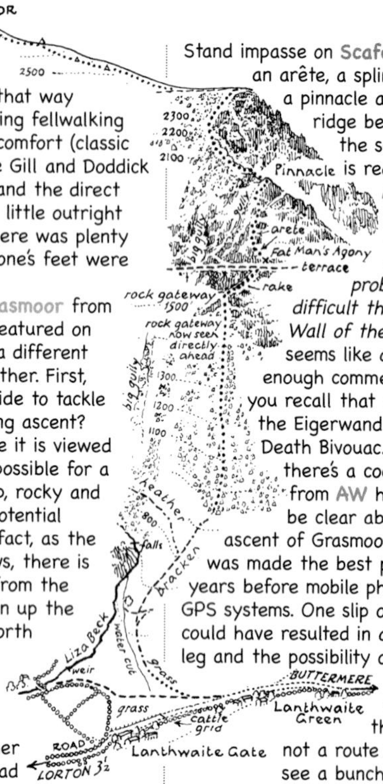

comforting (!) knowledge that someone had been that way before. This pioneering fellwalking meant plenty of discomfort (classic examples are Blease Gill and Doddick Gill on **Blencathra** and the direct ascent of Barf) but little outright danger, providing there was plenty of watching where one's feet were going, of course.

The ascent of Grasmoor from Lanthwaite Green, featured on Grasmoor 6, was a different kettle of fish altogether. First, what made AW decide to tackle this fearsome-looking ascent? From whatever angle it is viewed it just doesn't look possible for a fellwalker: too steep, rocky and rough, and full of potential (unseen) danger. In fact, as the diagram (right) shows, there is an ingenious route from the base of the mountain up the ridge dividing the north and west faces. It involves scree, a rock gateway, a terrace, a fat man's agony (there's another of these on the Broad

Stand impasse on Scafell), a rake, an arête, a splintered crag, a pinnacle and a curving ridge before (at last) the summit plateau is reached. AW famously describes the climb as On the whole . . . probably less difficult than the North Wall of the Eiger, which seems like a flippant enough comment – until you recall that a location on the Eigerwand is called Death Bivouac. I think there's a coded message from AW here. And let's be clear about this – his ascent of Grasmoor direct was made the best part of 40 years before mobile phones and GPS systems. One slip on this climb could have resulted in a fractured leg and the possibility of something far more serious than that – it was not a route likely to see a bunch of fellow

Diagram labels:
GRASMOOR
2500
2300
2200
2100
Pinnacle
arête
Fat Man's Agony
terrace
rake
rock gateway
1500
rock gateway
Now seen directly ahead
1300
1200
1100
Dove Gill
800
falls
bracken
Liza Beck
weir
grass
BUTTERMERE
Lanthwaite Green
water cut
cattle grid
ROAD
Lanthwaite Gate
LORTON 3½

THREE RIDGES: Perhaps it was this view from St Sunday Crag that gave AW the inspiration for the two direct climbs of Dollywaggon Pike and Nethermost Pike via their eastern ridges. He thought both climbs were the best way up the two fells.
12/10/10

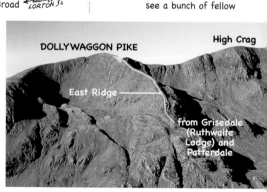

DOLLYWAGGON PIKE
High Crag
East Ridge
from Grisedale (Ruthwaite Lodge) and Patterdale

The ascent of Dow Crag via **South Rake**, the scree-filled way up beneath the foot of the fell's massive crag, is unique in that it is the only way up in the guidebooks described in the 'natural features' section of the chapter. A look at the pictures here reveals it's very much a *Jack's Rake lite*, even though it's steep and rocky enough for the tastes of most scramblers.

LEFT: A steep descent looking back towards a misty Goat's Water. 20/7/10
RIGHT: The climb is rough all the way, but safe with care. 22/9/08

walkers strolling along a few minutes later. If the worst had happened the remains of an intrepid walker and author most probably wouldn't have been found for many months, and we would have been left with a half-finished BOOK SIX and a never-started BOOK SEVEN. Chris Jesty would have had to compile that from scratch!

It is climbs such as Grasmoor Direct that add yet another layer of excellence and interest to the guidebooks; such pages stand out like beacons among the more established ascents as evidence that there is far more to Lakeland than dusty tourist paths and crowds of people.

This individualism is probably why AW loved 'striding-out' places such as the **High Street** range and just about any walk among THE OUTLYING FELLS (except, perhaps, poor Ponsonby Fell!). The off-piste routes he sought out and climbed are another reason why his eight great Lakeland guidebooks have never been matched – and are never likely to be.

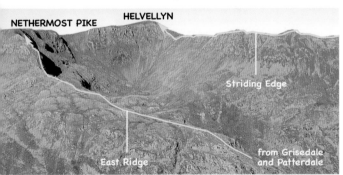

HELVELLYN
NETHERMOST PIKE
Striding Edge
East Ridge
from Grisedale and Patterdale

273

PASTORAL CHARMS

Lakeland's valley floors add much to its amazing beauty

The title of this section – THE HAND OF MAN – suggests some brutal treatment of Lakeland's glorious landscape by people determined to make a fast buck or two (and of that there has been plenty; we'll come on to that later). But it can also refer to the human influences that have shaped the Jaws of Borrowdale, the Curve of Great Langdale, the Head of Ullswater . . . the pastoral valley floors that contrast so dramatically with the crags and the waterfalls and the peaks high above. This, of course, was summed up by AW on page 4 of the Castle Crag chapter – the now-famous 'thick black line' map that must surely have been a labour of love, and about which he wrote: *The thick line forming a square has a special significance. It encloses one mile of country containing no high mountain, no lake, no famous crag, no tarn. But, in the author's humble submission, it encloses the loveliest square mile in Lakeland – the Jaws of Borrowdale.*

He listed seven other lovely square miles (all eight shown, below left), one more of which was in Borrowdale (Lodore-Ashness) and another just off the main valley (the Stonethwaite Valley), the start of which is right in the middle of the picture above. This was taken from Castle Crag looking south-east, and the distinctive shape of Eagle Crag can be seen further up the valley.

Personally, I'm surprised that AW only chose eight lovely square miles. It must surely have pained him to have omitted the **Newlands Valley** (Little

8 LOVELY SQUARE MILES

(and the books in which they feature)

The Jaws of **Borrowdale**
The Stonethwaite Valley
The head of Ullswater
Tilberthwaite to Brathay
Dovedale
Around Ry**dal Water**
The Buttermere Valley

274

THE MOST
BEAUTIFUL
OF VALLEYS:
A lot of
lovers of
Lakeland
would say
Borrowdale
was the top
valley – in
terms of
scenery – in
the district.
The view
from Castle
Crag to the
village of
Rosthwaite
(left) might
confirm that.
7/3/07
BELOW: Part
of the 'thick
black line'
map from
the Castle
Crag chapter
– the
loveliest
square mile
in Lakeland.

Town to Stair), about which he was so fulsome in his praise in the *personal notes* in BOOK SIX; **Martindale**, about which he was so enthusiastic in BOOK TWO; and the very lovely **Vale of Lorton**, (*sweet Lorton*), BOOK SIX.

There's no doubt that the idyllic beauty of the valley floors adds to the charm of the Lake District. All good there – but higher up the fells the noble hills bear the scars of an industry that didn't add to the beauty of Lakeland.

turn the page (if you can stand to) for the bad & ugly

275

SCARS OF THE MINES

The centuries man spent taking metal and minerals from the rocks of Lakeland have resulted in hundreds of caves and levels and quarries and unsightly spoil heaps all over the district – which is bad, yet, in a strange way, these scars of industry all add to the charm.

Somehow, they've made Coniston Old Man and its satellites prouder and stronger – as if shrugging off the injustice of having **Coppermines Valley** (above) spoil their foothills has only made them more determined to flaunt their beauty and charm; somehow they've made the disused **Force Crag Mine** beside Grisedale Pike seem a perfectly natural part of the local landscape – a kind of monument to man's insignificance in the greater scheme of things; somehow the **Honister Slate Mine** below Fleetwith Pike is a much better place now it has been reopened as Lakeland's only working mine rather than remaining a sad shadow of its former 'glory'. There is no 'somehow' about how the **Greenburn Lead Mine** beside Glenridding Beck and below **Sheffield Pike** (featured on pages 214-215) is now a great place to visit . . . This is the 'hand of man' at its most forgiving; the remnants of a once-thriving industrial operation that closed in 1962 have been reinvigorated now that the old mine buildings have been converted into a youth hostel, a bothy and an outdoor pursuits centre.

You can find mine workings and associated structures all across Lakeland; here's a breakdown of the main ones: **Dollywaggon Pike**: Copper mine, lead levels; **Raise, Sheffield Pike**: Greenburn lead mine. **Caudale Moor**: Caudale quarry; **Sour Howes**: Applethwaite quarry; **Wether Hill** and **Yoke**: Both quarries; Pavey Ark: Dam on Stickle Tarn; **Brim Fell**: Dam on Levers Water; Coniston Old Man, Brim Fell, Swirl How, Wetherlam: Coppermines Valley; Dow Crag: Blind Tarn quarry, Banishead quarry; Great Carrs, Swirl How: Greenburn copper works; Lingmoor Fell: Quarries; Wetherlam: Caves, levels; **Bannerdale Crags**: Lead mine; **Blencathra**: Gategill mine; **Carrock Fell**: Carrock mine; **Great Sca Fell, High Pike, Knott**: Roughtongill lead mines; Castle Crag: Quarry and levels; Catbells: Three disused mines; Dale Head: Copper mines and quarries; Grisedale Pike: Force Crag mine; High Spy: Rigghead quarries, Castlenook mine; Hindscarth: Goldscope mine; Fleetwith Pike: Honister quarries and slate mine; Grey Knotts: Plumbago mine; Haystacks: Dubs quarry; Whitbarrow: Iron ore drift mine; Walna Scar: Banishead quarry; Caw: Level and quarry.

SCOURGE OF THE FELLS

Not much can be said about people who wantonly destroy – except that they are the ugly face of Lakeland. The fools who leave litter on the fells are bad enough; the idiots who think it's cool to destroy the artistic labours of someone else are just morons – and that's being kind. To the right is an example of what I mean. The top picture is the drawing of the splendid summit cairn on Hallin Fell. AW called it a *permanent memorial* to its creator. A fat chance, as he was to find out two guidebooks later following the fate that befell the summit cairns of Lingmell and Pike o'Blisco. The photo above right shows the cairn on Hallin Fell as it is these days (30/5/07). The red line (right) shows the amount the cairn has diminished in 50 years thanks to people who think it's a good idea to remove or steal a stone or two from the cairn. Here's a message to them: you're not wanted in Lakeland – get lost (and don't bother taking a compass or GPS).

SHRUGGING OFF THE SCARS: Coppermines Valley (above) remains an eyesore, but the strength and beauty of the fells around and above it far outweigh the unsightly nature of its immediate environs. 15/11/07 *BELOW: A copper level on Wetherlam.*

277

FEATS FOR FEET...

Why the ancient routes across the mountains still have a significance in the age of the automobile

Esk Hause, Sty Head, Sticks Pass, Grisedale Hause, Coledale Hause, Garburn Pass, Walna Scar, Nan Bield, Black Sail . . . these Lakeland passes read like a list of mystical destinations on the way to higher objectives. The passes of Lakeland hold special significance for walkers, just as they did for traders and farmers and smugglers through the centuries before the arrival of paved roads and, later, motorised transport. These are key places high up in the fells where, in mist and without a compass, one false turn could lead to a weary walker arriving in the wrong valley. Which is why throughout the PICTORIAL GUIDES AW goes to great pains to make it clear where each path leads – particularly when there is a localised problem such as the 'false' Esk Hause or the Wythburn valley (from Greenup Edge), which can easily give the impression that it leads to Grasmere (it doesn't).

This chapter identifies all the important routes in the guidebooks that could be described as a pass (usually ending in the words *pass* or *hause/hawse*), and looks at what AW had to say about all of these routes. NOTE: It could help you NOT get lost on the fells one day!

BOOK BY BOOK: All the key passes across the fells

Grisedale Hause: A complicated pass on the southern flank of **Dollywaggon Pike** close to **Fairfield**, **St Sunday Crag** and **Seat Sandal**. A path from Grasmere-Patterdale crosses here (the Coast To Coast Walk), as do well-trod paths from St Sunday Crag and Fairfield to Dollywaggon Pike/Seat Sandal.

Deepdale Hause: Depression between **Fairfield** and **St Sunday Crag** with a path across the flank of Cofa Pike linking to Grisedale Tarn and nearby Grisedale Hause.

Scandale Pass: A little-used pass between Scandale (south-west) and

THE BEST ZIGZAGS IN LAKELAND: Above, the perfect Nan Bield Pass built for packhorses. (19/4/10) Compare this to the awful modern equivalent on Sail (right) leading up from Sail Pass. 2/6/11

These zig-zags are delightful

Caiston Beck (north-east).

The Hause: Motor road (above 1200ft) on the south side of Great Mell Fell.

Sticks Pass: So named because wooden posts used to mark the (now little-used) route between Stanah and Glenridding. At 2420ft it's the highest pass in Lakeland (so AW says; more on that later). Nearby fells are Raise and Stybarrow Dodd.

Boredale Hause: Important depression between Place Fell and Angletarn Pikes, carrying paths between Patterdale and Boredale/Martindale.

Garburn Pass: Historic 'road' between Troutbeck and Kentmere, passing just

north of summit of Sallows.

Gatesgarth Pass: An ancient link between Mardale and Longsleddale, well made with plenty of zigzags. Major depression between Harter Fell and Branstree.

Low Moss: Important 'crossroads' at a depression on Place Fell (the Mecca of lost pilgrims on the extensive north-eastern slopes).

Nan Bield Pass: AW's favourite pass, scenically (The sharp-crested Nan Bield is the finest of Lakeland passes); see above. It links Mardale and the Kentmere Valley and is a major depression between Harter Fell and

AND SOLID SLOPES FOR MOTOR VEHICLES

Kirkstone Pass is the Lakeland's highest pass (1489ft) that is open to motor traffic. The A592 connects Ambleside and Patterdale and peaks at the Kirkstone Pass Inn (no drinking and driving, please); it is where BOOK ONE and BOOK TWO link. The two toughest passes for drivers are generally thought to be **Hardknott Pass** and **Wrynose Pass** – both are in sight of each other and (rather amazingly) both summit at 1289ft. **Honister Pass** (Buttermere-Borrowdale) is 1168ft, and is the closest link between fells in BOOK SIX and BOOK SEVEN. **Newlands Hause** (Newlands Valley-Buttermere, the quickest way from Keswick to the Buttermere Valley) is 1093ft. **Whinlatter Pass** (Braithwaite-Cockermouth) is 1043ft.

Mardale Ill Bell.

Stile End-Sadgill: South of Shipman Knotts, this is a cart track linking Kentmere and Longsleddale.

Threshthwaite Mouth: A depression between Thornthwaite Crag and Caudale Moor, linking the Troutbeck Valley and Pasture Beck (leading to Hartsop).

Greenup Edge: A pass, at just over 2000ft, linking Borrowdale with Grasmere (via Far Easedale), and with Thirlmere (via Wythburn). Confusing in mist. Best described in AW's A COAST TO COAST WALK (page 26, the Wythburn trap), also Ullscarf 10. Depression between High Raise and Ullscarf.

High Tove: The summit (1690ft) acts as a pass between Watendlath and Thirlmere, the shortest way across Lakeland's central ridge. AW writes: *This oddity arises because the depressions either side are not only insignificant but even wetter than the way over the top.*

Stake Pass: Ancient an important pass (1576ft) linking Borrowdale (via Langstrath) with Great Langdale. Depression between Pike o'Stickle and Rossett Pike.

Three passes: All linking Grasmere and Great Langdale in the vicinity of Chapel Stile, all crossing Silver How (two paths, one road via Red Bank). See Silver How 3 and 9.

Burnmoor Pass: Not named, but featured in the Ill Crag and Scafell maps. Highest point on route between Wasdale Head and mid-Eskdale.

Esk Hause: One of the most important (and confusing) passes in Lakeland, on a tilted shelf between Esk Pike, Great End and Allen Crags (see facing page).

Goat's Hawse: More of a col than a pass. Between Dow Crag and Coniston Old Man.

Red Tarn: Depression between Cold Pike and Pike o'Blisco; a route between Great Langdale and Wrynose Pass and a popular way of ascending Crinkle Crags.

Rossett Pass: Well-used way from Mickleden (Great Langdale) to Esk Hause and Scafell Pike. Features the infamous Rossett Gill (see Rossett Pike chapter).

Sty Head Pass: One of the busiest and most important walkers passes in Lakeland. Between Great End and Great Gable, it is a crossroads of routes from Borrowdale, Wasdale, Great Langdale and the Corridor Route to Scafell Pike. Details on Great End 5, where AW writes . . . *it is doubtful whether Sty Head is without a visitor on any day of any year* [this was the assessment in 1959, remember]; *and on most days scores, and, in high summer, hundreds of walkers pass this way.*

Swirl Hawse: Between Swirl How and Wetherlam, and a little-used link from Little Langdale to Coniston. AW was partial to this depression: *Swirl Hawse is true mountain pass, a neat and narrow defile with a small summit marked by a big cairn.*

Three Tarns: A 2320ft depression between Bowfell and Crinkle Crags, crossed by a path from Great Langdale to Eskdale.

Walna Scar Pass: Highest point of an ancient 'road' from Coniston to Seathwaite in the Duddon Valley. Between south ridge of Dow Crag and Walna Scar, the highest of THE OUTLYING FELLS. In recent years, efforts have been resisted to

FAMOUS NAMES: A sign at the head of Mickleden, looking to Rossett Pass, another legendary crossing. 4/6/09

Ridge to ESK PIKE

2490ft The real Esk Hause

GREAT END

2386ft The false Esk Hause

Ridge to ALLEN CRAGS

THE MOST CONFUSING PASS IN LAKELAND: But hopefully not if you memorise this view from Rossett Pike of the 'two' Esk Hauses. 11/2/10

ESK HAUSE: IT NEEDED TWO PAGES TO EXPLAIN

Two pages of BOOK FOUR are devoted to a description of Esk Hause in the Esk Pike chapter, including a drawing that shows – as does the picture above – the curious lie of the land, accompanied by a succinct explanation of this tilted grass plateau high in the hills . . . *two passes have their summits on the plateau . . . If these routes crossed at the highest point of the plateau there would be a simple 'crossroads', but they do not: one is a hundred feet higher than the other and 300 yards distant.* The real Esk Hause, the higher pass, is a shallow depression between Great End and Esk Pike and is the highest point on a path between Borrowdale and Eskdale; the false Esk Hause, a much busier pass, is the depression between the real Esk Hause and Allen Crags, and is the much-used path between Great Langdale and Wasdale.

FALSE SUMMIT: The cross-shaped shelter marks the (2386ft) summit of the false Esk Hause. The picture is taken looking towards Allen Crags. 17/10/06

Incidentally: It's clear that the false Esk Hause (2386ft) has almost assumed the real title. How else would you explain why Sticks Pass (2420ft) is said to be the highest pass in Lakeland (even by AW, it has to be pointed out, in the Stybarrow Dodd chapter), when the real Esk Hause (2490ft) tops it by 70ft?

designate this route as a BOAT (byway open to all traffic), in effect opening it to 4x4 vehicles. Well done the National Park!

Glenderamackin col: High-level crossing between three Bs: **Bowscale Fell, Blencathra** and **Bannerdale Crags.**

Trusmadoor: A gap between **Meal Fell** and **Great Cockup** carrying paths

from Longlands and Orthwaite. Hardly significant, but AW clearly likes it: *The neat little pass of Trusmadoor is the Piccadilly Circus of sheep in that locality, a busy thoroughfare in popular use when changing pastures, progression always being in parties, and in single file. The place is also well known to the shepherds and their*

FROM PASS TO PASS ... VIA A TRAVERSE

ASCENT FROM ENNERDALE
(BLACK SAIL YOUTH HOSTEL)

BECK HEAD: From the slopes of Great Gable looking to Kirk Fell and, in the distance, Pillar. The path linking Beck Head with Black Sail Pass runs below Boat How Crags (right edge of Kirk Fell).   4/11/08

Kirk Fell is at the centre of a strange Lakeland phenomenon – a traverse linking two passes. Usually a fell occupies the ground between passes and thus must be crossed to get from one to the other. But, as the ascent of Kirk Fell shows (above), a path on the north flank links **Beck Head** and **Black Sail Pass**, bypassing the mountain.

dogs, and to various species of mutton-eating birds that hover morbidly overhead, waiting for somebody to die.

Coledale Hause: A high-level crossing of the north-west fells between Braithwaite and Lanthwaite Green at a point where four nearby mountains – Eel Crag, Grasmoor, Grisdale Pike and Hopegill Head – all turn their backs on the pass.

Hause Gate: The depression between Catbells and Maiden Moor is also a way over the ridge between Newlands (Little Town) and Borrowdale (Manesty and Grange).

Rigg Head: A significant depression between High Spy and Dale Head that carries two paths from Newlands (both from Little Town) to Honister Pass and to Borrowdale at Seatoller (variation to Rosthwaite).

Rigg Beck: More of a high-level valley walk, linking Newlands (Keskadale) with Buttermere to the north of the Ard Crags–Knott Rigg ridge; part of this route also links with . . .

Sail Pass: A named coined by AW to describe the depression between Scar

Crags and Sail crossed by a path from Stair (Newlands) and one from Braithwaite (via Barrow Door or Low Moss) that links with Buttermere using part of the Rigg Beck route.

Beck Head: Big drop between Kirk Fell and Great Gable carrying the Moses' Trod path (Honister to Wasdale). See above for its interesting link to . . .

Black Sail Pass: Between Kirk Fell and Pillar carrying path from Mosedale (Wasdale Head) to Black Sail Youth Hostel (Ennerdale), then on to Scarth Gap and Buttermere.

Floutern Pass: Between Great Borne and Gavel Fell, a seldom-used crossing from Ennerdale Bridge to both Buttermere and Loweswater.

Gillercomb Head: Best crossing from Borrowdale to Ennerdale; see Grey Knotts chapter.

Scarth Gap: Links Buttermere Valley with Ennerdale. Between High Crag and Haystacks.

Windy Gap: Crossing between Great Gable and Green Gable linking head of Ennerdale with Sty Head Pass (details on page 280).

Birks Bridge

AW just loved his
stone bridges – and
here's the evidence

RIGHT OUT
OF THE TOP DRAW

DUDDON'S FINEST: Birks Bridge looks absolutely splendid in the June summer sunshine. 4/6/10 Inset: Drawing in the Harter Fell (BOOK FOUR) chapter.

It took 22 years – from the first completed page of BOOK ONE on 9 November 1952, until the publication of THE OUTLYING FELLS OF LAKELAND in 1974 – before AW really waxed lyrical about a stone bridge. That's not to say we didn't know how much he liked them; from the number of drawings that appeared in the guidebooks it's clear he had a soft spot for a bit of well-crafted stone.

The Low Pike 4 page in BOOK ONE should have given the game away. And if the penny hadn't dropped by then, how about the dedication to BOOK TWO . . . *to the memory of the men who built the stone walls, which have endured the storms of centuries and remain to this day as monuments to enterprise, perseverance and hard work.* The stone walls are, of course, a wonderful part of the fabric of Lakeland – the man-made ingredient that binds the landscape together. However, continuing the metaphors, the packhorse bridges are another thing altogether – the icing on the stone cake.

The bridge drawn on page 4 of the **Low Pike** chapter is **High Sweden Bridge**, a magical place on a summer's day. The first time I saw this bridge was the first time I walked the

FAVOURITE: Matty Benn's Bridge.

Fairfield Horseshoe (possibly the most overrated ridge 'round' in Lakeland, in my opinion); it was a sultry June morning with verdant bracken shimmering like emerald gemstones on the fellsides and Scandale Beck gurgling and twinkling in the speckled sunlight. To be honest, it was very difficult to press on up the steepening ridge to Low Pike; High Sweden Bridge

LINGCOVE BRIDGE: 21/5/07

HIGH SWEDEN BRIDGE: 9/6/06

ASHNESS BRIDGE: 22/10/9

on a perfect day is one of those places where it's almost impossible to leave.

I'm sure you all have your favourite stone bridge; **Lingcove** in Eskdale, perhaps. Or maybe the beautiful **Ashness** or **Watendlath** or iconic **Stockley**. AW's was the little-known **Matty Benn's Bridge** way out on the western edge of Lakeland. In the Cold Fell chapter of THE OUTLYING FELLS he calls it *the most charming of Lakeland's packhorse bridges*. On the facing page is a drawing. And he really did love this bridge – there are two drawings of it in the Lank Rigg chapter as well.

STOCKLEY BRIDGE: 26/6/07

COVE BRIDGE: 12/12/11

GO WITH THE FLOW

When it came to running water, AW was a pen-and-ink genius – and a great explorer

Just like tarns, a waterfall can be a highlight of a Lakeland ascent – and AW recognised this by drawing a total of 88 in his eight guidebooks, six of which each occupied a whole page. However, he didn't just sketch the usual suspects – **Aira Force**, **Sourmilk Gill** (the Easedale version; there are three with this name), **Taylorgill Force**, etc – but sought out shy cascades hidden by trees or ravines, many of them without names.

As with tarns, I suppose we've all got our favourites. If you've ever had a holiday based in Buttermere you probably will be partial to the three splendid waterfalls nestled among the skirts of Red Pike – **Far Ruddy Beck**, **Scale Force** (Lakeland's highest not far from the wettest path) and **Sourmilk Gill** – which make Red Pike the fell with the most named waterfalls in separate locations (different streams). Many tourists only ever see the likes of **Aira Force**, **Stockghyll Force** and **Lodore Falls**, but personally, I prefer waterfalls away from the low-level trails. I remember one scorching July day descending from one of my favourite walks (Wall End, Pike o'Blisco, Crinkle Crags, Bowfell, the Great Slab, Climber's Traverse, Hell Gill) and arriving at **Whorneyside Force** at about three in the afternoon . . . hot, bothered and dusty. There is a beautiful circular pool some 20ft in diameter at the base of the main cascade that just begs to be

LITTLE AND LARGE: Tiny sketch (ringed red), on Haycock, and full-page of The Forces, Howes, an outlying fell.

MILKING THE MOMENT: *The amazing Sourmilk Gill in Easedale, still flowing while all around it is ice and snow.*
30/11/10

BELOW: *Drawing in the Tarn Crag (Book Three) chapter showing the full extent of the waterfalls. The portion of the falls occupies just the top third of the sketch.*

swum in, and I wasn't about to disappoint it. These are the days you remember; the ones where something special stands out – such as a sudden parting of the clouds on a misty ridge to reveal a sun-drenched valley far below; or turning a corner to see a vision of an unexpectedly blue tarn. But even better are the days when you seek out something different. What is behind that rocky tor? Does that grassy shelf offer a new way up? Is that ravine worth checking out?

One ravine that AW did deem worthy of investigation was **Dungeon Ghyll**, on the southern flank of the Langdale Pikes overlooking the business end of Great Langdale. That's

not strictly correct, because Dungeon Ghyll's zig-zagging ravine is so deeply sunk into the fellside that you can't see what's in it from ground level; so it could hardly be overlooking anything, could it! In fact, it's not that easy to see into it even from the best vantage point of the Langdales, Lingmoor Fell, the other side of the valley. There was only one thing AW could do when it came to BOOK THREE – he had to boldly go where no man (well, perhaps no guidebook writer from Blackburn at any rate) had gone before, and find out the secrets of the deep valley that gave its name to two hotels on the valley floor below.

He discovered that beyond the

SECOND OBSTACLE
Choke of boulders in floor of ravine

INSET PICTURE TAKEN FROM HERE: Looking in the direction of the arrow. 21/4/09

FIRST OBSTACLE
40ft cascade

DUNGEON GHYLL RAVINE: The middle section, seen from Lingmoor Fell. 19/8/10

frequently visited **Dungeon Ghyll Force** at the lower end of the ravine (out of picture below right of the main photo above) was a **40ft cascade** (clearly seen at the foot of the inset picture above), which he dubbed the *First Obstacle*. This is avoided by taking the steep slope to its left after which the ravine may be rejoined. A little further up (about three-quarters of the way up the inset photo) is the *Second Obstacle*, a choke of big boulders through which, with trial and error, a way may be found. The *Third Obstacle* is around the left bend of the ravine (out of sight in inset photo), *a beautiful 50ft waterfall*, which ends the ravine, with an exit up a steep rib or gully to the left.

All this is revealed on Harrison Stickle 8. The upper waterfall is visible from the Pike Howe route, and AW describes it as *certainly one of the most attractive in Lakeland*. He drew it (above right). If you want to see it in

THE 50ft WATERFALL: Getting here will require scrambling, says AW.

all its glory (and not just from the flank of Pike Howe) you'll have to get stuck into the ravine. Go on, you know you want to! Reward yourself with a refreshing glass of something on your return to one of the hotels below.

THE PEN DOESN'T LIE: Two views of Aira Force: an AW classic and a great Sean picture. 22/9/11

FLOWING DRAWINGS
BOOK BY BOOK

Dollywaggon Pike: Ruthwaite; **Dove Crag:** Dove Falls; **Fairfield:** Tongue Gill; **Gowbarrow Fell:** Aira Force, High Force; **Great Rigg:** Greenhead Gill; **Helvellyn:** Helvellyn Gill, Whelpside Gill; **Nethermost Pike:** Birkside Gill (x3); **St Sunday Crag:** Coldcove Gill; **Seat Sandal:** Raise Beck; **Stybarrow Dodd:** Stanah Gill; **White Side:** Brund Gill, Fisherplace Gill (x2).

Gray Crag: Haweswater Gill; **High Raise:** Whelter Beck; **Mardale Ill Bell:** Dodderwick Force, River Kent; **Wansfell:** Stockghyll Force; **Wether Hill:** Hawes Beck, Measand Beck.

Armboth Fell: Launchy Gill (x2); **Calf Crag:** Far Easedale Gill; **Harrison Stickle:** Dungeon Ghyll (x2); **High Seat:** Ashness Gill; **Silver How:** Megs Gill; **Steel Fell:** Greenburn Valley; **Tarn Crag:** Sourmilk Gill; **Ullscarf:** Wythburn Valley; **Walla Crag:** Cat Gill.

Bowfell: Browney Gill, Hell Gill, Whorneyside Force; **Coniston Old Man:** Church Beck; **Glaramara:** Tray Dub; **Great Carrs:** Greenburn Beck; **Hard Knott:** Lingcove Beck; **Scafell Pike:** Taylorgill Force.

Bakestall: Dash Falls (x2); **Blencathra:** Roughten Gill (x2); **High Pike:** Roughton Gill (x2); **Great Sca Fell:** Roughton Gill; **Mungrisdale Common:** Sinen Gill; **Skiddaw Little Man:** Whit Beck; **Souther Fell:** River Glenderamackin.

Eel Crag: Rannerdale Beck; **Grasmoor:** Cinderdale Beck (x3); **Graystones:** Spout Force; **Grisedale Pike:** High Force, Low Force; **Hindscarth:** Little Beck; **Maiden Moor:** Ellers Beck; **Robinson:** Moss Force; **Whiteside:** Gasgale Gill (x2).

Base Brown: Sourmilk Gill (x2), Taylorgill Force; **Burnbank Fell:** Holme Force; **Grey Knotts:** Hause Gill; **Haycock:** Nether Beck (x2); **Kirk Fell:** Sail Beck; **Middle Fell:** Nether Beck, Tongues Gills (x2); **Red Pike (B):** Far Ruddy Beck, Scale Force, Sourmilk Gill; **Starling Dodd:** Red Gill; **Steeple:** High Beck; **Yewbarrow:** Ritson's Force.

Walna Scar: The Big Hole (Banishead Quarry); **Stainton Pike:** Rowantree Force; **Howes:** The Forces (x3); **The Wet Sleddale Horseshoe:** Sleddale Beck.

A NORTHERN SOUL

Skiddaw

This, then, is Skiddaw, a giant in stature. But an affable and friendly one.

And a benevolent one. Keswick people have an inborn affection for Skiddaw, and it is well earned. The mountain makes a great contribution to the scenic beauty of this most attractively-situated town, shelters it from northerly gales, supplies it with pure water, feeds its sheep, and provides a recreation ground for its visitors. Throughout the centuries Skiddaw's beacon has warned of the town's troubles and alarms – "the red glare on Skiddaw raised the burghers of Carlisle" – and today shares in its rejoicings.

Skiddaw's critics have passed on, or will soon pass on. Their span of life is short. Skiddaw has stood there in supreme majesty, the sole witness to the creation of Lakeland, for millions of years and will be there to the end of time, continuing to give service and pleasure to the insignificant and unimportant mortals.

Let us at least be grateful.

MAJESTIC: Skiddaw (above Keswick and the morning mist), seen from Catbells.   1/11/10

AN ENGLISH LESSON

The extract from BOOK FOUR shown on the facing page comes from the Bowfell chapter and describes the ascent via The Band. It is not in the second edition of the book because the footpath variation went out of fashion sometime between 1959 and 2008. It's a pity because it's a wonderful

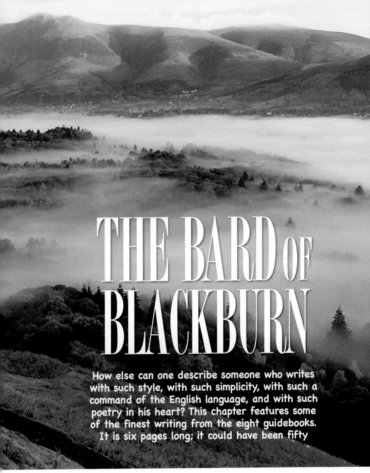

THE BARD OF BLACKBURN

How else can one describe someone who writes with such style, with such simplicity, with such a command of the English language, and with such poetry in his heart? This chapter features some of the finest writing from the eight guidebooks. It is six pages long; it could have been fifty

example of AW's command of the English language and his dry sense of humour; the last word – *with* – is, of course, a preposition. And this explanation actually made as much impact on my English language studies at my senior school as anything ever uttered by my teachers – I'm not

←This variation on the higher part of the Band is not well known — it avoids the wetter patches on the main path, from which its bifurcation, at both ends, is indistinct and must be watched for carefully. *The word 'carefully' is added to avoid ending the sentence with a preposition, which should never be used to end a sentence with.*

kidding you. That's why it is such a shame it is no longer in BOOK FOUR – and I guess you can blame fickle (or possibly decisive) walkers for that!

THE MAGNIFICENT ONES

Great End: Natural features

The vast northern fall of the mountain is one of the finest scenes in the district, awe-inspiring in its massive strength and all the more imposing for being eternally in shadow. The summit breaks immediately in a long cliff seamed by dark gulleys, below which a broad shelf holds Sprinkling Tarn and continues as Seathwaite Fell, but a shoulder (the Band) also fiercely scarped and severed from the main fell by the deep ravine of Skew Gill, runs down to Sty Head.

When mist wreathes the summit and clings like smoke in the gullies, when ravens soar above the lonely crags, when snow lies deep and curtains of ice bejewel the gaunt cliffs, then Great End is indeed an impressive sight. Sunshine never mellows this grim scene but only adds harshness.

This is the true Lakeland of the fellwalker, the sort of terrain that calls him back time after time, the sort of memory that haunts his long winter exile.

It is not the pretty places – the flowery lanes of Grasmere or Derwentwater's wooded bays – that keep him restless in his bed; it is the magnificent ones.

Places like Great End . . .

GREAT NORTHERN FACE: Great End is the kind of mountain that can keep fellwalkers warm inside during their long winter exile from Lakeland.
1/4/09

SHORT CUTS

Great Dodd from Dockray: *All routes from Dockray are uninspiring and dreary . . .*

Hart Side from Dockray: *The joy of this walk is . . . in the splendid high-level route to it [from Dockray].*

High Seat: Ridge to Bleaberry Fell: *This is a walk to wish on one's worst enemy, especially after rain.*

Ridge to High Tove: *This is not a pleasant walk, either. The hags of rich deep peat may be wonderful stuff for growing rhododendrons but seem singularly unattractive to walkers with soaking feet.*

Hallin Fell: *In choosing Hallin Fell as their weekend picnic-place and playground, the Penrith and Carlisle motorists show commendable discrimination, for the rich rewards its summit offers are out of all proportion to the slight effort of ascent.*

Watson's Dodd: *Whoever Mr. Watson may have been, it is a very odd Dodd that has been selected to perpetuate his name.*

Great Gable: *. . . the name is good, simple yet subtly clever. If Great Gable were known only as Wasdale Fell fewer persons would climb it.*

DELIGHTFUL OUTLIERS

Beacon Fell: **Introduction**

Beacon Fell ranks amongst the most delectable of the lesser heights of Lakeland. It is an epitome of all that appeals to fellwalkers. The approach is a joy: lovely and colourful terrain rich in trees and dense thickets of juniper relieved occasionally by marshy flats of myrtle and dry banks of bracken. Higher, grey rocks outcrop in haphazard array and heather and bilberry carpet the rough ground. The paths are enchanting, full of little surprises, while the streams are crystal clear. There is a tarn, too, hidden in a fold of the hills. But it is the summit, abrupt and rocky, and the far-reaching view that make the ascent so worth while. One can recline in comfort here and almost feel sorry for youngsters who, at this moment, are toiling up Great Gable.

Orrest Head: **Introduction**

Orrest Head, for many of us, is "where we came in" – our first ascent in Lakeland, our first sight of mountains in tumultuous array across glittering waters, our awakening to beauty . . . It is a fitting finale, too, to a life made happy by fellwandering. Dare we hope that there will be another Orrest Head over the threshold of the next heaven?

SHORT CUTS

Armboth Fell: *Walkers of a contrary turn of mind will summarily reject the advice to leave Armboth Fell alone and may indeed be strengthened in their determination to climb it . . . They would be further outraged if, having already paid for this book, they found it did not cater for their idiosyncrasies by offering some details of routes of ascent.*

Birks: *Although this spur lacks a distinctive summit it is sufficiently well-defined to deserve a separate name; but, being an unromantic and uninteresting fell, it has earned for itself nothing better than the prosaic and unassuming title of Birks.*

Raven Crag: *Except in the matter of upward progression, there is no resemblance to fellwalking in this climb . . . The silence and gloom of the forest are too oppressive to be enjoyed.*

Little Mell Fell: *One feels sorry for Little Mell Fell, as for all who are neglected and forlorn, but at least it is beloved of birds and animals and it is one of the few fells that grouse select for their habitat, and not even the great Helvellyn itself can make such a claim!*

About a quiet corner of Lakeland . . .

The Vale of Lorton is one of the pleasantest of Lakeland's valleys. Quiet and serene, it has suffered little by modern developments. In comparison with other valleys it lacks interest in the shape of impending crags and cliffs (although there is no more compelling skyline than that formed by the Buttermere and Grasmoor fells just around the corner to the south), but this deficiency is more than redeemed by its velvet pastures and neat woodlands, the latter occurring everywhere and giving the appearance of a park. Those now gone who settled here, to whom it was home and therefore the fairest place on earth, who first planned these sheltered farmsteads and valley communities, were great lovers of trees; and those who followed have, to their credit, taken good care of their heritage. Sweet Lorton!

From
Graystones

Scafell Pike: **Soliloquy**

Why does a man climb mountains. Why has he forced his tired and sweating body up here when he might instead have been sitting at his ease in a deckchair at the seaside, looking at girls in bikinis, or fast asleep, or sucking ice-cream, according to his fancy. On the face of it, the thing doesn't make sense. Yet more and more people are turning to the hills; they find something in these wild places that can be found nowhere else. It may be solace for some, satisfaction for other: the joy of exercising muscles that modern ways of living have cramped, perhaps; or a balm for jangled nerves in the solitude and silence of the peaks; or escape from the clamour and tumult of everyday existence. It may have something to do with a man's subconscious search for beauty, growing keener as so much in the world grows uglier. It may be a need to readjust his sights, to get out of his own narrow groove and climb above it to see wider horizons and truer perspectives. In a few cases, it may even be a curiosity inspired by A. Wainwright's PICTORIAL GUIDES. Or it may be, and for most walkers it will be, quite simply, a deep love of the hills, a love that has grown over the years, whatever motive first took them there: a feeling that these hills are friends, tried and trusted friends, always there when needed. It is a question every man must answer for himself.

Personal view

In my opinion, this is AW's most poetic piece of writing in all of his eight guidebooks. Some people think it's pretentious, and they've got a point. But I still love it!

SHORT CUTS

Hopegill Head: The road to Scale Hill – *This was the way of the waggonettes and the carriages in the days when a speed of three or four miles per hour was considered to be appropriate for a due appraisal of beautiful scenery. (Some of us still think so). Eyes were more appreciative then and minds more receptive. Not one of the passengers along this highway would give a thought to nuclear bombs. Not one would be in a hurry. Those were the days of the artists and poets. The good days.*

Hard Knott: The Roman fort: *One wonders what were the thoughts of the sentries as they kept watch over this lonely outpost amongst the mountains, nearly two thousand years ago? Did they admire the massive architecture of the Scafell group as they looked north, the curve of the valley from source to sea as they looked west? Or did they feel themselves to be unwanted strangers in a harsh and hostile land? Did their hearts ache for the sunshine of their native country, for their families, for their homes?*

Rannerdale Knotts: *This is Rannerdale Knotts, a mountain in miniature, and a proud one. Not even Gable has witnessed a real battle! And, what's more, our side won!!*

Grey Crag: *One looks east, and the heart is soothed; west, and it is stirred . . . the vast skyscapes deserve the brush of a Turner.*

Skiddaw: *Ask a Barkbeth sheep what the north-west ridge of Skiddaw is like and it will reply without hesitation "C'est magnifique" (if it is French, which is unlikely) – which just shows how tastes differ, for most walkers, less easily satisfied, will consider it disappointing.*

ANCIENT SITE: The top of High Street, looking west.   12/11/08

High Street: The summit

The summit is barren of scenic interest, and only visitors of lively imagination will fully appreciate their surroundings. Any person so favoured may recline on the turf and witness, in his mind's eye, a varied pageant of history, for he has been preceded here, down the ages, by the ancient Britons who built their villages and their forts in the valleys around; by the Roman cohorts marching between their garrisons at Ambleside and Brougham; by the Scots invaders who were repulsed on the Troutbeck slopes; by the shepherds, dalesmen and farmers who, centuries ago, made the summit their playground and feasting-place on the occasion of their annual meets; by racing horses (the summit is still named Racecourse Hill on the large-scale Ordnance Survey maps) . . . and let us not forget Dixon of immortal legend, whose great fall over the cliff while fox-hunting is an epic in enthusiasm. Nowadays all is quiet here and only the rising larks disturb the stillness. A pleasant place, but – to those unfortunate folk with no imagination – so dull!

> NOTE: AW urged us 'not to forget' then failed to add in any detail about this story! According to **W.P. Haskett-Smith** (*Climbing in the British Isles, 1894*), the legend was that a fox-hunter named Dixon fell off Blea Water Crag in the year 1762: *Perhaps no one ever fell so far and yet sustained so little permanent injury. As an instance of 'the ruling passion strong in death,' or at least in appalling proximity to death, it may be mentioned that, on arriving at the bottom, he got on his knees and cried out: 'Lads, t'fox is gane oot at t'hee end. Lig t'dogs on an' aa'l cum syun.' He then fell back unconscious, but recovered, and lived many years after.*

Latrigg: The summit

The top of Latrigg is a grand place, especially for fellwalkers on the retired list: here they can recline for hours, recalling joyful days when they had energy enough to climb to the tops of all the mountains in view. Strange how all the best days of memory are to do with summit cairns . . . Will there be mountains like this in Heaven . . . or is this heaven, before death, and will there never again be hills to climb? Is Latrigg the last of all? But no, it needn't be – there's still Orrest Head, even easier . . . Funny, that's where we came in . . .

A to Y

The only alphabetical guide to AW's 330 Lakeland fells (214 from **BOOKS ONE** to **SEVEN**, 116 **OUTLYING FELLS**). Not an X or Z in sight... and just one Q!

To paraphrase a well-known introduction: any index of the 214 Wainwrights and 116 Outliers in the PICTORIAL GUIDES TO THE LAKELAND FELLS and THE OUTLYING FELLS must necessarily be arbitrary, and he who takes it upon himself to say what details should be included in such an index (or not) – for example, whether Abbey Buttress (the lower part of Eagle's Nest Ridge on the Great Napes) warrants a separate entry – must not expect his pronouncements to be generally accepted.

Not every topographical feature contained within the eight guidebooks – whether it be a gill, a cascade, a hillside, a boulder etc. – has been included here. Indeed, a subjective approach has been adopted; what may not warrant a second glance in a chapter such as Coniston Old Man may well be a significant feature in the chapter on Blawith Knott. So please don't assume any such omissions to be a . . . ahem . . . **Great Cockup**: they are more than likely to be because a subjective opinion (that of this author) has been exercised.

If readers find any significant errors or omissions in this index, I would appreciate it they posted them on the Facebook page for this book. The address is **The Wainwright Companion**.

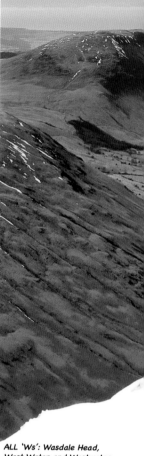

ALL 'Ws': Wasdale Head, Wast Water and Wastwater Screes from Westmorland Cairn on Great Gable (all Gs!).
3/2/10

HOW THE INDEX WORKS

Entries for every one of the 330 fells include its height and its main features. The main features are given a separate entry which includes a reference to the fell (and its book). There are no cross-references between the features. An example: **Lingcove Bridge** may be cross-referenced to **Esk Pike**, **Bowfell**, **Crinkle Crags**, etc., but not to the **River Esk**, and vice versa. The COLOUR CODING is as usual:

E = Eastern FE = Far Eastern C = Central S = Southern
N = Northern NW = North-Western W = Western O = Outlying

Outlying fells, if they are not the main (named) fell in the chapter, are linked to the *(MAIN FELL)* as indicated in capital letters. Features cross-referred to Outlying fells are referred to the *CHAPTER* name, not the specific summit. Outlying fells where there is a chapter name (such as **Potter Fell**) but no summit of that name (or with multiple summits) are listed in **BOLD CAPITAL** letters, with a cross-reference to each separate summit within the chapter.

Sorry if that's confusing. Blame AW! He devised THE OUTLYING FELLS.

Aaron Crags | S
  Seathwaite Fell.
Aaron Slack | W
  Great Gable,
  Green Gable.
Abbey Buttress | W
  Great Gable.
(The) Abominable Snowman (AW's footsteps) | NW
  Outerside.
Abbot's Bay | NW
  Catbells.
Adam-a-Cove | S
  Crinkle Crags.
Adam Seat | FE
  Harter Fell.
Addacomb Beck | NW
  Wandope.
Addacomb Hole | NW
  Wandope.
aeroplane memorial | E
  Helvellyn.
aeroplane wreckage | S
  Great Carrs.
aeroplane wreckage | O
  Black Combe.
Aik Beck | C
  Loadpot Hill.
Aiken Beck | NW

  Broom Fell.
Aiken Plantation | NW
  Lord's Seat.
Aira Beck | E
  Gowbarrow Fell, Great Dodd, Hart Side.
Aira Force | E
  Gowbarrow Fell, Hart Side.
Alcock Tarn | E
  Heron Pike, Nab Scar.
Allan Bank | C
  Silver How.
Allan Tarn | C
  Top o'Selside.
Allen Crags | 2572ft | S
  Allen Gill, Esk Hause, Grains Gill, High House Tarn, Ruddy Gill, Seathwaite, Sprinkling Tarn, Stockley Bridge.
Allen Gill | S
  Allen Crags.
Ambleside | E C
  Dove Crag, High Pike, Loughrigg Fell, Low Pike, Wansfell.
amphitheatre | C
  Loughrigg Fell.
Anglers' Crag | W

  Crag Fell.
Angle Tarn | FE
  Angletarn Pikes, Brock Crags, Rest Dodd.
Angle Tarn | FE
  Bowfell, Esk Pike, Rossett Pike.
Angletarn
Pikes | 1857ft | FE
  Angle Tarn, Boredale Hause, Heck Crag, Martindale, Patterdale.
Anna Crag | O
  BLACK COMBE.
Applethwaite | N
  Latrigg.
arch, quarry | S
  Holme Fell.
Ard Crags | 1906ft | NW
  Keskadale, Keskadale Beck, Rigg Beck.
Armaside | NW
  Graystones.
Applethwaite | N
  Skiddaw, Skiddaw Little Man.
Applethwaite
Common | FE
  Sour Howes.
Applethwaite Quarry | FE

Styhead Tarn | S W
Great End, Great Gable, Green Gable, Scafell Pike, Seathwaite Fell.

Stythwaite Steps | C
Calf Crag, Gibson Knott, Helm Crag, Tarn Crag.

Sulphury Gill | FE
The Knott.

Summit seat | N
High Pike.

Surprise View | C
High Seat.

Swallowdale (fictional) | O
WOODLAND FELL.

Swan Dub | S
Glaramara.

Swan Hotel | E
Great Rigg, Heron Pike, Nab Scar, Stone Arthur.

Swarthbeck Gill | FE
Arthur's Pike, Bonscale Pike, Loadpot Hill.

Swinburne Park | E
Gowbarrow Fell.

Swinburn Gill | N
Great Sca Fell.

Swindale | FE O
THE NADDLE HORSESHOE, SEAT ROBERT, Selside Pike.

Swindale Tunnel | O
THE NADDLE HORSESHOE.

Swindale Head | FE O
Selside Pike, HOWES.

Swine Crag | FE
High Street.

Swineside Knott | E
Hart Side.

Swinside | NW
Catbells.

Swinside | NW
Hopegill Head.

Swinside Plantation | NW
Hopegill Head.

Swinsty Gill | S
Crinkle Crags.

Swirl Hawse | S
Swirl How, Wetherlam.

Swirl How | 2630ft | S
Coniston, Coniston Copper Mines, Great How Crags, Greenburn Beck, Greenburn Reservoir, Hawse Beck, Levers Hawse, Levers Water, Little How Crags, Little Langdale, Little Langdale Tarn, Paddy End Copper Works, Prison Band, Simon's Nick, Swirl Hawse.

Swirral Edge | E
Catstycam, Helvellyn.

Symonds Knott | S
Scafell.

(The) Tale of Peter Rabbit | NW
Catbells.

Tarn at Leaves | S
Rosthwaite Fell.

Tarn Beck | S O
Caw, Dow Crag, Grey Friar.

(Valley of) Tarn Beck | S
Grey Friar.

Tarn Crag | 1801ft | C
Cockley Crag, Codale Tarn, Deer Bield Crag, Easedale, Easedale Tarn, Far Easedale, Grasmere, Greathead Crag, Sourmilk Gill, Stythwaite Steps.

Tarn Crag | 2176ft | FE
Buckbarrow Crag, Great Howe, Greycrag Tarn, Longsleddale, Mosedale, Sadgill.

Tarn Crag | S
Green Crag.

Tarn Crag (three gullies) | E
Dollywaggon Pike.

Tarn Crag | C
Harrison Stickle.

Tarn Hill | 920ft | O
(DUNNERDALE FELLS).

Tarn Hill | 1183ft | O
(STICKLE PIKE).

Tarn Riggs | O
WOODLAND FELL.

Taylorgill Force | S W
Base Brown, Green Gable, Scafell Pike, Seathwaite Fell.

Terrace Route | S
Scafell, Slight Side.

Tewit How | W
Scoat Fell.

Tewit Tarn | W
Scoat Fell.

Thackthwaite | W
Fellbarrow, Low Fell.

Thackthwaite | E
Little Mell Fell.

Thief Gills | N
Knott.

Third Gill | NW
Wandope, Whiteless Pike.

Thirdgillhead Man | NW
Wandope, Whiteless Pike.

Thirlmere | C E
Armboth Fell, Calf Crag, Helvellyn, High Tove, Raven Crag.

Thirlmere aqueduct | E
Great Rigg.

Thirlmere dam | C
Raven Crag.

Thirlspot | E
Helvellyn, Raise, White Side.

Thorn Crag | C
Harrison Stickle, Loft Pike.

Thornholme | W
Lank Rigg.

Thornhow End | E
Birks.

Thornthwaite | NW
Barf, Grisedale Pike, Lord's Seat.

Thornthwaite Beacon | FE
Thornthwaite Crag.

Thornthwaite Crag | 2569ft | FE
Gavel Crag, Hayeswater, (River) Kent, Kentmere Reservoir,

*TWOBARROW: (facing
page) Two views of
Yewbarrow, the
2058ft fell that
punches above its
weight in the Wasdale
landscape. It's steep,
it's rocky (at both
ends), it looks great
beside Great Gable
and Lingmell in views
of West Water (top
picture) and, by a
quirk of nature, you
can see all four
Lakeland 3000-
footers from its
summit. That makes it
worthy of two
pictures in this index
to AW's eight Lakeland
guidebooks.* 23/6/09

QUIZ ANSWERS

A1: Eel Crag (also known as Crag Hill); **A2:** Gowbarrow Fell (the attraction is Aira Force); **A3:** Stickle Tarn; **A4:** Froswick; **A5:** The Chair (Red Pike, Wasdale); **A6:** Wet Side Edge (Great Carrs); **A7:** Cold Pike Tooth (Cold Pike); **A8:** Claife Heights; **A9:** Longlands Fell; **A10:** Grey Crag (not THE Borrowdale and Wasdale!).

B1: High Rigg (ascent from St John's in the Vale); **B2:** Mellbreak; **B3:** Bowscale Tarn; **B4:** Heron Pike; **B5:** Thirdgillhead Man (right is Wandope); **B6:** High Crag (ascent of Sheepbone Rake); **B7:** Oak Howe Needle; **B8:** Newton Fell (Newton Fell North); **B9:** Harrison Stickle; **B10:** Blencathra via Blease Gill.

C1: Binsey; **C2:** Hopegill Head; **C3:** Sprinkling Tarn; **C4:** Bonscale Pike; **C5:** Belles Knott, 'the Matterhorn of Easedale'; **C6:** St Sunday Crag; **C7:** Catbells Pinnacle; **C8:** Beacon Fell; **C9:** Scafell; **C10:** Middle Fell and Seatallan.

D1: Robinson; **D2:** Harrison Stickle (2415ft), Pike o'Stickle (2323ft), Pavey Ark (2288ft), Loft Crag (2270ft); **D3:** Small Water; **D4:** Starling Dodd; **D5:** Bonscale Pike; **D6:** Pike o'Blisco; **D7:** Gladstone's Finger on Crinkle Crags; **D8:** Hampsfell; **D9:** Low Pike; **D10:** Bakestall (Dash Falls).

E1: Great Carrs; **E2:** Bakestall, Dodd, Carl Side, Latrigg, Longlands Fell, Long Side, Skiddaw Little Man, Ullock Pike; **E3:** Blackbeck Tarn (Haystacks); **E4:** Broom Fell; **E5:** Seathwaite, Duddon Valley; **E6:** Mardale Ill Bell; **E7:** The Split Boulder (Blea Rigg); **E8:** Irton Pike; **E9:** Pillar (Walker's Gully); **E10:** Great Dodd.

F1: Causey Pike; **F2:** Blake Fell, Burnbank Fell, Gavel Fell, Hen Comb and Mellbreak; **F3:** Blea Water; **F4:** Raise; **F5:** Trusmadoor (Meal Fell); **F6:** Thunacar Knott; **F7:** Eskdale Needle, a.k.a. The Steeple (Hard Knott); **F8:** High Knott (a.k.a. Williamson's Monument); **F9:** High Spy (a.k.a. Eels Crags, Lobstone Band and Scawdel Fell); **F10:** Caudale Moor (a.k.a. John Bell's Banner; summit known as Stony Cove Pike).

G1: Kirk Fell (Wasdale Head); **G2:** Nab Scar, Heron Pike, Great Rigg, Fairfield, Hart Crag, Dove Crag, High Pike and Low Pike; **G3:** Dalehead Tarn and Launchy Tarn (Dale Head); **G4:** High Tove; **G5:** Cairn on Artlecrag Pike, Branstree; **G6:** Grange Fell; **G7:** Badger Rock, a.k.a. Brock Stone (Yoke); **G8:** Whitbarrow; **G9:** Great Calva; **G10:** Row of ten cottages, Sheffield Pike.

H1: Grisedale Pike; **H2:** Coniston Old Man (2633ft), Swirl How (2630ft), Brim Fell (2611ft); Great Carrs (2575ft); Dow Crag (2555ft), Grey Friar (2536ft) and Wetherlam (2502ft); **H3:** Dock Tarn (Great Crag); **H4:** High Raise; **H5:** Goats Water; **H6:** Base Brown; **H7:** The Needle, Black Crag, Pike o'Blisco; **H8:** Black Combe; **H9:** Wandope; **H10:** Great Mell Fell.

HOW DID YOU DO?

80pts:	You are an absolute AW genius.
75-79pts:	You know the guidebooks and Lakeland like the back of your hand.
70-74pts:	Your knowledge is very impressive – you must read a lot!
60-69pts:	You've read the guidebooks and a lot of it has sunk in.
50-59pts:	You're a bit of a fan and you like your Lakeland.
40-49pts:	You've read the guidebooks, but not all of it has sunk in.
20-39pts:	Maybe you haven't got the complete set of eight guidebooks.
15-19pts:	Maybe you've only got two or three.
10-14pts:	And you haven't even read them.
5-9pts:	Can you read?
1-4pts:	You can't read, and you're not good at the picture questions either.
0pts:	The closest you've been to the Lake District is probably Blackpool's North Beach . . . but it's never too late for redemption!

the WAINWRIGHT companion

Some personal notes in conclusion

I guess we all can trace our love of Lakeland back to one or two moments earlier in life. In my case, I can thank the public library in my home town, plus the two authors whose work I had the pleasure of reading from an early age whose books they stocked: first, Arthur Ransome, whose Lakeland tales of *Swallows and Amazons* and *Swallowdale* captivated me; then A.H. 'Harry' Griffin, whose books about Lakeland, *Inside The Real Lakeland* and *In Mountain Lakeland* (both published 1961, both first read by me in 1965), really whetted my appetite.

So much so, that the following year I begged my parents (the 'begging' largely consisted of sulks and tantrums) to go to the Lake District for the summer holidays. My dad being my dad, of course, the chosen destination was Cornwall. And to add insult to injury (the 'injury' being a gruelling overnight drive from the Home Counties to near Penzance in an era when dual-carriageways were as common as manual typewriters are now), we missed the 1966 World Cup Final. Well, not quite. My parents had an afternoon nap in our second-hand frame tent during the whole period of Geoff Hurst's finest two hours in football but not before pointing out to me that they'd chosen the camp site because it had a clubhouse equipped with the latest in television technology (that's how they sold it to me). Looking back, I'm pretty sure they weren't far wrong. A 17-inch black-and-white telly probably WAS the state-of the art equivalent to a 48-inch plasma back then. And, if it had been in our home (the small telly) I'm sure it would have offered just as good a viewing experience as that we had four days earlier when two Bobby Charlton goals helped England beat Portugal 2-1 in the semi-final. Ahhh, but I was barely ten feet away from the screen then . . . On final Saturday when I marched into the clubhouse ten minutes before kick-off I found myself at the back of a very large (and very big, vertically) crowd. My best estimate was I was a cricket pitch-length from the screen, so Bobby Moore was, at best, about a quarter-of-an-inch high (from my perspective) when he collected the Jules Rimet Trophy – which made that about a sixteenth of an inch (please note: no metrication appears in this book, although for readers who only know 'new money' a sixteenth of an inch is probably something in the region of one-and-a-half millimetres).

All that leads me on to the following summer holidays where, naturally, I was in a strong position to call the shots: we ended up in the Peak District! Actually, it wasn't bad: Edale and Mam Tor, Blue John caves and the rest. The decision was sold to me on the grounds of 'we wanted to make sure you like mountains before we drive all the way to the Lake District' (my dad) and 'it's still very pretty, so they say' (my mum). 'But it isn't the Lake District, mother. Grrrrrrr.'

Needless to say, the following summer I finally did hold ALL the aces. I wanted Borrowdale or Great Langdale: we spent two weeks in the Newlands Valley. "We've done some research," said my mum (not sure how she managed that in the pre-internet era), "and we've decided to start off with the nursery slopes." Which meant Catbells and Causey Pike instead of the Langdale Pikes or Scafell Pike – but try telling that to parents. In fact, the Newlands Valley WAS (and probably still is) the perfect place for an introduction to Lakeland's fells. But don't just take my word for it. Here's what AW wrote in his personal notes in conclusion to BOOK SIX: *Newlands is a privileged valley, not only extraordinarily pleasant in itself but ringed by grand fells; for a quiet fellwalking holiday there is no better centre.*

Actually, it wasn't quite so quiet (we'll come on to that later) but the mountains around Newlands, while not aspiring to the lofty heights of the eastern, southern or western fells, foot-for-foot are right up there with the very best of Lakeland.

We pitched the frame tent at a camp site in the tiny hamlet of Skelgill, just a little way from Stair, and in the balmy sunlight of a July early evening decided to climb the pointy hill that loomed over us by way of a green avenue framed by verdant bracken. This was Catbells, and less than 30 minutes later we emerged on the watershed to a wondrous vision of Derwent Water backed by Skiddaw, Keswick and, away to the right, Blencathra. It was like that moment in *Jerry Maguire* when Renée Zellweger says to Tom Cruise: 'You had me at hello.'

The route we chose is outlined on Catbells 7 and is alongside another diagram, via Hause Gate, under which AW writes: *Up one way and down the other is a nice idea.* Of course it is, but not being equipped with A PICTORIAL GUIDE TO THE LAKELAND FELLS - BOOK SIX: THE NORTH WESTERN FELLS we were in no position to know that. This was remedied a day later when we strolled into the George Fisher store in Keswick and asked if there were any books that showed the best mountains and how to climb them, and emerged with BOOK FIVE and BOOK SIX, both necessary for a fulfilling stay in the Keswick area, we were told. A couple of days later we added BOOK THREE and BOOK FOUR to our burgeoning collection of Wainwrights (by then, we even knew the term!) and we were well equipped to tackle any challenge. A day trip to Buttermere swiftly put paid to that notion, however, and it was back to George Fisher for BOOK SEVEN, by which time I had used up all my previous two summers' worth of capital (and a large chunk of my father's) in about four days and that was the end of our guidebook purchasing for that year. This was, of course, pre-decimalisation when, if I recall correctly, the books sold for 12 shillings and sixpence (I think that's 62.5p in today's money).

Well, our 'quiet' Newlands holiday turned out to be noisier than we thought, thanks to a car-load of hippies who pulled up in a bright-yellow Hillman Minx (that's a car, by the way) and made camp about 30 yards away. They liked to play guitars and sing around an illegal camp fire until past midnight, but they were a cheerful bunch – and useful, too, when our Morris Oxford got stuck in a mud rut and they very kindly pushed us out.

We climbed Skiddaw that summer, and Blencathra (just my dad and me – mum had by then decided she preferred Friar's Crag), plus a whole bunch of fells around Newlands . . . and apart from one morning when it was cloudy and it drizzled, every day was a glorious sunny experience that has stayed with me all my life.

I managed to finagle my way back to the Lakes for the next two summers (aged 13 and 14) before August 1971's spectacular trip to Camber Sands in East Sussex (I'm not joking), but by 1972 – aged 16 and mature enough (so I told the folks) to go away on my own – I was ready for another dose of Lakeland. I had a willing accomplice (my mate Kev) who was only too eager to head north for two weeks away from his younger sister (personally, I would have preferred to bring her, but that's not in the remit of this book!). Kev, being ignorant of anything to do with the fells, left all the organising to me, which I proceeded to do with (for me) highly-unusual efficiency. I planned the route, booked the youth hostels, bought the bus tickets (Luton-Ambleside on the midnight special) and generally did everything in 1972 that AW did back in 1931 when he and three friends from Blackburn made a week-long excursion to the Lakes (see Ed Geldard's interesting book *Wainwright's Lost Tour* for all the details).

We got off the bus at Ambleside around 7.45 in the morning, had some breakfast in a 'greasy spoon', hitch-hiked up to the Dungeon Ghyll Old Hotel, and then hauled our backpacks up Rossett Gill and over the 'false' Esk Hause with the day's destination being Wasdale Youth Hostel, which (rather unfortunately) is at the wrong end of Wast Water. Somewhere around Sty Head we fell asleep in the noon sunshine for a couple of hours and woke up looking like refugees from a beetroot farm, but apart from that (painful) mishap we got to the hostel unscathed.

The rest of the holiday was a blur of steep walks, northern girls, frothy beer (we both looked 18 and, when asked, engaged in some clever reverse psychology by claiming our real ages to be 19) and great pubs (one drinking session we had at The Fish Inn in Buttermere before a return walk – or should that be 'stagger' – to Wasdale Youth Hostel via Honister Pass and Moses' Trod is particularly embossed on my brain!).

We returned with another friend the following year, and at various times over the 38 years since I've been back to meet all my old friends (the fells, not Keswick drinking buddies). You never stop going back, as they say.

But not as often as I would have liked, and the nearest I ever came to living in Lakeland was a particularly depressing sojourn in Darlington (where I worked as a designer and sub-editor on *The Northern Echo* newspaper). Still, it was close enough for me and my pal Mike Chapple from Liverpool to make a mad dash across the Pennines on Midsummer's Eve in 1984 and commence a moonlit ascent of Helvellyn from Patterdale in the early hours. We actually had to wait an hour at the start of Striding Edge because some clouds came over, and we were 30 minutes late getting to the summit in time for sunrise. Imagine our surprise to find a mini-encampment of Druids who were all up and about wearing Druid gear and doing Druid things. That's Helvellyn for you.

But enough about me and Lakeland, and on to more important things: seven things, in fact, *alWainwright's* PICTORIAL GUIDES TO THE LAKELAND FELLS, which are the veritable Seven Wonders of the Publishing World. And number eight isn't half bad, either (when you're getting on a bit!).

This is a paragraph I've been able to quote, verbatim, for 40 years (from *Great End* 2): *It is not the pretty places – the flowery lanes of Grasmere or Derwent Water's wooded bays – that keep him* [the fellwalker] *restless in his bed; it is the magnificent ones. Places like Great End…*

Throughout my various periods of exile from Lakeland, it is not the Pouchers and it is not the Ordnance Survey maps that have kept me sane while being hundreds or thousands of miles from heaven; it is the magnificent ones: the sublime; the poetic; the literary; the typographically superb; the everlasting; the absolutely wonderful great guidebooks that pay homage to the 'Wainwrights' contained within their pages.

Now on to my lists. No need to turn over!

I'll follow AW's footsteps here by choosing some 'best sixes', starting with drawings. In my opinion, the best six full-page (or double-page) drawings of a mountain scene (not in order of merit) are:

CAMBRIDGE CRAG / BOWFELL BUTTRESS (Bowfell 10, BOOK FOUR)
DOVE CRAG (High Hartsop Dodd 3, BOOK ONE)
DOW CRAG AND GOATS WATER (Dow Crag 12, BOOK FOUR)
GREAT SLAB, BOWFELL (Bowfell 13-14, BOOK FOUR)
PAVEY ARK FROM STICKLE TARN (Pavey Ark 10, BOOK THREE)
WASTWATER SCREES (Whin Rigg 9-10, BOOK FOUR)

My favourite 'lower-level' full-page drawings, that capture the atmosphere of Lakeland, are:

BELLES KNOTT, EASEDALE (Sergeant Man 12, Book SIX)
CASCADES, RUTHWAITE (Dollywaggon Pike 11, Book ONE)
HAWESWATER AND A.W. (Harter Fell 10, BOOK TWO)
GOAT CRAG (High Spy 12, BOOK SIX)
SOURMILK GILL (Tarn Crag 10, BOOK THREE)
ULLSWATER AND WOMAN (St Sunday Crag 8, BOOK ONE)

My favourite small drawings, for quality of drawing, relevance and humour (those sheep on High Sweden bridge are like something from *Toy Story*!), are:

BISHOP OF BARF, REAR VIEW (Barf 5, BOOK FIVE)
HEARTS IN BOOTS (Scafell Pike 20, BOOK FOUR)
HIGH SWEDEN BRIDGE (Low Pike 4, BOOK ONE)

PERFECT MOUNTAIN TARN (Allen Crags 7, BOOK FOUR)
TOP OF CONISTON OLD MAN (Coniston Old Man 11, BOOK FOUR)
WHICHAM MILL (Black Combe, THE OUTLYING FELLS)

My favourite chapter 'page one' drawings, that capture the essence of the fell concerned, are:

DOW CRAG (BOOK FOUR)
FLEETWITH PIKE (BOOK SEVEN)
GRANGE FELL (BOOK THREE)
EAGLE CRAG (BOOK THREE)
PILLAR (BOOK SEVEN)
ST SUNDAY CRAG (BOOK ONE)

Now on to my favourite CHAPTERS. Now this doesn't mean they are my favourite mountains, just that I feel AW has done full justice to the fells concerned in his own, inimitable style. For instance, I don't feel able to include any BOOK ONE chapters because the first guidebook in the series had some features that were never seen again (poor treatment of views, strange way of showing the ascents of Helvellyn, etc.). My best six, after much thought, are:

BLENCATHRA (BOOK FIVE)
SCAFELL PIKE (BOOK FOUR)
GREAT GABLE (BOOK SEVEN)
HAYSTACKS (BOOK SEVEN)
LOUGHRIGG FELL (BOOK THREE)
PILLAR (BOOK SEVEN)

Best of all is Blencathra, with a wonderful explanation about the structure of this magnificent mountain. Note that there are three from BOOK SEVEN (I think he was getting the hang of this by then!).

Now to the best DIAGRAMS (ridges/ascents). Again, these are not in order of merit:

BLENCATHRA VIA HALL'S FELL (Blencathra 17-18, BOOK FIVE)
BOWFELL via Climber's Traverse/Great Slab (Bowfell 5-6, BOOK FOUR)
BOWFELL-CRINKLE CRAGS ridge (Crinkle Crags 11-14, BOOK FOUR)

EEL CRAG via Shelf Route and Tower Ridge
(Eel Crag 7-8, BOOK SIX)
PAVEY ARK via Jack's Rake (Pavey Ark 5-6, BOOK THREE)
PILLAR via High Level Route (Pillar 10-11, BOOK SEVEN)

Finally, my best dust-jackets (first and second editions) – no 'best six' this time. First edition:
BOOK SIX: Hopegill Head, The Notch

This was my first book, and for me the rugged nature of the drawing made it look like the Alps! And for the second edition, it has to be:
BOOK SEVEN: Haystacks and Buttermere

It has to be because ... well, you know why.

CH
May 2012